Creating a **Digital** Home Entertainment System

with Windows®

Media Center

Michael Miller

800 East 96th Street,
Indianapolis, Indiana 46240

Creating a Digital Home Entertainment System with Windows Media Center

International Standard Book Number: 0789735423

Library of Congress Catalog Card Number: 2006920614

Printed in the United States of America

First Printing: March 2006

09   08   07   06   4   3   2   1

Trademarks

Warning and Disclaimer

Bulk Sales

Que Publishing offers excellent discounts on this book when ordered in quantity for bulk purchases or special sales. For more information, please contact

U.S. Corporate and Government Sales
1-800-382-3419
corpsales@pearsontechgroup.com

For sales outside of the U.S., please contact

International Sales
international@pearsoned.com

Associate Publisher
Greg Wiegand

Managing Editor
Charlotte Clapp

Acquisitions Editor
Neil Rowe

Development Editor
Sean Dixon

Project Editor
Seth Kerney

Copy Editor
Mike Henry

Proofreader
Leslie Joseph

Indexer
Chris Barrick

Team Coordinator
Cindy Teeters

Designer
Anne Jones

Page Layout
Nonie Ratcliff

Contents at a Glance

Introduction

PART I: Planning Your Media Center System

1   Why You'd Want a PC in Your Living Room 7

2   Media Center System #1: The Digital Audio Server 23

3   Media Center System #2: The Digital Video Recorder 41

4   Media Center System #3: The Whole House
       Entertainment System 57

5   Buying or Building: Choosing the Right Media Center
       System for You 69

PART II: Setting Up Your Media Center PC

6   Making the Connections 91

7   Configuring Windows XP Media Center Edition 121

PART III: Using Your Media Center PC

8   Getting to Know Windows XP Media Center Edition 147

9   Using Windows XP MCE for Audio Storage and Playback . . 167

10   Using Windows XP MCE for Television Viewing
       and Recording 209

11   Using Windows XP MCE for DVD Playback and
       Recording 245

12   Using Windows XP MCE for Digital Photos 261

13   Using Windows XP MCE for Computer Tasks 277

PART IV: Extending Your Media Center PC

14   Using Your Media Center PC with a Media Center Extender 293

15   Exploring the Online Spotlight 303

16   Finding and Using Other Media Center Applications 327

17   Customizing Windows XP Media Center Edition 349

18   Troubleshooting Media Center Problems 365

       Index 379

Contents

Introduction 1

Who Should Read This Book 2

How This Book Is Organized 3

Special Features in This Book 3

Navigating Media Center 4

PART I: PLANNING YOUR MEDIA CENTER SYSTEM

1   Why You'd Want a PC in Your Living Room 7

Things You Can Do with a PC in Your Living Room 8

Why a Living Room PC Is Different from a Desktop PC 15

Controlling the Living Room PC—With Windows XP Media Center Edition 19

Alternatives to a Living Room PC 20

2   Media Center System #1: The Digital Audio Server 23

The Goal: Listening to Your Music Collection, Digitally 24

The Plan: Configuring Your System 32

3   Media Center System #2: The Digital Video Recorder 41

The Goal: Watching and Recording Television and Movies 41

The Plan: Configuring Your System 50

4   Media Center System #3: The Whole House
Entertainment System 57

How a Media Center Extender Works 58

Goal #1: Sharing Audio/Video Entertainment Throughout the House 61

Plan #1: Placing Multiple Media Center Extenders Throughout Your Home ... 62

Goal #2: Accessing Audio and Video Files Stored on Another PC—On
Your Living Room System 63

Plan #2a: Placing a Media Center Extender in Your Home Theater System ... 64

Plan #2b: Using an Xbox Game Console As a Media Center Extender 65

Using Windows Media Center via a Media Center Extender 67

**5   Buying or Building: Choosing the Right Media Center
      System for You** **69**

Different Types of Media Center PCs 69

Shopping for a Living Room Media Center PC 73

Building a Media Center PC from Scratch 77

Build or Buy: Comparing the Options 88

PART II: SETTING UP YOUR MEDIA CENTER PC

6   Making the Connections **91**

How Connecting a Media Center PC Is Different from Connecting
    a Desktop PC 91

Connecting the Antenna Input 94

Connecting the Video Output 101

Connecting the Audio Output 108

Connecting to a Network 114

Connecting the Keyboard, Mouse, and Remote Control 117

Connecting External Peripherals 118

7   Configuring Windows XP Media Center Edition **121**

Dealing with Windows XP 121

Setting Up MCE for the First Time 122

Configuring Other Settings 141

PART III: USING YOUR MEDIA CENTER PC

8   Getting to Know Windows XP Media Center Edition **147**

Basic Operation 148

The Start Page 149

Getting Help in Media Center 151

The Menus 152

Launching and Exiting Media Center 162

9   Using Windows XP MCE for Audio Storage and Playback **167**

Setting Up Media Center for Audio Use 168

How to Play CDs 173

How to Copy CDs to Your Hard Drive 176

How to Download Digital Music to Your PC 177

Managing and Playing Digital Audio Files 179

How to Work with Playlists 192

How to Burn Your Own Music CDs 205

10   Using Windows XP MCE for Television Viewing and Recording 209

How to Use the Program Guide 209

How to Watch Live Television 217

How to Record Television Programs 224

How to View Programs You've Recorded 239

11   Using Windows XP MCE for DVD Playback and Recording 245

How to Play DVDs 245

How to Record DVDs 248

How to Rip DVDs to Your Hard Drive 255

How to Play Other Video Files 258

12   Using Windows XP MCE for Digital Photos 261

Configuring Your Photo Slideshows 262

How to View Digital Photos 263

How to Manage Your Digital Photos 265

How to Edit Your Digital Photos 268

How to Burn Your Photos to a CD 271

How to Play a Photo Slideshow 274

How to Listen to Music While Playing a Slideshow 275

13   Using Windows XP MCE for Computer Tasks 277

Chatting with Other Users via Media Center Messenger 277

Checking Your Email with Hotmail Plus Reader 281

Managing Your Schedules, Contacts, and Email with MCE Outlook 283

Managing Your Files with My File Manager 287

PART IV: EXTENDING YOUR MEDIA CENTER PC

14   Using Your Media Center PC with a Media Center Extender 293

Connecting a Media Center Extender 293

Configuring a Media Center Extender 297

Using Your Media Center Extender 298

Tricks for Improving Media Center Extender Performance 299

15 Exploring the Online Spotlight **303**

  Understanding Online Spotlight 303

  TV & Movies in the Spotlight 305

  Music & Radio in the Spotlight 311

  News & Sports in the Spotlight 318

  Games in the Spotlight 321

  Lifestyle Options in the Spotlight 323

16 Finding and Using Other Media Center Applications **327**

  News Programs 328

  Weather Programs 331

  Entertainment Programs 332

  DVD-Burning Programs 335

  Lifestyle Programs 337

  Home Automation Programs 339

  Caller ID Programs 340

  Internet Phone Utilities 340

  Computer Applications 341

  Remote Control Utilities 343

  Media Center Utilities 344

  Games 346

17 Customizing Windows XP Media Center Edition **349**

  Tweaking Windows Media Center with Tweak MCE 350

  Customizing Windows Media Center with MCE Customizer 357

18 Troubleshooting Media Center Problems **365**

  Keeping Your Media Center System Up-to-Date 365

  Where to Go for Help 367

  Common Problems—And Probable Solutions 369

  All These Problems—Is It Worth It? 377

INDEX **379**

About the Author

Michael Miller is a successful and prolific author with a reputation for practical advice, technical accuracy, and an unerring empathy for the needs of his readers.

Mr. Miller has written more than 75 best-selling books over the past 17 years. His books include *How Home Theater and HDTV Work, Microsoft Windows XP for Home Users, Absolute Beginner's Guide to Computer Basics,* and *Making a Living from Your eBay Business.* He is known for his casual, easy-to-read writing style and his practical, real-world advice—as well as his ability to explain a wide variety of complex topics to an everyday audience.

You can email Mr. Miller directly at mediacenter@molehillgroup.com. His website is located at www.molehillgroup.com.

Dedication

To the memory of Dr. Richard French.

Acknowledgments

Thanks to the usual suspects at Que, including but not limited to Neil Rowe, Mike Henry, Sean Dixon, and Seth Kerney. Additional thanks to Garry Weil for performing the technical edit, and to our mutual friend Jordan Gold for introducing us. Thanks also to the gang at The Green Button, and to all the site's users—it's the best place on the Web for Media Center news and information!

We Want to Hear from You!

As the reader of this book, *you* are our most important critic and commentator. We value your opinion and want to know what we're doing right, what we could do better, what areas you'd like to see us publish in, and any other words of wisdom you're willing to pass our way.

As an associate publisher for Que Publishing, I welcome your comments. You can email or write me directly to let me know what you did or didn't like about this book—as well as what we can do to make our books better.

Please note that I cannot help you with technical problems related to the topic of this book. We do have a User Services group, however, where I will forward specific technical questions related to the book.

When you write, please be sure to include this book's title and author as well as your name, email address, and phone number. I will carefully review your comments and share them with the author and editors who worked on the book.

Email: feedback@quepublishing.com

Mail: Greg Wiegand
           Associate Publisher
           Que Publishing
           800 East 96th Street
           Indianapolis, IN 46240 USA

For more information about this book or another Que Publishing title, visit our website at www.quepublishing.com. Type the ISBN (excluding hyphens) or the title of a book in the Search field to find the page you're looking for.

Introduction

Let me tell you about my new home theater system.

About six months ago I replaced my 12-year-old home theater with all new components, a from-the-ground-up makeover that touched virtually every component. I started with a Sony 60" rear-projection television, added a B&K preamplifier and power amp, and topped it off with some really great-sounding Rocket speakers from AV123. The system looks great and sounds great; it is a significant upgrade over my old system.

When people first see the system, they're impressed by the big screen and the high-definition picture. Then they notice the great sound, first on surround sound movie soundtracks, and then when listening to my music collection. That's when they notice that there's no CD player to play the music; when they ask about it, I show them the most unique component of the entire system, my Media Center PC.

It's the Media Center PC that's the brains behind my entire system. My intent was to digitize my entire 1,000-disc CD collection, so I'd have the equivalent of a digital jukebox that could play any album or song at the press of a button. To that end, I purchased a high-performance, high-capacity Media Center PC from Niveus Media, with more than enough hard disk storage for my entire CD collection. When visitors see how easy it is to sort and display my music collection, and to play any single track or album, they're really impressed. "I need one of those things," is the comment I most often hear.

Indeed, most people would find "one of those things" quite useful. It doesn't matter whether your music collection is small or large, being able to organize it in this fashion— and to do away with all those clunky physical discs—is extremely attractive. Then, when I further show how the Media Center PC can display digital photo slideshows while an album is playing, how it can play back DVD movies, and how it can record television programming and then burn those programs to DVD, the deal is sealed. My Media Center PC is a multifunction digital entertainment device unlike anything we've seen before.

My appreciation for the concept of the living room PC is why I've written this book. *Creating a Digital Home Entertainment System with Windows Media Center* takes you from the discovery and education process, through the purchase of a Media Center PC, all the way through the connection, configuration, use, and customization of a Media Center system. It's the same process I went through a scant six months ago, so you're getting the benefit of my first-hand experience. It's real information from a real user—me.

You're also getting the benefit of the experience of the dedicated Media Center users who both manage and visit The Green Button website. The Green Button is a community of and for Media Center users. These folks, like me, use Media Center every day, and freely trade advice and opinions with anyone who visits. If you're serious about Media Center, I recommend you visit The Green Button site, located at www.thegreenbutton.com; it's on my daily "must see" list.

Who Should Read This Book

If you're considering the purchase of a Media Center PC, this book is for you. If you've just purchased a Media Center PC and are learning how to set it up and use it, this book is also for you. And if you've been using Media Center for awhile and want to learn how to get more out of your system, guess what—this book is for you, too.

In other words, your level of experience or expertise doesn't matter; if you're serious about putting a Media Center PC in your home entertainment system, there's something in this book that you'll find useful.

By the way, I don't assume that you have any prior experience with Windows XP Media Center Edition, nor that you're a computer wizard. All the instructions and advice in this book should be easy enough for nontechnical readers to understand.

I think the material in this book is particularly applicable for those of you who already have a decent home audio or home theater system. In fact, that's the approach I took— that you'll be adding your Media Center PC to an existing entertainment system. (I am not a big fan of—or believer in—using Media Center Edition on a desktop PC.)

How This Book Is Organized

To make this book easy for you to use, I've organized its 18 chapters into four major sections, each focusing on a specific group of tasks or operations. This way, you can turn directly to that part of the book that contains the information you want—or you can read straight through, from front to back, to get the whole Media Center story.

- **Part I: Planning Your Media Center System** is the section to read before you purchase a Media Center PC. You'll discover just what a Media Center PC can do, find out what types of Media Center systems you need for specific uses, and then get some purchasing advice. (I even cover how to build your own Media Center PC from scratch!)

- **Part II: Setting Up Your Media Center PC** shows you how to connect your new Media Center PC to your existing home entertainment system, and how to configure Media Center for initial use.

- **Part III: Using Your Media Center PC** is all about the action. Here is where you'll find step-by-step instructions for using Media Center to store and play back digital music, to view and record television programs, to play and record DVDs, to view digital photos, and to perform computer-related tasks.

- **Part IV: Extending Your Media Center PC** shows you how to get even more out of your Media Center system, by using Media Center Extenders, the subscription services in Media Center's Online Spotlight, and dozens of third-party Media Center add-on applications. I even show you how to customize your Media Center PC, and how to troubleshoot potential problems.

Read the book straight through from Chapter 1 to Chapter 18, or dip in and out for specific information, whatever works best for you. You should find all the information presented quite useful, and directly applicable for how you're using your Media Center PC.

Special Features in This Book

Besides the main text in this book, you'll find several extra features that give you even more information about getting the most out of Windows Media Center.

Tips

These are pieces of advice—little tricks, actually—that help you use Media Center more effectively.

tip Most newer TVs come with at least one HDMI connection. If your Media Center PC has only a DVI output, you can use a DVI-to-HDMI converter to un-mismatch the connection.

Notes

Notes provide information that is generally useful but not specifically needed for what you're doing at the moment. Some are like extended tips—interesting, but not essential.

note A standard-definition TV tuner is called an *NTSC* tuner. A high-definition TV tuner is called an *ATSC* tuner.

Cautions

These tell you to beware of a potentially danger-ous act or situation. In some cases, ignoring a Caution could cause you significant problems—so pay attention to them!

caution Searching large digital music collections can be a very time-consuming process. The more files Media Center has to search, the longer the search will take. If you have 1,000 or more albums stored, be prepared for some serious lag time when searching.

Navigating Media Center

In describing how to find your way around Media Center, I use some specific language and shortcuts that you should become familiar with. In most cases I start you at the Media Center Start screen (this is the screen you see when you press the Green Button on your remote control), and then direct you to make selections on that screen and subsequent screens. The shorthand I use is to detail each selection you make, one after another, separated by the ">" character. So, for example, if I say to go to the Start screen and select **My Music > Artists**, you would press the Green Button to go to the Start screen, select **My Music**, and then when the next screen appears, select **Artists**. As you'll discover, navigating Media Center is pretty easy.

Planning Your Media Center System

1 Why You'd Want a PC in Your Living Room

2 Media Center System #1: The Digital Audio Server

3 Media Center System #2: The Digital Video Recorder

4 Media Center System #3: The Whole House Entertainment System

5 Buying or Building: Choosing the Right Media Center System for You

1

Why You'd Want a PC in Your Living Room

Personal computers are fickle things. Notoriously unreliable. Difficult to use. Prone to crashes and freezes and likely as not to be infected with some sort of nasty computer virus or spyware. Definitely less than user friendly.

You might put up with this erratic behavior in a corporate office, where you have a tech support person on perennial call, or even in your home office, where you've grown used to rebooting and disinfecting and spending half your time doing basic maintenance. But why, in the name of all that's righteous, would you want to introduce such an inherently capricious device into your living room?

Why, indeed.

Putting a PC in your living room might sound like one of the worst things you could do for your overall peace of mind. The living room just isn't the place for a piece of equipment this technical. Besides, a PC is a big, ugly thing, not the sort of device you'd want to place next to a fancy vase or expensive couch. And how to explain away the keyboard, or the mouse, or all the wires and cables and peripheral devices that tag along with the main machine? Or the *noise*?

Nope, you'd have to be a little bit light in the head to put a personal computer in your living room. Computers are creatures of the office environment; they just don't belong in the wide open spaces that you share with the rest of your family.

Unless, that is, there was something really useful that the living room PC could do. Or if the PC didn't look like a normal PC—or act like one, either. Maybe, if the thing looked more like a typical audio or video component, and maybe if it offered some unique functionality for your entertainment pleasure, maybe—just maybe—you might want to consider putting it in your living room, next to your television set and the rest of your home theater system. Maybe.

It might come as some surprise, then, to discover that hundreds of thousands consumers are already putting PCs in their living rooms. These people aren't insane; they wouldn't be doing this if there wasn't a good reason to do so. And there are lots of good reasons; these new living room PCs are designed to fit within the traditional living room environment, to connect to your television display and home theater system, and to provide the functionality of several existing components—and a few you probably don't have yet.

We call this new breed of living room PC the *Media Center PC*—and it's guaranteed to be a component of the next generation of digital home entertainment systems.

> **note** The term *Media Center PC* is used specifically to refer to a living room PC that runs Microsoft's Windows XP Media Center Edition operating environment. In more general terms, living room PCs are sometimes referred to as *home theater PCs* (*HTPCs*) or *entertainment PCs*.

Things You Can Do with a PC in Your Living Room

To justify putting a PC in your living room, it has to perform some fairly useful functions. After all, you're perfectly happy with your current home entertainment system, right? To augment that system with a personal computer, that computer would have to do something that your current system doesn't, or do it better, or do it cheaper. Or some combination of that.

Well, I'll tell you up front that a living room PC won't be any more cost-effective than your existing components, so you can check that one off the list right now. That leaves us with functionality—the things that a PC can do that your existing components can't. And there are quite a few.

CD/DVD Player

The first thing a personal computer can do is play audio CDs and movie DVDs, as shown in Figure 1.1. Now, I'll admit that this isn't a real impressive function. After all, you can buy a $60 DVD player from Wal-Mart that performs just as well as a $2,000 PC with built-in CD/DVD drive. So, replacing your inexpensive and perfectly functioning DVD player with a pricey personal computer for the sole purpose of playing CDs and DVDs wouldn't be a very smart thing to do.

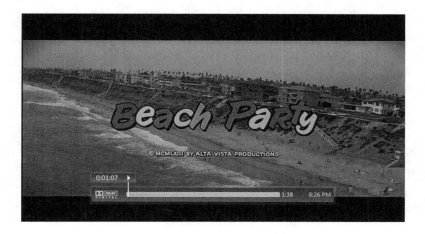

FIGURE 1.1

Playing a DVD movie on a Media Center PC.

Still, it's just one piece of functionality that a living room PC does offer. So, we'll file it away for future reference, and move on to something a little more substantial.

CD/DVD Recorder

Okay, now we're starting to make more sense. You need a personal computer when you want to burn your own music CDs, and there's no reason that a PC shouldn't be in your living room. In fact, putting together your playlists on the big TV screen and then burning custom CDs might be fun, as you can see in Figure 1.2. And it's something that your inexpensive Wal-Mart CD player can't do.

Your $60 Wal-Mart player also can't burn DVD copies of your home movies, or of television programs you've recorded. But a living room PC can do all this and a little more; any video that passes through the computer can be copied to a blank DVD disc. Use the right software and you can edit out any commercials you've recorded, edit in all sorts of transitions and special effects, and create professional-looking DVDs with custom menus and animations. This is definitely a check in the "plus" column for the living room PC. (Although, to be fair, you can buy more expensive standalone DVR/DVD recorder combos; expect to pay $350 or more, and not get the kind of program editing options you get with a living room PC.)

FIGURE 1.2

Burning a music CD on a Media Center PC.

Television Tuner—With Program Guide

Most Media Center PCs come with one or more built-in television tuners. Because the PC connects to your television display, you can use your living room PC to control what you watch on your TV.

This might not sound like much, especially considering the fact that just about every television sold today has its own built-in tuner. Why would you want to supplant your set's built-in tuner with an outboard one in a personal computer?

The answer to that question lies in three little words: *electronic program guide*. As you can see in Figure 1.3, an electronic program guide (or *EPG* for short) displays a grid of current and upcoming television program listings, complete with program titles and descriptions. When you want to watch a program, you locate it in the guide and then click the listing; the computer immediately tunes to the selected program.

Most EPGs display programming for at least 24 hours in advance; some store up to 14 days of future program listings. This is definitely a good thing because you can plan your viewing schedule multiple days in advance. You can even search for listings that meet a certain criteria; for example, you can search for all showings of your favorite programs, or for those programs that feature a particular star in the cast.

And here's where the EPG gets really useful. When you find a future program you want to watch, you can record it. That's because most living room PCs also function as digital video recorders, which we'll discuss next.

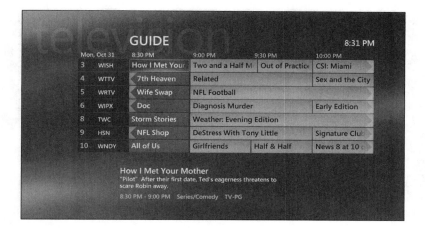

FIGURE 1.3

Using the electronic program guide to find and watch a television program on a Media Center PC.

(Once again, to be fair, it's worth mentioning that you don't have to buy a living room PC to get an EPG. If you're receiving your TV programming via a set-top cable box or satellite receiver, you already know the joys of electronic program guides. But few standalone TV sets come with built-in EPGs; you need an external box of some sort.)

Digital Video Recorder

You've heard all about TiVo. Maybe you've even checked out those digital video recorders (*DVRs*) offered by your cable or satellite company. You know how all those devices work? They use an EPG to help you select what you want to record, and then they record selected programs to a hard disk drive. That's right, the same type of hard disk contained within every personal computer. In fact, a TiVo or other DVR is really just a computer without a lot of extras—just a program guide, some sort of simple interface, and a hard disk.

If TiVo is just a simplified PC, why not use a real PC for the same tasks? That's the beauty of the living room PC; it provides TiVo-like DVR functionality, as you can see in Figure 1.4, but without TiVo's monthly fees—and with some interesting additional features.

> **note** TiVo is just one brand of digital video recorder. All DVRs offer similar recording and playback features; the important differences are hard disk size and the ease of use of the electronic program guide.

First, the fees. There aren't any. TiVo charges $10 or so a month for the use of its EPG. The EPG you get with a Media Center PC is free—and it's just as accurate and detailed as the TiVo guide. In my book, free is better than $10/month. But maybe that's just me.

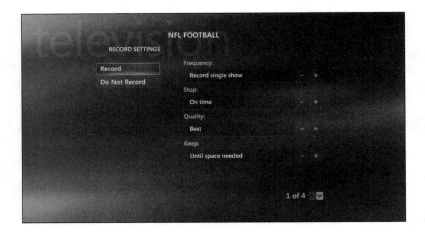

FIGURE 1.4

Getting ready to record a television program with a Media Center PC.

Next, consider the size of the hard disk. The hard disks in most TiVo and similar cable/satellite set-top boxes offer around 80–100GB of storage space. You might think 100GB is a lot of storage, and it is—if you're storing Word or Excel files. Digital video, however, is a lot more space intensive; an hour of standard definition video uses a little over 3GB of disc space (at the best possible picture quality), whereas the same hour of a high-definition program uses a whopping 10GB. Record an entire season of *Lost* or *Desperate Housewives* and you'll find that a 100GB hard disk fills up pretty fast.

Personal computers, however, offer lots of hard disk space for little additional cost. Fill up one hard disk and you can trade up to a larger one (or add an external auxiliary disk) for just pennies per gigabyte. It's not unusual to find Media Center PCs with 400GB, 500GB, even 1,000GB (that's called a *terabyte*) of available storage space. The more you record, the more you'll like the storage options of a personal computer.

Then there's the issue of creating a removable, portable, archival copy of the programs you record. I'm talking about burning your recorded television programs to DVD, which most TiVo and cable/satellite boxes don't let you do. You can, however, do this with a personal PC, where burning the occasional DVD is just part and parcel of the whole computing experience.

In other words, a living room PC is like TiVo on steroids. (That's another checkmark in the PC's plus column.)

note Learn more about using a Media Center PC as a DVR in Chapter 3, "Media Center System #2: The Digital Video Recorder."

Digital Audio Jukebox

So far we've concerned ourselves primarily with the PC's video-related functions. But a PC can also store and play back all manner of digital audio, as you're no doubt aware. Whether you're downloading music from the Internet or ripping songs from your favorite CDs, a PC's hard disk can store all your music in digital audio files. After the music is stored, you can use your PC as a digital audio jukebox, playing any and all songs from your collection in any order you want—one album after another, all the songs by a particular artist, in predetermined playlists, or just randomly.

In short, having a Media Center PC is like having a giant iPod in your living room, as you can see in Figure 1.5. The only difference is that the music stored on your PC can be of much higher quality that what is stored on an iPod or similar portable music player; choose the right digital audio format and the songs on your hard disk will sound identical to the original CDs. Which is what you want when you're listening to your music collection over a quality audio system.

FIGURE 1.5

Playing digital music on a Media Center PC.

Of course, the music on your living room PC isn't limited to what you download off the Internet or copy from your CD collection. You can also use your living room PC to listen to all manner of Internet radio stations, streaming audio, podcasts, you name it. If it's online, your PC can grab it—and play it back.

All of which are operations that traditional audio components simply can't do. It doesn't matter how expensive your CD player and audio/video receiver, they can't store music digitally, and they can't access the Internet to find even more music. Nor

note Learn more about using a Media Center PC as a digital audio server in Chapter 2, "Media Center System #1: The Digital Audio Server."

can they, generally, connect to your iPod to transfer songs back and forth between the living room and the road. This audio functionality is a definite plus over traditional components, something new and exciting to add to your home entertainment system.

Big-Screen Photo Slideshow

Here's something else you've probably never been able to do on your existing home entertainment system—view your digital photos. That's right, a Media Center PC lets you view your digital photos on your big-screen TV, as you can see in Figure 1.6, either one at a time or in a constantly-changing slideshow. High-resolution digital photography looks really sharp on a 50" or 60" screen, and it's a great way to show off your holiday photos to friends and family.

note Learn more about using a Media Center PC to create photo slideshows in Chapter 12, "Using Windows XP MCE for Digital Photos."

FIGURE 1.6

Viewing your digital photos on a Media Center PC.

Whole House Entertainment

If you're at all familiar with computers, you're also familiar with computer networks, whether it's the large corporate network or the small home network. The capability of computers to network together to share data and programs makes for some interesting possibilities *vis-à-vis* the living room PC.

note A Media Center Extender is a special device designed to connect to a computer network, access a Media Center PC connected to your network, and then connect to a television display and audio system for playback. Most Extenders not only connect to a main PC, but can also control media operation of that PC.

First of all, the living room PC doesn't actually have to be a PC. That is, you can store all your digital audio and video files on a desktop PC equipped with Windows XP Media Center Edition, and use a Media Center Extender, connected to your main PC via a home network, to take the place of the living room PC. Or you still use a living room PC, but put

note Learn more about using a Media Center PC to set up a whole house entertainment system in Chapter 4, "Media Center System #3: The Whole House Entertainment System."

Media Center Extenders in other rooms throughout your house, thus sharing the data stored on that main PC. And your living room PC can connect to your home network to play back files stored on any PC in your house. The possibilities are virtually endless.

Or Any Combination of the Above

Okay, so now you know that a living room PC can replace a DVD player, or a CD changer, or a TiVo box. But what's key is that the PC can replace not just one, but *all* of these devices—while adding new functionality to your system. So, if you have a living room PC, you can throw away your standalone CD/DVD player, CD changer, and DVR. That's one device in the place of three, which explains part of the appeal.

The rest of the appeal comes from those additional functionalities that a living room PC offers—digital audio jukebox, Internet radio tuner, digital photo slideshow, whole house entertainment, and so on. All of a sudden that $2,000 PC starts to look like a pretty good deal, all things considered. (And that's not even considering the convenience of having just one component in your system, instead of two or three.)

Why a Living Room PC Is Different from a Desktop PC

All that said, you can't just take a standard-issue desktop PC and plunk it down in the middle of your living room. A proper living room PC—what we'll officially call a *Media Center PC*—offers a combination of features, functionality, and form factor that is subtly different from that found on a traditional desktop PC.

It's Not for Writing Memos or Crunching Numbers...

First, you have to recognize that how you use your Media Center PC will be quite different from how you use your desktop PC. A desktop PC is perfect for typical office work; a living room PC is more of a home entertainment device. Although you can perform office tasks on a Media Center PC (and use a desktop PC for home entertainment purposes), each type of PC is purpose-built for different purposes.

If you're not sure what I mean by that, here's a list of tasks that are common on a desktop PC but you probably *won't* be doing on a living room model:

- Letter and memo writing in Microsoft Word
- Number crunching in Microsoft Excel
- Developing presentations in Microsoft PowerPoint
- Balancing your checkbook in Quicken or Microsoft Money
- Sending and receiving email in Microsoft Outlook or Outlook Express
- Surfing the Web in Internet Explorer

And so on. All these tasks are better done when you're sitting at a desk, with your computer keyboard, mouse, and monitor all at arm's length.

...But It *Is* for Listening/Viewing Home Entertainment

What a living room PC *is* good for is something else entirely. A Media Center PC is designed to connect to a big-screen television display and a home audio system—in other words, to be part of a complete home theater system. Here are the most common Media Center PC operations:

- Listening to music CDs
- Viewing movie DVDs
- Recording and viewing television programming
- Listening to digital audio files
- Viewing digital photographs

As you no doubt notice, most of these activities are better suited for a big room, rather than a small office. Hence the design of the Media Center PC to fit in with a traditional home entertainment system. The living room PC is less a personal computer than it is a home entertainment device.

The Ten-Foot Interface

Operating a computer in your living is a much different experience than operating a computer in your office. In your office, you're sitting 10 inches away from the computer screen; everything you see is small and compact yet still visible from the 10-inch level. In your living room, you're sitting 10 *feet* away from the television screen; all the onscreen icons and buttons need to be big enough to be seen from the extended distance. It's the difference between a 10-inch interface (shown in Figure 1.7) and a 10-foot interface (shown in Figure 1.8).

FIGURE 1.7

The traditional Windows interface is just fine for using at a 10-inch distance, but too small and cluttered to watch from 10 feet.

FIGURE 1.8

Windows Media Center Edition offers a true 10-foot interface; it's designed to be used from across a living room.

Remote Control Operation

The other big difference between a desktop and living room PC is how you operate it. You're accustomed to using a keyboard and mouse in your office, but both of those peripherals seem out of place in a typical living room environment. In your living room, you're used to using a remote control unit—just point it at the screen and click.

To this end, the living room PC has to be remote control operable. That 10-foot interface has to include big buttons and controls that you can operate with a click of the remote control, like the one shown in Figure 1.9. No fiddling about with diminutive buttons and sliders; in the living room, big is beautiful—and necessary. And forget about typing; anything you select on screen has to be done with a simple remote control, not a keyboard or mouse.

FIGURE 1.9

A typical Media Center remote control unit.

Silence Is Golden

The typical office environment is anything but quiet. You might be so inured to the sound that you don't even notice it, but trust me, it's there; noisy coffee machines, water coolers, copiers, and the like, augmented by ringing phones and chattering office workers. Even if you work in a home office, there's plenty of noise to go around.

Unfortunately, part of the overall office noise is the noise of your computer. Almost all desktop computers utilize one or more large fans, designed to keep the insides cool. Those fans are constantly whirring, generating a background of white noise. You get used to it, but it's there.

The sort of noise you tolerate in an office environment is completely intolerable in your living room—especially when you're trying to listen to music or watch a movie. That whirring computer fan becomes a big distraction very fast. How can you concentrate on the quiet passages when your computer is humming away in the corner?

This is why many home theater PCs are *silent* PCs. Manufacturers go to some lengths to reduce the noise levels of their living room PCs, by using quieter, slower-moving fans; surrounding the fans and hard drives with insulating materials; or removing the fans completely and going with water cooling or a heat-dissipating cabinet design instead. This quiet factor is one of the biggest differences between a typical desktop PC and one designed specifically for living room use.

Form Matters

You have to ask yourself the question, Do you really want to stick that ugly desktop PC in the middle of your living room? Does the typical beige-box computer fit in, style-wise, with your other audio and video components?

Of course not, which is why you don't want to stick your existing desktop PC in your component rack. Most home theater PCs are designed to look like traditional audio/video components. That means a horizontal design instead of the typical vertical tower, and black cases and faceplates instead of beige or white ones. Let's face it, you really don't want people to notice that you have a PC in your living room; you want your PC to fit in with your other components, as much as possible.

A/V Connections

Fitting in with your other components also means interfacing with them. The PC in your living room has to connect to your television display (instead of a small computer monitor) and to your audio/video receiver (instead of a pair of small desktop speakers). To do this, a home theater PC must have a full complement of audio/video connections in the back—component video, S-Video, digital audio, and the like. Most desktop PCs are not properly equipped to connect to traditional consumer electronics equipment; you need a PC specially designed for home theater hookup.

Controlling the Living Room PC—With Windows XP Media Center Edition

The other thing that most (but not all) living room PCs have in common is that they run Windows XP Media Center Edition. Media Center Edition is an interface that runs on top of the Windows XP operating system; it's designed as a 10-foot interface for use in the living room environment.

Media Center Edition is just one of many different interfaces available for home theater PCs; other companies offer similar 10-foot interfaces, some of which have particularly vocal adherents. But offered

note Windows XP Media Center Edition is a rather long moniker. (You'd think Microsoft's marketing department would be a little more name-savvy, wouldn't you?) This is why you sometimes see it referred to as *Windows Media Center*, or *Media Center*, or *Media Center Edition*, or just *MCE*.

as it is by Microsoft as an adjunct to Windows XP, Media Center Edition has become, far and away, the most popular interface for living room PCs. If Microsoft is behind it, it's bound to be heavily adopted. And, in the case of Media Center Edition, its popularity is well earned.

The Media Center interface lets you perform most common home entertainment operations with the click of a button on the included remote control unit. It's not designed for desktop applications; there's no built-in web browser, or word processor, or email client. If you want to do office work, shut down the Media Center interface and revert to plain old Windows. But if you want to listen to music, watch DVDs, or record television programs, Media Center is the perfect interface. It's simple, it's intuitive, it's easy to read from across the room; it's a computer interface that doesn't look like a computer

note Learn more about how Media Center Edition works in Chapter 8, "Getting to Know Windows XP Media Center Edition."

interface. And you don't need to take a training course to learn how to use it. It's easy enough to use that your parents (or grandparents!) can probably figure it out.

That doesn't mean that Media Center Edition is limited in functionality. There's quite a lot of fancy stuff you can do from the comfort of your couch, even if you have to hunt around for some of it. (And, to be honest, there are some things that *aren't* easy to do from within Media Center; there are even some things you have to revert back to Windows to do.)

Alternatives to a Living Room PC

All this functionality sounds great, but what if you really, truly, don't want a personal computer in your living room?

Several manufacturers make what they call *digital media servers*, which offer some of the same functionality as Media Center PCs. The typical digital media server contains a hard disk drive and a CD or CD/DVD drive, and connects to a home theater system in the same way that a living room PC does. Some digital media servers specialize in storing and playing digital audio; others also function as digital video recorders.

How, then, is a digital media server different from a Media Center PC? The answer is: not much. In fact, most digital media servers are personal computers in disguise; open up the box and you'll find random access memory, a hard disk drive, an Intel microprocessor, and all the other piece in parts you'd find in any other PC. The difference is that these boxes tend to use proprietary onscreen interfaces, and focus solely on audio/video functionality.

For example, the Escient FireBall Movie Manager, shown in Figure 1.10, can be used to store digital music, and to play back DVDs stored on connected DVD changers—but you can't use it to display digital photos, or instant message other computer users over the Internet, or write letters or memos in a word processor. It's strictly an audio/video entertainment device; it has no other functionality. And, as you can see, it uses a proprietary onscreen interface designed by Escient, not a universal interface that all users will be familiar with.

FIGURE 1.10

The Escient FireBall digital media server.

If a proprietary digital media server is just a home theater PC in a closed box, why would you go that route over a more fully-featured Media Center PC? There are a few reasons, although I'm not sure they're completely valid.

First, some custom home theater installers prefer working with proprietary systems that are supported by a company that they're used to working with. For these installers, a dedicated digital media server offers fewer surprises than does a Media Center PC. (And maybe a bigger profit, too; most digital media servers are on the pricey side.)

Second, some consumers just don't want a PC in their living room. Never mind that a digital media server is a PC in all but name only, it still isn't a PC. The closed nature of a media server means you don't have to worry about the security and reliability issues that you sometimes have with Microsoft's Windows operating system; because you can't install other software on the media server, there are no upgrade and compatibility issues, either.

Those issues aside, in my opinion you get a lot more bang for your buck with a Media Center PC than you do with a dedicated digital media server. A Media Center PC does everything a digital media server does—and a lot more.

But don't take my word for it. In the next few chapters we'll examine different types of Media Center systems, each focused on a specific audio/video task. It all starts in Chapter 2, where we look at "Media Center System #1: The Digital Audio Server."

2

Media Center System #1: The Digital Audio Server

As you learned in the previous chapter, there are many uses for a Media Center PC. Some people use their Media Center PCs solely to listen to music; others, to record television programs; still others, to share music and movies in other rooms throughout the house. What type of digital home entertainment system you need depends on how you intend to use it.

Of course, a Media Center PC isn't limited to a single purpose; this versatility is one of the reasons to go with a PC instead of a dedicated digital media server. But different uses have different requirements, so over the course of the next few chapters we're going to look at these uses separately. This chapter, then, focuses on using a Media Center PC primarily as an audio component; Chapter 3, "Media Center System #2: The Digital Video Recorder," focuses on video-related uses; and Chapter 4, "Media Center System #3: The Whole House Entertainment System," focuses on multiroom operation. If you want to use your PC for multiple uses, combine the advice given in these separate chapters.

In this chapter, then, we'll discuss just what you need to do to use a Media Center PC as a digital audio server. I can tell you from experience that it's great to have a big ol' digital jukebox in your living room—and it's all made possible by a properly tricked-out Media Center PC, running Windows XP Media Center Edition.

The Goal: Listening to Your Music Collection, Digitally

The goal for our digital audio system is simple. We want to store all the music we own on a Media Center PC so that we can listen to it at any time, in any order. It doesn't matter whether our music is on CD or in a digital audio file, we want our Media Center PC to facilitate access to that music. And, of course, we want the best sound quality available; none of this compressed MP3 file nonsense.

That's it in a nutshell. But before we proceed, let's take a closer look at each of the individual things we want this system to do.

note Learn more about using Media Center to store and play digital music in Chapter 9, "Using Windows XP MCE for Audio Storage and Playback."

Playing CDs

If you're a typical music lover, you have the bulk of your music collection on compact discs. That means, first and foremost, you need your Media Center PC to be able to play back all your CDs. Achieve this goal and you can remove your current CD player from your home entertainment system; the Media Center PC will function as your system's CD player.

Standard Audio CDs

Playing a CD on a Media Center PC is one of the easiest operations. All you have to do is insert the CD into your PC's CD drive, and playback starts automatically. As you can see in Figure 2.1, the CD cover appears onscreen, along with the track list. If you don't do anything, the CD plays from start to finish. You can also choose to play individual tracks, to shuffle through the tracks in random order, or to copy the CD to your PC's hard disk.

note The display of the CD's cover art depends on you having a live connection to the Internet—and on your Media Center PC sharing that connection. When a CD is inserted, Media Center connects to an online database and retrieves both the album art and the track information.

SACD and DVD-Audio Discs

Although Media Center is great for playing regular audio CDs, most Media Center PCs can't play back audio discs recorded in the higher-quality SACD or DVD-Audio formats. That's both a drawback of the system and a function of digital rights management technology.

Not only are SACD and DVD-Audio discs recorded in a different format than standard CDs, these discs are also encoded in such a way that the digital audio is protected from copying. To do that, the digital audio signals are pretty much placed off-limits, which really gums up the works when you're dealing with an all-digital music reproduction system, as you have in a Media Center PC.

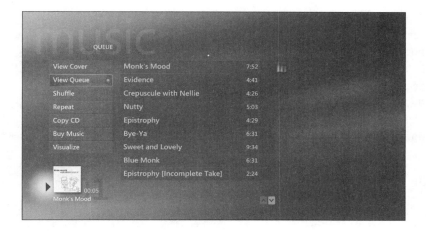

FIGURE 2.1

Playing a CD in Windows Media Center—the cover art and track listing are displayed.

As an example of this, note the back-panel connections of a typical SACD or DVD–Audio player; there are no optical or coaxial digital connections, only six separate analog connections (for 5.1-channel surround sound). The powers that be assume that if you had access to the digital data stream you'd make a bit-perfect copy of the disc, hence they block any access to the digital data stream. Because a Media Center PC needs access to that digital data stream (and could, then, be used to copy the digital data to the PC's hard disk), SACD/DVD–Audio playback is a no-no.

There are currently no Media Center PCs on the market that offer SACD playback. Only one audio card on the market, the Sound Blaster Audigy Z 2S, offers DVD–Audio playback. So unless your Media Center PC features the Audigy Z 2S audio card (with the corresponding six analog channel outputs), you'll have to limit your playback (and ripping, as discussed next) to standard audio CDs.

Ripping and Storing Your CDs in a Digital Library

Listening to CDs is just the first step in creating a digital audio system. If you have hundreds (or thousands) of CDs in your collection, you know what a pain it is to store all those discs, and then pick out the CD you want to hear, insert it into the CD player, and then skip to a specific track. A better solution is to digitize all your CDs so that you're dealing with digital versions of your CDs, instead of the physical discs themselves.

In this system, every CD in your collection is ripped to the Media Center PC's hard drive. The music on the physical disc is converted into digital audio files, which can then be played back from the Windows Media Center interface. When all your music is stored digitally, it's a lot easier to select a given album or song to listen to; moving from track to track, or from CD to CD, is almost instantaneous. Plus, of course, you no longer have to store all those old CDs out in the open.

The ripping process is surprisingly easy. We'll discuss it further in Chapter 9, but in essence all you have to do is insert the CD you want to rip into your PC's CD drive, and then choose Copy Music from the available options. As you can see in Figure 2.2, each track is copied to your hard disk as a separate audio file; cover art is also stored for each CD you download. When the entire CD is copied, your PC ejects the disc from the drive.

tip
After I ripped all my CDs to my Media Center PC, I stored the original CDs in boxes in my garage. This enabled me to remove the large CD storage cabinets I had been using, which freed up significant floor space in my living room. I kept the original CDs as back up for my newly digital collection; if anything ever happens to my PC or hard disk, I still have the original CDs to work with.

FIGURE 2.2

Copying a CD to a PC's hard disk.

Ripping Takes Time

When you rip your CDs to a PC's hard disk, there are a few issues you'll have to deal with. First, there's the time involved. It takes about 3–4 minutes to rip an entire CD to hard disk; that doesn't take into account the time it takes to locate the CD, remove the disc from the jewel case, insert the disc into your computer's CD drive, and afterward remove the CD from the computer, reinsert the disc into the jewel case, and return the CD to storage. If we say the whole process takes 5 minutes per disc, that's 500 minutes, or almost 8 1/2 hours, to rip 100 discs. If you have 500 CDs, we're talking close to 42 hours; if you have 1,000 discs, that's 85 hours or so. With this in mind, assume that you won't do your ripping in one marathon session. (For what it's worth, I ripped my 1,000-CD collection in bits and pieces over a period of six weeks.)

There are companies that will do your CD ripping for you. For example, MusicShifter charges about a buck a disc to rip your CDs to either an external hard drive or to multiple DVD data discs (which can then be copied to your PC's hard disk). The way it works is you box up your entire CD collection and ship it to the company; a week or so later you get your CDs back, along with the hard disc or DVDs to which they were ripped. This type of service, however, is only for those who won't get nervous shipping their entire music collection cross-country. (You can learn more about the MusicShifter service, shown in Figure 2.3, at www.musicshifter.com.)

FIGURE 2.3

Let MusicShifter rip your CD collection for you—for a buck a disc.

Ripping Takes Space

Another important consideration is hard disk space. The more CDs you have, the more hard disk space it takes to store them in digital format. Also a factor is the quality level of the digital files; the higher the quality, the larger the resulting audio files.

Let's look at audio quality first. When you rip CDs in Windows Media Center, you're actually using Windows Media Player (WMP) to do the ripping, in the background. WMP can copy files to a number of different file formats, and by default uses Microsoft's Windows Media Audio (WMA) format. WMA is an okay format, similar in many ways to the industry-standard MP3 format. What WMA and MP3 have in common is that they compress the original music to save file space; the sound quality is lowered to create smaller files.

Now, if you're listening to ripped music on a portable audio player, you probably won't notice the compressed sound quality. But when you're listening to music on a quality home audio system, you'll definitely notice the compromised audio in WMA and MP3 files. Listening to an WMA file on a quality audio system is like watching a VHS video-tape on a high-definition TV set; all the flaws inherent in the format are magnified. On a good audio system, WMA and MP3 files sound tinny, with a noticeable lack of high and low frequencies, and without a lot of "punch." If you do an A–B comparison between the original CD and the ripped WMA or MP3 file, you can easily tell the difference.

All of this is a prelude to advising that you don't copy your CDs to WMA-format files. Instead, you should use the WMA Lossless file format. WMA Lossless uses lossless compression to reduce the original file size just a smidgeon, but doesn't remove any important information from the music file. The result is a file that's about half the size of what it was on the original CD, but with sound quality identical to the original.

note Turn to Chapter 9 to learn how to configure Windows Media Player to rip CDs to WMA Lossless format.

Here's the upshot of all the technical stuff. When you rip your CDs to WMA Lossless for-mat, the resulting files take up around 300MB of hard disk space. That means if you rip 100 CDs, you'll need 30GB of hard disk space to store the digital audio files. If you have 500 CDs, you'll need 150GB of hard disk space; 1,000 CDs will take up 300GB.

Thus you'll need to purchase a Media Center PC that has a big enough hard disk to store all your CDs in digital format. And remember, you have more than just digital music files to worry about; the Windows operating system itself (along with the Media Center inter-face) takes up space, as do any other programs you have installed. Factor at least 50GB for operating system/program files, more if you have a lot of other programs on your system.

My recommendation? If you have 250 CDs, go with a 160GB hard drive. If you have 500 CDs, go with a 250GB drive. If you have 1,000 CDs, go with a 400GB drive. This way you'll have some hard disk space left over for all those new CDs you buy.

Downloading Digital Music from the Internet

In this modern world, not all the music you listen to is purchased on physical media. If you're a music lover, chances are you download a fair amount of music from the Internet, either via commercial online music services or via peer-to-peer file trading networks. If you have a Media Center PC connected to your home audio system, you can now listen to all your downloaded music over your main system—assuming that you have your Media Center PC connected to the Internet, of course.

If you plan on downloading digital music to your Media Center PC, there are a few points to keep in mind.

First, the file format offered by the download service is critical. Windows Media Center can play back files encoded in the MP3, WMA, WMA Lossless, and WAV formats. Media Center will not play back files encoded in the AAC format—which happens to be the file format used by Apple's iTunes Music Store.

note The notable exception to this non-AAC playback is HP's line of Media Center PCs. These PCs come with a Media Center application called HP Tunes that enables you to access your entire iTunes library. At this time, only HP offers this cross-platform compatibility.

What does this mean? Well, if you're downloading from a file-sharing network, you're probably okay because those files are typically encoded in MP3 format. You're also okay if you're using Napster or similar online music services because these services tend to encode their files in WMA format. But if you're an iTunes subscriber, you're out of luck—the files you download from iTunes cannot be played in Windows Media Center. (Not without a fair amount of high-tech tinkering, anyway; more on this in Chapter 9.) So, feel free to sign up to Napster and its ilk, but skip iTunes and anything Apple; instead, look for a service that displays Microsoft's PlaysForSure logo, which ensures WMA compatibility.

caution Apple's iPod is also a sore point because the iPod can play AAC and MP3 files, but not WMA files. So, your iPod will be most incompatible with your Media Center PC. (Competing portable audio players don't have this problem because almost all non-Apple players play WMA-format files.)

Downloaded digital audio files are stored in Windows Media Center the same as those files you rip from CD. The bigger issue, however, is sound quality. As noted previously, WMA and MP3 files are compressed, which means they've had some of the music sucked out to reduce file size. Depending on the amount of compression, the quality of your home audio system, and how golden your ears are, these files will sound anywhere from subtly different to totally unlistenable when played on your Media Center system.

Let's put it this way. If you have a $500 audio system (speakers included), you probably won't mind listening to WMA and MP3 files in this fashion. But if you have a $5,000 (or higher) audio system, why in the world would you want to listen to inferior-quality WMA/MP3-quality music over it? I'm a bit of an audiophile, and would *never* listen to compressed music on my system. But I know lots of other folks who are less picky than I am, who don't mind the slight degradation in sound quality. Ultimately, it's your ears that have to live with whatever choice you make. But don't automatically assume that all the digital music you download is suitable for playback on your home audio system—because it isn't.

Listening to Internet Radio

Assuming that your Media Center PC is connected to a broadband Internet connection, there's another source of music available to you: the thousands of available Internet radio stations. Windows Media Center includes a Radio application for listening to

Internet radio; as you can see in Figure 2.4, you can choose from any of the stations listed in the built-in application, or go directly to any Internet radio website to listen from there.

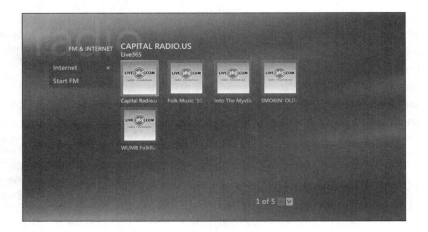

FIGURE 2.4

Listening to Internet radio in Windows Media Center.

Internet radio is another of those "good news/bad news" applications. The good news is that you can find stations playing just about every type of music imaginable, from all around the world. (There's even an application to listen to XM satellite radio in Media Center, as shown in Figure 2.5—assuming that you're a paid subscriber, that is.) The bad news is that audio quality is variable—probably not as good as listening to a CD.

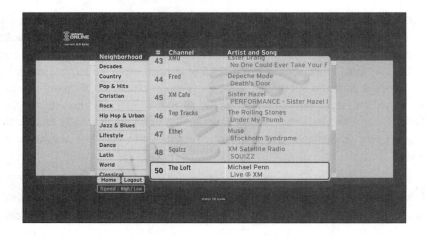

FIGURE 2.5

Listening to XM Radio Online in Windows Media Center.

The substandard audio quality comes from the fact that, like MP3 files, Internet radio is encoded in a compressed format. Compressed audio means a more limited frequency range, which means that it sounds a tad tinny, especially over a quality audio system. In addition, Internet radio relies on a constant (and constantly fast) Internet connection. If your connection is slow or prone to interruptions, you'll hear it as stuttering or stopped audio. And this applies to the entire audio path, from the initiating website to your PC; interruptions anywhere along the line will affect your listening pleasure.

All that said, it's kind of cool to listen to Internet radio in your living room. It's certainly a good thing to have more programming choices available—most of them for free.

Listening to FM Radio

In addition to Internet radio, some (but not all) Media Center PCs come with built-in FM tuners. If your PC is so equipped, you can use Media Center's Radio function to listen to local FM radio stations, as shown in Figure 2.6. Again, the more music programming, the merrier.

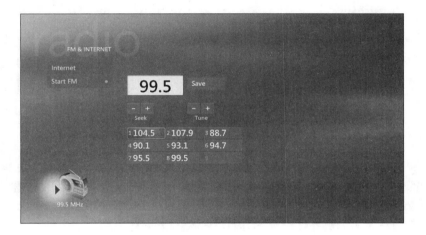

FIGURE 2.6

Listening to FM radio in Windows Media Center.

Burning Your Own Custom CDs

When you have your entire music collection stored in digital format on your Media Center PC, you have lots of options available to you. You can listen to your music one CD at a time. You can listen to all the music recorded by a specific performer. You can listen to all the songs in your collection of a particular genre, such as country or R&B. You can listen to playlists of songs that you create. You can even shuffle randomly through all the songs in your entire collection, which is really cool.

And, of course, you can burn any of the songs in your collection to CD. When all your music is digital, it's relatively easy to assemble a playlist of your favorite songs, and then burn those songs to a custom music CD, as shown in Figure 2.7. It's certainly easier to assemble a multiartist CD like this than it was when all your music was on physical CDs, which required a lot of inserting and removing of discs during the process. With your music all digital (and all in one place), all you have to do is point and click to the songs you want to copy, and then burn the selected songs to CD, using your Media Center PC's CD burner drive.

FIGURE 2.7

Burning a playlist of songs to CD in Windows Media Center.

We'll discuss this CD-burning function in more detail in Chapter 9; suffice to say, it's a lot more convenient to burn your CDs in your living room than it is from a desktop PC.

The Plan: Configuring Your System

Now that you have an idea of what your want your digital audio system to do, how do you assemble a system that can do it all? Well, it's all a matter of choosing the right Media Center PC, connecting it to your home audio system, and then supplementing your system with any necessary third-party software. Read on to learn more.

Choosing the Right Media Center PC

The first step in planning your system is to choose the right Media Center PC for audio use. Choose wrong and you won't have enough hard disk space for all your digital music, or you might not be satisfied with the resulting sound. Choose right and everything comes together like clockwork.

When choosing a Media Center PC for audio use, you'll want one that meets the following minimum specifications detailed in Table 2.1.

TABLE 2.1   Media Center PC/Digital Audio Server Specifications

Component	Recommended Minimum Specification
Microprocessor	Intel Celeron or Pentium 4 running at 2.4GHz
Memory	512GB
Hard disk drive	160GB (stores 250 CDs) or 250GB (stores 500 CDs) or 400GB (stores 1,000 CDs)
Optical drive	CD burner (CD+R, CD-R)
Audio output connections	Analog audio (R/L RCA jacks) or Digital audio (optical or coaxial)
Video output connections	S-Video
Networking	802.11g Wi-Fi (wireless) or ethernet (wired)
Optional components	FM radio tuner
Optional peripherals	External hard disk

Let's examine each of these specifications separately.

Microprocessor

For an audio-based Media Center PC, the microprocessor is the least important part of the equation. That's because you really don't need a powerful microprocessor to play back digital audio files. In this instance, you can go with the least expensive microprocessor available, if that's your wont. (You'll need a more powerful processor if you're viewing and recording television programming because processing video is more demanding than processing audio.) That said, a faster processor is able to rip audio files from CDs quicker than a slower processor, so if you have a lot of CDs to rip, you might want to go with a faster chip.

I like Intel chips for Media Center use because they support RAID arrays—useful if you have more than one hard disk drive. In addition, higher-end chips (starting with the Pentium 4 915) offer 7.1-channel High Definition Audio, which is desirable for high-quality audio playback.

Memory

For our purposes, random access memory (RAM) is slightly more important than microprocessor power, but not much. Playing audio files simply doesn't require massive amounts of memory. (Unlike video playback, which is a memory hog.) Although you could theoretically get by with 256MB, I recommend moving up to 512MB, which should provide plenty of headroom for your audio processing needs.

Hard Disk Drive

Now we come to something important. The size of the hard disk is critical in an audio system because digital audio files—especially those stored in lossless format—consume copious amounts of disk space. If you only have a moderate-sized CD collection (fewer than 250 discs), you can get by with a modest 160GB hard drive. But if you have 500 or so CDs, you should beef up your drive to a 250GB model, and if you have a 1,000-CD collection, go with the biggest hard drive you can find—400GB should do the job.

Naturally, your hard drive requirements get larger if you plan on doing more than storing digital audio files. If you're going to be recording television programming in addition to listening to music, double the necessary hard disk space.

Which leads us to an option that serious users should consider: using dual hard drives. If you put two hard drives in your machine, you can dedicate the first one to system files and television recording, and the second to digital audio files. My system has two 400GB drives, which lets me do just that; the second drive contains my entire digital music collection, and nothing but.

Also worth considering are the mega hard drives offered by LaCie (www.lacie.com) and similar companies. For example, LaCie's Bigger Disk Extreme drive (shown in Figure 2.8) offers up to 2 terabytes (TB) of storage, using multiple hard disks chained together in what is known as a *RAID array*. This might be a more effective way to provide storage for extra-large digital music collections—and provide space to grow.

> **note** RAID stands for *Redundant Array of Independent Disks*; a *RAID array* is a collection of multiple disk drives that work together as if they were a single drive.

Optical Drive

By optical drive, I mean CD drive. If all you plan on doing is playing music, you can go with a CD-only drive. But if you plan on burning the occasional music disc, you'll need a CD drive that both reads and writes—what is sometimes called a *CD burner*. Most CD burners can handle all three current recordable/writeable CD formats: CD-R, CD+R, and CD-RW. If you plan on playing your homegrown CDs on other CD players, you'll want to use either the CD-R or CD+R formats. Blank discs are readily available for either format.

Another way to go is with a combo CD/DVD drive. This is the preferred option if your entertainment needs encompass both audio and video. The key thing here is that a combo drive does everything a CD-only drive does, except it also plays back (and sometimes records) DVD discs. It's a slightly more expensive way to go, but the versatility might be worth it.

FIGURE 2.8

LaCie's Bigger Disk Extreme external hard drive provides up to 2TB of storage space.

Audio Output Connections

Your Media Center PC has to connect to your home audio/video system. As such, you need to make sure that the rear panel includes the appropriate connections.

Most important, of course, are the audio connections. At a bare minimum, you'll need right and left RCA audio output jacks. You'll connect a cable between these jacks and the right and left input jacks on your audio/video receiver. These connections are analog, and are pretty much industry standard.

Better quality sound, however, can be had from digital audio connections, of either the optical or coaxial type. These are single-cable connections that carry the audio signal in digital format to your audio/video receiver. In addition to higher quality sound in a single cable, optical and coaxial digital connections also carry the digital surround sound found on DVD movies; if your system is also going to be used for watching DVDs, a digital audio connection is necessary.

Note that we're talking about connecting your Media Center PC to a stereo or surround sound receiver, or perhaps to a separate preamplifier/processor unit (on high-end audio systems). You do not connect speakers directly to the PC; the speakers connect to your receiver, which is

note Optical and coaxial digital audio connections are almost identical in sound quality. Optical cables are a little better for longer connections, whereas coaxial cables are a little better for runs with sharp curves. Either cable is acceptable for most installations.

then connected to your Media Center PC. This is different from a typical desktop PC installation, where powered speakers are connected directly to the PC. Note the word *powered*; all speakers have to receive power from somewhere. In a desktop PC system, the powered speakers have their own built-in amplifiers. In a home audio system, the speakers' power comes from a separate amplifier or from the amplifier built into the audio/video receiver. That's why you won't find speaker outputs on the back of Media Center PCs designed for living room use.

Video Output Connections

The video output connection is less critical for an audio-based system than it is for a video-based one (like what we'll discuss in Chapter 3). For that reason, you can go with a lower-quality S-Video connection, as opposed to a higher-quality (and higher-priced) component video connection. All you'll be viewing onscreen will be track listings, album graphics, and the Windows Media Center interface itself—none of which needs high resolution reproduction.

If, on the other hand, you'll also be using your system to watch DVDs and television program, you should go with a component video connection (or better). You'll learn more about video connections in Chapter 3.

Networking

Networking capability is important on a Media Center PC primarily because you need to connect to the Internet. Because your Internet connection probably comes into a different room of your house, and is connected to your main desktop PC, you need to network your Media Center PC to that main PC (or to the Internet router) to connect.

There are two ways to connect to your home network. The most convenient, for most people, is a Wi-Fi wireless connection. Assuming that you'll be downloading your share of digital music files, go with the faster 802.11g Wi-Fi connection, either through a built-in Wi-Fi access point or an external one, connected to your PC via USB.

Alternately, and if the wiring isn't too much of an issue, you can connect your Media Center PC to your home network via ethernet. Most PCs come with a built-in ethernet connection; you can also add ethernet functionality via an external device, which connects to your PC via USB.

Optional Components

There's not a whole lot extra you need inside the case of your Media Center PC, although you might want to consider a unit that offers a built-in FM tuner. This will let you listen to local FM radio stations via Media Center; of course, you probably have an FM tuner in your audio/video receiver, so this might be a redundant function.

Optional Peripherals

As to external peripherals, the one you definitely want to consider is an external hard disk—for backup. When your entire music collection is stored digitally on your computer's hard drive, what do you do if that hard drive crashes? Short of kissing your entire music collection bye-bye, a good insurance policy is to back up your music collection every night on an external hard drive. These external drives are increasingly affordable and surprisingly easy to use; most connect to your PC via USB or FireWire and come with their own automatic backup software. In my system, I have a 400GB external drive that backs up my 400GB internal drive. If my PC fails, I can simply transfer the backup files from the external drive to a new PC and have my entire music library intact.

Other Considerations

For most audiophiles, the look of the Media Center PC is an important consideration. You don't want the PC to look out of place in your A/V component rack; for that reason, you probably want to go with a unit that mirrors traditional audio component design, in both size (17" wide × 4" high) and color.

Also important is the noise factor, especially when you're listening to softer music. The best audio system in the world will be rendered ineffective if your Media Center PC is whirring and humming off to the side. This is why it's important to look for a PC that offers quiet or totally silent operation. This is typically achieved by using a lower-speed cooling fan; by insulating the cooling fan; or by eliminating the cooling fan completely, instead using an alternative cooling scheme, such as water cooling or external heat sinks. Whenever possible, listen to the PC before you buy; there is a big difference in noise level among different models.

Other Audio/Video Components

Of course, a Media Center PC is only one component of a complete digital audio entertainment system. You probably have a system assembled already, but if you're starting from scratch, here's what you'll need:

- Media Center PC, as spec'd earlier in this chapter
- Audio receiver, audio/video receiver, or separate preamplifier and amplifier
- Speakers: two for strictly stereo listening, five plus a subwoofer for surround sound
- Television set (to display the Media Center interface)

The resulting system should like the one in Figure 2.9.

note Even though your system is for listening only, you still need a television screen to navigate the Media Center interface—and select what music you want to listen to.

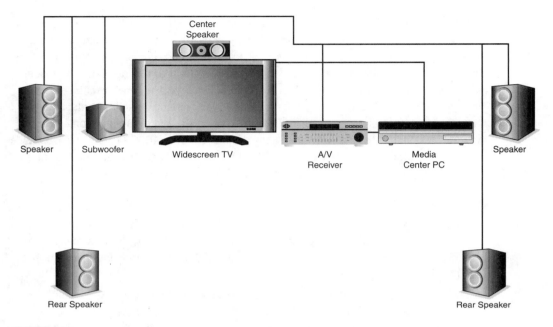

FIGURE 2.9

Connecting a Media Center PC to a home audio system.

What type of receiver you use depends on whether you're listening strictly to music, or whether your system also doubles as a home theater system for movie watching. If you're listening to music only, all you need is a stereo receiver. If you throw video into the mix, you'll want a surround sound audio/video receiver with at least five channels of amplification. You'll run the receiver in two-channel mode for music, of course, but you'll need the other channels when playing back surround sound DVDs.

Connecting Your System

After you purchase your new Media Center PC, you have to connect it to your home audio/video system. Although specific connections differ from system to system, here are the general connections to make:

- Connect the audio output(s) of the Media Center PC to a free audio input(s) on your receiver.

- Connect the video output of the Media Center PC to a free video input on your television display.

In other words, your Media Center PC should be connected the same way you'd connect a DVD player to your system.

As noted previously, you can use either R/L RCA audio connections or optical/coaxial digital audio connections. You can use either S-Video or component video connections (component is better, but not necessary); you should avoid using a single-cable composite video connection. Naturally, your

note Learn more about connecting your Media Center PC in Chapter 6, "Making the Connections."

stereo or surround sound receiver should then be connected to all the speakers in your system.

And that's that. You can learn more about operating the audio-specific functions of Media Center in Chapter 9, "Using Windows XP MCE for Audio Storage and Playback"; there's a lot Media Center can do, and a few tricks you need to learn, as well.

3

Media Center System #2: The Digital Video Recorder

In the last chapter we discussed a Media Center system designed primarily for audio-related uses. Media Center isn't limited to just audio, of course, and there are plenty of video-related activities that make a Media Center system worthwhile.

In this chapter, then, we'll discuss the various ways you might use a Media Center PC to watch various types of video—from DVDs to live television to recorded television. Then we'll look at what type of Media Center PC is best for these activities, and how it fits in with your existing home theater system.

The Goal: Watching and Recording Television and Movies

If you have a home theater system, big or small, you watch a lot of video programming. You watch movies on DVD, television programs via cable or satellite (maybe even a few in high definition), and recorded programming from a digital video recorder. The thing is, you can do all this—and a little more—from a Media Center PC, and save yourself a box or two in the component rack.

Watching DVD Movies

If your Media Center PC includes a DVD drive (and most do), you can throw out your current DVD player and replace it with the Media Center PC. As you can see in Figure 3.1, DVD playback from a Media Center PC is every bit as good as what you get from a typical $100–$200 standalone DVD player—and it only costs ten times as much! Okay, so you probably wouldn't add a Media Center PC to your system solely to replace a DVD player, but it's one more reason to make the Media Center PC worthwhile. And if you have a Media Center PC, you don't need to duplicate functionality with a separate DVD player. Buy a Media Center PC, throw out the DVD player.

Chapter 29 of 33: "That's My James!"
1 hour 50 minutes   11:50 PM

FIGURE 3.1

Playing a DVD movie on a Media Center PC.

Controlling a DVD Changer

Any PCs running Windows Media Center Edition with Update Rollup 2 installed can also control playback of separate DVD changers. Now we have something that you couldn't do before: utilize a 200-disc DVD changer and control it from your Media Center PC. When you connect a compatible DVD changer to your Media Center PC, the Play DVD function changes to a My DVDs function, as shown in Figure 3.2. All the DVDs in the changer appear on the My DVDs screen, complete with DVD artwork and information about the movie. Play any individual DVD by clicking on the DVD cover in My DVDs; your PC sends a signal to the DVD changer to select the appropriate disc and begin playback.

note Update Rollup 2 is a midstream update for Windows XP Media Center Edition. Most newer Media Center PCs come with Update Rollup 2 installed; if you have an older Media Center PC, Update Rollup 2 should be downloaded as part of Microsoft's Windows Update feature, or you can download it manually from Microsoft's website.

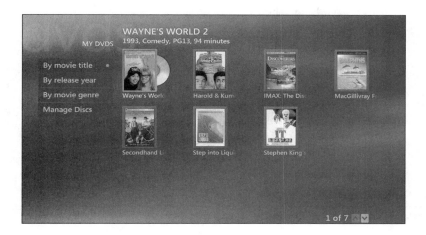

FIGURE 3.2

Controlling the contents of a DVD changer via the My DVDs screen in Windows Media Center.

The only hitch to this is that you can't hook up just any DVD changer to your Media Center PC; it has to be a special Media Center-capable changer. What makes this type of changer special is that it has a FireWire connection on the back—and that's all. No video outputs, no audio outputs, just that FireWire connector, which connects to a similar FireWire connector on your PC.

In this configuration, the changer is controlled exclusively by the PC. Control commands flow from the PC through the FireWire cable to the changer; audio/video signals flow from the changer through the FireWire cable to the PC, and then from the PC's outputs to your television display and A/V receiver.

Some companies, such as Niveus Media, sell these Media Center DVD changers separately. Niveus' Ice Vault 200 Disc Changer, shown in Figure 3.3, holds up to 200 DVDs or CDs, and sells for $2,499. What I really like about the Ice Vault is that you can daisy-chain multiple units together to handle extra-large DVD collections; if you have 1,000 discs, just connect five changers together. You can find more information at www.niveusmedia.com.

Other companies bundle the DVD changer with a compatible Media Center PC. For example, Sony's VAIO XL1 Digital Living System packages a 200GB Media Center PC (in a sleek horizontal living room form factor) with a 200-disc DVD/CD changer; the changer also features CD- and DVD-burning functionality, activated from Sony's proprietary My Changer menu in Media Center. The whole system costs $2,299.99; learn more at products.sel.sony.com/xl1/.

note Sony's Digital Living System is discussed in more detail in Chapter 5, "Building or Buying: Choosing the Right Media Center System for You."

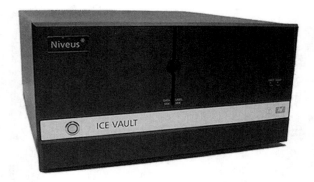

FIGURE 3.3

Niveus Media's Ice Vault 200 Disc Changer.

Adding a DVD changer to your Media Center system is a great way to manage medium-sized DVD collections. Just load all your DVDs into the changer, and use the Media Center PC to decide what movies you want to watch. Playback is via the Media Center interface.

Ripping DVDs to Your Hard Drive

Although it's nice to have all your DVDs handy in an attached DVD changer, why wouldn't you want to store your DVD collection digitally, as can with your CD collection? Well, this is something that's technically possible—although it takes a bit of technical wizardry to kludge together a solution.

First, it should be obvious that copying the digital contents of a DVD to your PC's hard drive is technically possible. Digital files are digital files, whether they're stored on a DVD, CD, or hard drive. But there's a problem in copying a DVD's files to another storage device—a little something called digital rights management, or DRM.

You can think of DRM as a complex copy protection scheme. When you try to copy a DVD to a hard drive, the DRM scheme prevents the copying from happening. It's more complex than that, but you know what the results are.

Fortunately, there are technological solutions to this technological problem. There are several programs available that let you bypass the DRM scheme to copy your DVD files directly to hard disk. When you use one of these programs to rip the contents of a DVD to your hard drive, that DVD now appears in the My Videos section of Windows Media Center, you can play that DVD as you would any other digital video file. It's not a particularly elegant solution (nor is it an officially endorsed one, or one that is strictly legal), but it is possible.

The bigger problem with storing your DVDs digitally is the sheer amount of disk space required. A typical dual-layer DVD contains up to 8.5GB of data;

note Learn more about playing back, ripping, and recording DVDs in Chapter 11, "Using Windows XP MCE for DVD Playback and Recording."

storing 100 DVDs requires 850GB of hard disk space. If you have a 200-disc collection, we're now talking about 1.7 *terabytes* of storage—much more than any current Media Center PC offers. (Unless, that is, you recompress your ripped DVDs to save disc space—which also sacrifices picture quality, of course.)

Of course, you could go with a really big external hard drive, such as one of LaCie's Biggest S2S five-disc, 2.5TB RAID tower, but that will set you back a cool $3,500—more expensive than all but the highest-priced Media Center PCs.

The bottom line is that until hard disk storage comes down in price (which it will), and until DVD-to-hard disk copying becomes officially supported (which it might—or might not), storing your DVDs digitally probably isn't a viable option for the average consumer. For techie videophiles, however....

Downloading Videos from the Internet

DVDs aren't the only nonbroadcast source of video programming. There are many sites on the Internet that let you download music videos, short-form programming, documentaries, and the like. (And I won't even talk about the illegal file swapping of television shows and the like over the Internet—although it's a pretty big deal, if you're into that sort of thing.) There are even several services provided within Windows Media Center, such as MTV Overdrive and TVTonic (shown in Figure 3.4), that provide various types of video programming for download to your Media Center PC. When you're searching for unique video programming, a Media Center PC (hooked up to a fast broadband Internet connection) is a major boon.

FIGURE 3.4

Watching news clips downloaded from the Internet via TVTonic.

Watching Videotaped Home Movies

You can also use your Media Center PC to watch home movies you've recorded with a video camcorder. Most camcorders feature a FireWire connection, as do most Media Center PCs. (On some Media Center PCs, the FireWire connection is on the front panel, typically behind a decorative door.) Just connect a FireWire cable between your camcorder and your PC, and you can watch the movies you've recorded. You can watch the movies in real time, or copy the movies from your camcorder to your PC's hard drive.

From there, you can play back the recorded videos at any time, or use a third-party movie-editing program (outside of Media Center) to edit your movies and apply transitions and special effects. After they're edited, you can use Media Center to copy your videos to DVD, to distribute to all your friends and family.

note A PC television tuner receives broadcast television signals. It can also receive analog cable signals, but if you have digital cable, you'll still need to use the cable company's set-top box. The same with satellite broadcasts, which are all digital; the satellite tuner box is still necessary. You can, however, connect the output from a cable or satellite box to the PC's TV tuner, but then you're faced with controlling the set top box via an infrared transmitter "bug," which is less than ideal.

Watching Live Television

Many (but not all) Media Center PCs come with one or more television tuners built-in. A TV tuner in a Media Center PC lets you watch local television broadcasts via the Media Center interface, as shown in Figure 3.5.

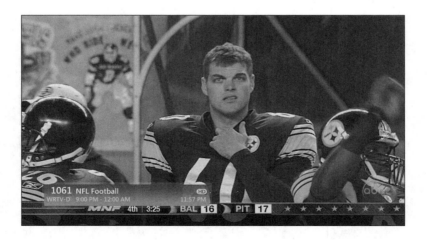

FIGURE 3.5

Watching TV on a Media Center PC.

Given that virtually all television sets in use today come with a built-in tuner, why would you want or need to use the tuner in a Media Center PC to watch television? Well, you wouldn't. Except that the tuner in the Media Center PC utilizes an electronic program guide, like the one in Figure 3.6, which displays the programming schedule for all available stations up to 14 days in advance. That alone might be a good reason to watch TV via your Media Center PC; your regular TV doesn't have a built-in program guide. (Although, to be fair, your cable or satellite set-top box probably does.)

> **note** Learn more about using Media Center for watching and recording TV in Chapter 10, "Using Windows XP MCE for Television Viewing and Recording."

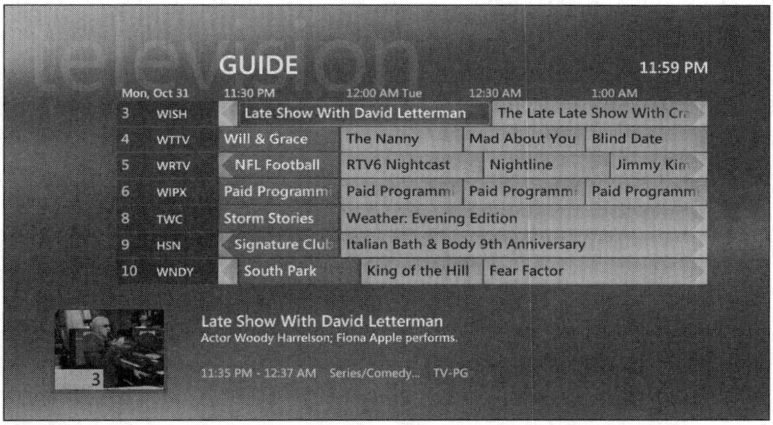

FIGURE 3.6

Viewing programming schedules with Media Center's electronic program guide.

An even better reason to use your Media Center PC to watch TV is that it centralizes *all* your TV viewing—not just TV broadcasts, but also DVD viewing and the viewing of recorded programs. Why switch from box to box when you can settle on a single box and a single interface for all your viewing?

Watching High-Definition Television

Here's another reason to watch TV on your Media Center PC. Some high-end Media Center PCs include tuners for both standard-definition and high-definition broadcasts. That's right, you can watch HDTV programming on a Media Center PC so equipped. If your television doesn't have its own built-in HDTV tuner, use the one in your HDTV-capable Media Center PC, instead.

> **note** A standard-definition TV tuner is called an *NTSC* tuner. A high-definition TV tuner is called an *ATSC* tuner. (And if you're reading this book in Europe or Asia, your TV tuner isn't NTSC or ATSC, it uses the *PAL* standard.)

Recording Television Programming

Some low-end Media Center PCs don't come with a TV tuner. Some mid-priced Media Center PCs come with a single NTSC TV tuner. But some higher-priced Media Center PCs come with two or more tuners; some even come with dual NTSC and ATSC tuners.

Why do you need more than one TV tuner in your PC? It's simple. A PC with a TV tuner can not only watch live television programming, it can also record that television programming direct to hard disk. That's right, your Media Center TV can function as a digital video recorder (*DVR*), kind of like a TiVo on steroids. And if you have two tuners in your PC, you can watch one program while you record another—or record two programs at the same time. You get the picture.

Here is where Media Center's electronic program guide really comes in handy. Use the guide to locate a program you want to record, and then schedule the recording right from the guide, as shown in Figure 3.7. It's a whole lot easier than manually programming the timer on a VCR!

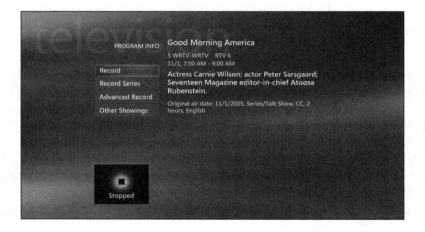

FIGURE 3.7

Scheduling a television recording in Windows Media Center.

Watching a recorded program is a snap. As you can see in Figure 3.8, Media Center lists all the programs you've recorded. Just click a program to begin playback. And the program is stored on your PC's hard disk until you erase it—or until the hard disk fills up.

Burning Recorded Programs—and Home Movies—to DVD

Any video file stored on your computer's hard disk can be copied to DVD—assuming that your Media Center PC includes a DVD burner drive, of course. That means you can burn a DVD containing last week's episode of *Desperate Housewives*, or a full week's worth of

The Daily Show, or that video you shot of your niece's wedding. It's one of the great things about having a computer in the living room; you're not limited solely to watching your video entertainment, you can also copy it to other media, as shown in Figure 3.9.

caution Not all TV programs can be burned to DVD, unfortunately. Some premium programming is content-protected so that you can record it to hard disk, but can't burn it to DVD.

FIGURE 3.8

Viewing a list of all recorded television programs in Media Center.

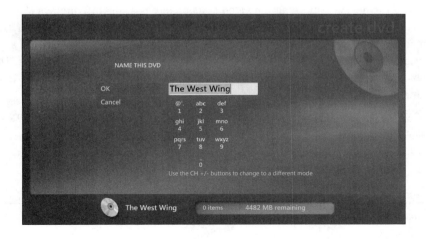

FIGURE 3.9

Getting ready to burn a video file to DVD.

Know, however, that the DVD-burning functionality built into Windows Media Center is fairly rudimentary. In most cases, you're limited to burning your video files to a data DVD, not to a regular movie DVD. Although some standalone DVD players (and all computers) will play data DVDs, some standalone players won't. A better solution, which we'll discuss in Chapter 11, is to use a third-party application (outside of Media Center) to burn movie DVDs that can play in any DVD player. It's a little kludgy, but it's doable.

note Some hardware manufacturers include their own DVD-burning software with the Media Center PCs they sell. For example, Sony integrates its Click-to-DVD software into the Media Center interface on its Media Center PCs, eliminating the need to use a third-party program for that activity.

The Plan: Configuring Your System

You have to admit, all this sounds pretty cool. When you add a Media Center PC to your home theater system, you add all sorts of functionality—DVD playback, DVD recording, digital video recording, downloading Internet videos, and so on. Assuming, of course, that you buy the right type of Media Center PC.

Choosing the Right Media Center PC

It helps to know what you need before you go shopping. This is especially true when it comes to any Media Center PC you intend to use for video viewing and recording. Not every Media Center PC on the market offers the same video-related features; you'll definitely be shopping for a unit in the mid- to upper-price range.

Here's the deal. To utilize all the video functionality possible in Windows Media Center, you need a PC with enough horsepower to handle those functions (video playback and recording are very demanding operations), enough hard disk storage to hold all your recorded programs, and at least one—possibly two or more—television tuners. This will not be a cheap PC. Expect to spend at least $2,000, and possibly twice that, to get the functionality you need.

So, what do you need? Table 3.1 details the minimum specifications necessary for acceptable video functionality.

TABLE 3.1 Media Center PC/Digital Video Recorder Specifications

Component	Recommended Minimum Specification
Microprocessor	Intel Pentium 4 *or* AMD Athlon running at 3GHz or higher
Memory	1GB
Hard disk drive	200GB (stores 45 hours of SDTV programming) *or* 400GB (stores 100 hours of SDTV programming or 35 hours of HDTV programming)

Component	Recommended Minimum Specification
Optical drive	DVD burner (DVD-R, DVD+R)
TV tuners	2 SDTV (NTSC) tuners 1 HDTV (ATSC) tuner (optional)
Audio output connections	Digital audio (optical or coaxial)
Video output connections	Component video *or* HDMI
Networking	802.11g Wi-Fi (wireless) *or* ethernet (wired)
Optional peripherals	External hard disk

Let's examine each of these specifications separately.

Microprocessor

It takes a bit more horsepower to process video material than it does to process audio material, so a Media Center PC for video applications is going to need a slightly faster microprocessor than one designed for audio applications. To that end, go with a Pentium 4 or AMD Athlon 64 running at 3GHz or more. If you're going to be recording HDTV programming, I'd bump that up to at least 3.4GHz. (HDTV material is more processor-intensive than is SDTV material.)

Memory

Again, you need more memory to handle video material than you do to handle audio. I recommend starting with 1GB of RAM, perhaps more if you're into HDTV.

Hard Disk Drive

A Media Center PC functioning as a DVR needs lots of hard disk space. The more programs you record, the bigger the hard disk you need. Assuming that you reserve 50GB or so for the operating system, key system files, and other essential applications, you need a 200GB hard drive to store 45 hours of standard-definition programming. To put that in perspective, we're talking about recording one entire season of two hour-long shows; anything more, and you'll run out of hard disk space.

Move up to a 400GB hard drive and you can store up to 100 hours of standard-definition programming. Or, if you're recording in high definition, that same 400GB drive will hold about 35 hours of HDTV programming.

You see the issue; you can never have enough hard disk space.

For this reason, you might want to consider a system with two separate internal hard drives. You can reserve one hard drive for system files and for storing digital photos and digital audio files, and devote the second drive exclusively for recorded TV programming.

If you have an entire 400GB drive to work with, with no system files taking up space, it will hold around 120 hours of SDTV programming, or 40 hours of HDTV programming. Move up to a 500GB drive (the largest available as I'm writing these words) and you can store 150 hours of SDTV and 50 hours of HDTV.

Then there's the option of using an external hard drive for archival purposes. Instead of storing older programs on your main hard drive, offload them to the external disk. This keeps the main hard drive free to record new programs; last year's collection of *CSI* in high definition can be stored on the external drive.

Optical Drive

Obviously, if you're going to watch movies on your Media Center PC, you need to purchase a unit with a built-in DVD drive. And if you intend to burn your own DVDs (and you will), make sure that you get a DVD+/-R drive. And don't forget the DVD changer option; if you have a medium-sized DVD collection (fewer than 200 discs), this is a great way to store and access all your movies from within Media Center.

TV Tuners

Here's where you have to shop carefully. Many lower-priced Media Center PCs don't come with a TV tuner; still more include only a single tuner. That's not good enough. Assuming that you will, at some point in time, want to either watch one program while you record another or record two programs that air at the same time, you'll need a unit that has two TV tuners built in. (For example, you'll need two tuners if you want to record both *Desperate Housewives* and *Law and Order: Criminal Intent* on Sunday evenings.)

But don't stop there. If your home theater system is HDTV-capable, you'll want to be able to record programs in high definition. That means that you need your Media Center PC to include at least one HDTV (ATSC) tuner—and possibly two, if you want to record both *Desperate Housewives* and *L&O:CI* in high definition.

Start adding it up. Two NTSC (standard definition) tuners, plus one or two ATSC (high-definition tuners). Get two of each and you can record *four* different programs at the same time. Amazing!

Audio Output Connections

When you're using your Media Center PC to watch TV or DVDs, you need to pass the sound from the PC to the audio/video receiver in your home theater system. Because we're talking surround sound, that means using either a digital optical or digital coaxial connection. Either one is good. (And don't even bother with the right and left RCA audio jacks; if you're connecting digital audio, these jacks are not used.)

Video Output Connections

For serious video viewing, skip the single-plug composite video connection, as well as the S-Video connection. Instead, step right up to the three-cable component video connection, which delivers much better picture quality. (Component video is also the minimum connection for HDTV.)

tip Most newer TVs come with at least one HDMI connection. If your Media Center PC only has a DVI output, you can use a DVI-to-HDMI converter to unmismatch the connection.

Even better, go with a digital DVI or HDMI connection. HDMI is preferred here, as it's quickly replacing the older DVI connection. HDMI can also carry both digital video and digital audio, which in some systems can let you eliminate a separate audio cable. (This isn't feasible if you send the video from your PC to your TV and the audio to your A/V receiver.)

In any case, the digital-to-digital HDMI connection delivers the best possible picture quality. It's my recommended video connection type.

Networking

Downloading videos from the Internet requires an Internet connection. So does using Media Center's electronic program guide; the guide data is downloaded once a day via the Internet.

The easiest way to connect your Media Center PC to the Internet is to first connect it to your home network. Assuming that your network is connected to the Internet, there you have it.

You can connect your PC to your home network via wired ethernet or wireless Wi-Fi. For most purposes, Wi-Fi works just fine (and is easier to install). However, if you plan on transmitting recorded videos throughout your house via Media Center Extenders, ethernet is probably the better bet because it's faster and more reliable than any current wireless connection. Transmitting video moves a lot of bits and bytes; ethernet is designed to do just this.

note Learn more about sharing video throughout the house in Chapter 4, "Media Center System #3: The Whole House Entertainment System."

Optional Peripherals

As with the audio-focused system we discussed last chapter, you might want to consider adding an external backup drive to your video system. Use the external hard drive to back up all your recorded videos, and you'll be safe if anything ever happens to your main disk or PC. Obviously, the bigger your internal drive, the bigger the external disk you'll need to mirror it.

Other Considerations

Most people want their Media Center PC to look and feel like the other components in their home theater system. That means a box that's about 17" wide, and either 4" or (for systems with more internal storage) 8" tall.

Don't forget the noise factor, either. Absolute quiet isn't quite as necessary when watching a movie, as opposed to listening to music, but still. Look for those units that offer some sort of fan-quieting or no-fan operation.

Other Audio/Video Components

Your Media Center PC is just part of your complete home theater system. Although the configuration of a home theater system is a personal choice, there are some key components that are essential to every system:

- Media Center PC, as spec'd earlier in this chapter
- Audio/video receiver, or separate preamplifier/processor and amplifier
- Speakers: five plus a subwoofer (for 5.1 systems)
- Television set

You can augment this basic system with a 6.1- or 7.1-channel receiver (instead of the basic 5.1-channel model), one or two more rear speakers, and a universal remote control to operate all the components. Obviously, you'll also need some sort of source for your television programming—either an over-the-air (*OTA*) antenna for broadcast television, a set-top cable box for cable TV, or a satellite receiver for digital satellite systems.

Whatever source you choose for your television programming, your system should look at least a little like the one in Figure 3.10.

Connecting Your System

Connecting a Media Center PC to a home theater system can be a little tricky. That's because you have some choices to make. Do you connect the video directly to the TV, or do you go through the A/V receiver? Are you using the TV's speakers for sound (and if so, why?), or do you have a proper surround sound receiver? And what types of connections do you use?

You'll have to make some of these decisions yourself; there aren't always right and wrong answers. That said, here are the general connections to make:

- Connect your television antenna or cable/satellite feed to the tuner input(s) on the Media Center PC.
- Connect the digital audio output of the Media Center PC to a corresponding digital audio input on your audio/video receiver.

- Connect the component or HDMI video output of the Media Center PC to a corresponding component or HDMI input on your television display or receiver.

note Learn more about connecting your Media Center PC in Chapter 6, "Making the Connections."

Naturally, your A/V receiver should then be connected to all the speakers in your system—and if you ran your video signal to the receiver, it should also be connected to the television display.

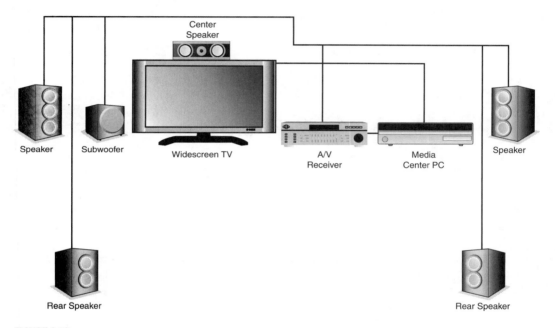

FIGURE 3.10

Connecting a Media Center PC to a home theater system.

After everything is connected, you can use your Media Center PC to view and record television programs (as discussed in Chapter 10), and to play DVDs (as discussed in Chapter 11). And, if you have one or more Media Center Extenders (as discussed in Chapter 4), you can also feed your recorded programs to other TVs in your house. It sounds complicated, but when you get it all connected, you can actually simplify your system—by throwing out your old DVD player and DVR. Your Media Center PC is the one device that does it all!

4

Media Center System #3: The Whole House Entertainment System

The previous two chapters highlighted the most common uses of a Media Center PC—to play back audio and video programming. But there's another increasingly popular use of Media Center PC, which can apply both audio and video entertainment. I'm talking about sharing your audio/video files between computers, in different rooms of your house. That's right, you can have a single PC feed television programs and music to TVs and audio systems in other rooms. If you want whole house entertainment, you don't have to put a Media Center PC in each room; instead, you can install one main PC and use it to feed signals to multiple Media Center Extenders placed throughout your house.

What is a Media Center Extender? Put simply, it's a device that lets you access digital files stored on another PC on your home network, and then display that programming on a connected TV and audio system. It's kind of like a remote Media Center PC, but without its own processor. Read on to learn more.

How a Media Center Extender Works

A Media Center Extender is a simple device, really; it's a set top box that connects to any television or audio system anywhere in your house. An Extender also connects to your home network (via either wired ethernet or wireless Wi-Fi), and thus to your main Media Center PC, on which all your audio and video files are stored. You control the Media Center Extender through its own remote control unit; the interface on the secondary TV is practically identical to the regular Media Center interface, which means you can choose what music or television programs you want to watch and listen to on your secondary TV. You can watch one thing on your main Media Center PC and another thing on each Media Center Extender you have installed. And you can use up to five Media Center Extenders simultaneously.

note The Media Center Extender must be connected to a PC running Windows XP Media Center Edition. It won't work if connected to a PC not running Media Center Edition.

It's important to note that Media Center Extenders are not PCs. A Media Center Extender does not include a hard disk drive or a CD or DVD drive. An Extender is a network device that connects to your main PC; it doesn't store any data itself.

Uses for a Media Center Extender

There are two main uses for a Media Center Extender. They're both based on the fact that you use the Extender to play back files stored on another PC.

The most common use is to stream music and television programming to multiple rooms in a whole house entertainment system. In this scenario, you install a Media Center PC in your main home entertainment system, and then place multiple Media Center Extenders in different rooms throughout your house.

The other way to use a Media Center Extender is in lieu of a living room PC. In this scenario, it's the Media Center Extender that you install in your living room's home entertainment system. The Extender gets its audio/video programming by connecting to another PC on your network, typically a large desktop PC with plenty of hard disk storage space. Theoretically, this type of setup provides Media Center functionality without the hassle of installing a PC in your living room.

Media Center Extenders can be used to play back the following types of media:

- Live television programming (SDTV only)
- Recorded television programs (SDTV only)
- Stored video files (WMV and MPEG formats)
- Digital audio files (MP3, WMA, and WMA Lossless formats)
- Digital photographs

Media Center Extenders can also perform instant messaging via the built-in Windows Messenger application.

Different Types of Media Center Extenders

Most Media Center Extenders are small boxes that can sit on top of any TV, or alongside other audio/video components. For example, the Linksys WMCE64AG Dual-Band Wireless A/G Media Center Extender, shown in Figure 4.1, looks like a small DVD player, but without a DVD slot. Its faceplate is rather plain; all the functions are controlled via remote control. Pricing is typically in the $250 range.

FIGURE 4.1

The Linksys Media Center Extender.

In addition, if you have a Microsoft Xbox videogame console, you can use it as a Media Center Extender. The original Xbox requires a special Media Center Extender add-on to function as an Extender; the new Xbox 360, shown in Figure 4.2, has Media Center Extender functionality built-in. For game players, this is a great way to add Media Center functionality to their main TV—without placing a bulky Media Center PC in their living room. Just use your desktop PC to store your music and video files; the Xbox connects to the PC via your home network, and plays back your audio/video programming via the Media Center interface.

Both types of Extenders—the standard type and the type built-into the Xbox console—feature some sort of network connection on the back. This might be a wired ethernet connection, or a wireless Wi-Fi connection. A wireless connection is fine for listening to music and for viewing digital photos, but not always fast enough to stream television and video programming. If you want to use your Extender for video, it's best to use the faster ethernet connection.

FIGURE 4.2

Microsoft's Xbox 360, with built-in Media Center Extender technology.

Media Center PC Requirements

The Media Center Extender connects (via your home network) to your main Media Center PC. Because playing back programming on multiple devices simultaneously requires additional processing power, you might need to beef up your PC to use it with one or more Extenders. For example, if you're connecting a single Media Center Extender, you can probably get by with a bare minimum 2.8GHz PC with 256MB of memory. But if you connect a second Extender, you definitely need 512MB memory—and if you connect three or more Extenders, you'll need a PC running at 3.4GHz or more with at least 1GB memory. Plan accordingly.

note Hard disk capacity isn't affected by Media Center Extender use. The Extender itself doesn't have a hard disk drive; it merely accesses the hard disk on your main PC—and no new files are installed on your hard disk.

Goal #1: Sharing Audio/Video Entertainment Throughout the House

As just discussed, there are two primary ways to use a Media Center Extender. Let us first examine the first use: to create a whole house audio/video system. In this type of system, you start with a traditional Media Center PC in your living room, and then install Media Center Extenders in up to five other rooms in your house. It's a great way to share your music and recorded television programming without installing duplicate systems throughout your home.

Listening to Music in Other Rooms

Let's take the goal of creating a whole house audio system. This type of system used to be the province of the rich and famous, utilizing a central CD jukebox, a multizone distribution amplifier, and in-wall controllers and remote speakers in each room. This type of system required a professional home theater installer, and could cost tens of thousands of dollars. Ouch!

That's what makes using a Media Center Extender so attractive. It's extremely easy to install, no professionals required, and it costs you only a few hundred dollars. (Plus the expense of a small TV and audio system in each room, of course.) You can connect the Media Center Extender to any audio system, from a simple boom box to a bookshelf system to a high-end audiophile-quality system. Use the system you have, or buy a cheap system to extend your system to additional rooms.

After it's installed, using the system is a breeze. Use the Media Center interface to select and play back any and all music files stored on you main PC. You can play back individual songs, complete albums, or any of the playlists you've previously recorded. And you don't have to listen to the same music that you're playing on your main PC; the selections you make on the Media Center Extender are independent of whatever you've selected on the Media Center PC.

Watching TV Programs in Other Rooms

Just as you can use a Media Center Extender to listen to music in other rooms, you can also use it to watch live television and recorded TV programs throughout your house. (You can't use the Extender to watch DVDs from your main PC, however.) Any other videos stored on your hard drive (such as videos downloaded from the Internet, or home movies you've recorded) can also be shared via the Extender. Selection of video programming is via the standard Media Center interface.

caution A Media Center Extender can play back only standard definition television programming. The Extender can not play back HDTV programs.

Plan #1: Placing Multiple Media Center Extenders Throughout Your Home

To implement a whole house entertainment system, you need one main Media Center PC (connected to your main home theater system) and a Media Center Extender for each room you want to include. The main Media Center PC, of course, should be connected to an incoming television signal, to your home network (via ethernet or Wi-Fi), and to your main home theater system. Each Extender must be connected to a television display and (optionally) an audio system.

Table 4.1 details all the components you need.

TABLE 4.1   Necessary Components for a Whole House Media Center System

Living Room	Each Auxiliary Room
Media Center PC	Media Center Extender
Television	Television
Receiver	Stereo system (bookshelf or floor-standing)
Speakers	Television antenna or cable/satellite feed

Naturally, you need a network connection of some sort in your living room and in each room in which you install a Media Center Extender. The connection between each Extender and the main PC can be via either ethernet or Wi-Fi. You can connect up to five Media Center Extenders in total. The entire system should look something like the one in Figure 4.3.

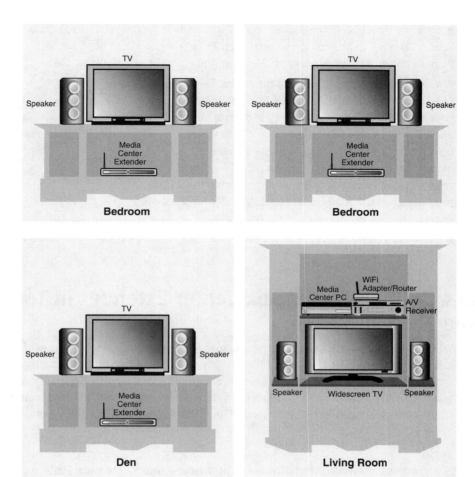

FIGURE 4.3

Using multiple Media Center Extenders in a whole house entertainment system.

Goal #2: Accessing Audio and Video Files Stored on Another PC—On Your Living Room System

An alternative reason to use a Media Center Extender is to connect it your main home theater system, instead of using a Media Center PC for this purpose. This type of setup is ideal if you have a lot of music or movie files stored on your existing desktop PC, and don't want to duplicate that storage on a separate living room PC. In addition, a Media Center Extender is less conspicuous in a living room setting than are most Media Center PCs; a thin set top box is easier to deal with than a bulky Media Center PC.

With this type of system, you use the Media Center Extender to access audio and video files stored on your desktop PC. (Your desktop PC, of course, has to be running Windows XP Media Center Edition.) You rip all your CDs to your desktop PC, and use the desktop PC to record television program. When you want to listen to digital music or view recorded TV programs, you use the Media Center Extender for playback.

> **tip** If you're using a Media Center Extender in your living room, you can still install additional Extenders in other rooms in your house.

The big drawback to this type of system is that you can't use your Extender to play back DVDs. So, if you go this route, you'll have to keep a standalone DVD player connected to your TV.

Plan #2a: Placing a Media Center Extender in Your Home Theater System

When planning for a living room Media Center Extender system, there's not a lot of setup involved. Your main Media Center PC is already installed and up and running, so all you have to do is connect and configure the Media Center Extender. The Extender connects to your television display and (optionally) to your audio system. Table 4.2 details all the components you need; as you can see in Figure 4.4, there's nothing fancy about this sort of setup.

TABLE 4.2   Necessary Components for a Living Room Media Extender System

Living Room	Office
Media Center Extender	Media Center PC (with monitor)
Television	Television antenna or cable/satellite feed
Audio/video receiver	
Speakers	
DVD player	

Assuming that you'll be streaming recorded TV programs from your main PC to the Media Center Extender, you should probably opt for an ethernet connection to your home network. Although you could go with an 802.11a or 802.11g Wi-Fi connection, it might not be fast enough or stable enough to

> **note** You'll need a separate DVD player in this system because the Media Center Extender does not play DVDs, nor can it stream DVD movies from your main PC.

convey uninterrupted video. If you go with a wireless connection and then find you get a lot of stuttering and stopping and starting when playing back television programming, that's a good sign that you need a faster, more stable ethernet connection.

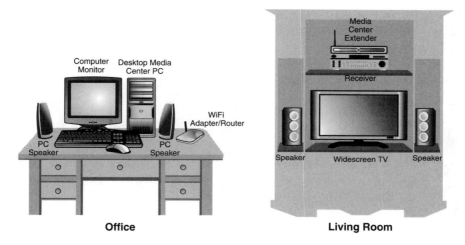

FIGURE 4.4

Using a Media Center Extender in place of a living room PC.

Plan #2b: Using an Xbox Game Console As a Media Center Extender

As an alternative to using a traditional Media Center Extender in your living room, you can get the same Media Center functionality from a Microsoft Xbox videogame console. That's right; if you already have an Xbox connected in your living room, you also have a Media Center Extender revved up and ready to go.

Table 4.3 details the components you need for this sort of system.

TABLE 4.3   Necessary Components for a Living Room Xbox/Media Center System

Living Room	Office
Xbox 360 *or*	Media Center PC (with monitor)
Xbox (original) with Media Center Extender software	Television antenna or cable/satellite feed
Television	
Audio/video receiver	
Speakers	

Whether you have the original Xbox or the new Xbox 360, your system should like the one shown in Figure 4.5.

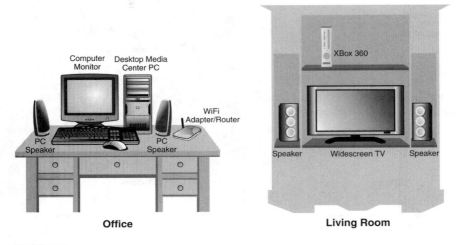

FIGURE 4.5

Using an Xbox console as a Media Center Extender in your living room.

Connecting the Original Xbox

Microsoft's original Xbox console is more accurately described as "Media Center–ready" because the Media Center technology isn't completely built in. To use your Xbox as a Media Center Extender, you'll need to purchase the Media Center Extender add-on software. This software also has a hardware component, in the form of a infrared dongle that plugs into one of the Xbox's controller ports, and a corresponding Media Center remote control; the remote control operates the Xbox via the infrared dongle.

The Xbox Extender software comes on a DVD that you play in your Xbox console; you have to insert the disc every time you want to use your Xbox in Media Center Extender mode. You'll also need to connect the Xbox console to your home network, via the built-in ethernet connection or an optional Wi-Fi connection.

Connecting the Xbox 360

If you own a new Xbox 360 console, you don't have to purchase anything additional to use it as a Media Center Extender; the Extender technology is built into the console. Just select the Media Center option from the Xbox 360 menu, as shown in Figure 4.6, and the screen switches to the Media Center interface that you know and love. Again, you'll need to connect the console to your home network, via either ethernet or Wi-Fi.

FIGURE 4.6

Switching the Xbox 360 into Media Center mode.

Using Windows Media Center via a Media Center Extender

After everything is connected, using your Media Center Extender is pretty much identical to using a regular Media Center PC. The Extender uses the same Media Center interface that you have on the PC, minus the Play DVD menu—an omission dictated by our old pal, digital rights management (DRM), which won't let you stream DVD content across a home network. DVD playback aside, just scroll through the onscreen menus using the Extender's remote control unit, and make your selections as you would normally.

note Learn more about connecting, configuring, and using Media Center Extenders in Chapter 14, "Using Your Media Center PC with a Media Center Extender."

Remember, whatever you select to play on your Media Center Extender is completely independent from what's playing on your main Media Center PC—or on other Extenders.

Each device operates independently from the others, so you could have up to six different songs or programs playing on five separate Extenders plus the main PC. It's a great way to share all those songs you've downloaded from the Internet or ripped from CD—and all the television programs you've recorded.

caution Although connecting five Extenders is possible (according to Microsoft), I wouldn't recommend it. With that many Extenders connected, it's likely that your main PC won't have enough horsepower to drive them all without some deterioration in performance.

5

Buying or Building: Choosing the Right Media Center System for You

If you're in the market for a new Media Center PC for your living room, you have several different directions in which you can go. If form factor isn't an issue (if your PC will be behind cabinet doors, for example), you can go with a traditional desktop PC, with Windows XP Media Center Edition loaded. If you want your PC to better fit in with your other audio/video components, you can go with a component-like Media Center PC. Or, if you're not comfortable with any of the prebuilt options (or want to save a few bucks), you can build your own Media Center PC from scratch.

Which option is for you? Well, that's what this chapter is all about—choosing the right Media Center PC for your own digital home entertainment system.

Different Types of Media Center PCs

First, let's look at the many different types of Media Center PCs available. As you'll see, not every Media Center PC is designed specifically for living room use. Strictly speaking, a Media Center PC is simply a personal computer running Microsoft's Windows XP Media Center Edition software. The Media Center interface can be applied to any type of PC—living room or otherwise.

The Notebook Media Center PC

As a case in point, many notebook PCs are now coming with Windows XP Media Center Edition already installed. Obviously, these are not computers designed for living room use. Instead, the notebook Media Center PC is designed for students in dorm rooms who need a compact all-in-one computing/entertainment solution, and for business travelers who want to watch movies on the plane

note Another option, of course, is to forego the living room PC completely, and go with a Media Center Extender instead. Learn more about Media Center Extenders in Chapter 4, "Media Center System #3: The Whole House Entertainment System."

and in their hotel rooms. The Media Center interface is perfect for both these uses; it might be a 10-foot interface, but it still works at the 10-inch level.

For example, HP's zd8230us, shown in Figure 5.1, is a high-end notebook PC that comes preloaded with Windows XP Media Center Edition. As a portable PC, it's a little feature-heavy—and just plain physically heavy, at 9.4 lbs. It comes with a 17" widescreen display, 1GB RAM, a 100GB hard drive, CD/DVD burner, and built-in TV tuner. Place it in a dorm room or small apartment and it functions quite well as a desktop replacement—and a complete entertainment system. Use the standard Windows XP interface for your traditional computing and web-surfing needs, and then switch to the Media Center interface to watch TV and listen to music. Price is $2,250; learn more at www.hp.com.

FIGURE 5.1

HP's zd8230us portable PC with Windows Media Center Edition loaded—great for students and business travelers.

You won't find Media Center Edition loaded on low-priced notebooks, so don't expect too many bargains. This sort of Media Center configuration is typically limited to higher-priced desktop replacement machines in the $1,500–$2,300 price range. Look for models from Alienware, Dell, HP, and Toshiba.

The Desktop Media Center PC

Take the traditional desktop PC, preload Windows XP Media Center Edition, and then add a couple of television tuners, a huge hard disk, and a big monitor, and you have a desktop computer that can do double duty as a complete audio/video system. Here, again, the target audience is college students, as well as young urban dwellers in small apartments. The idea is that where space is a premium (such as a small dorm room or studio apartment), one device that does it all is preferable to several devices that take up much more desk space. The desktop Media Center PC can function as a computer (using the normal Windows XP interface), and can switch over to the Media Center interface for home entertainment use.

tip If you're using a desktop PC for Media Center use, get as big a monitor as you can afford—bigger is better for watching live and recorded TV programs. (Widescreen is also good.)

A good example of this type of PC is Dell's Dimension E510, shown in Figure 5.2. This affordable machine (priced at $799) looks like a traditional desktop PC and acts like a traditional desktop PC, but when you push the big Green Button on the Windows Start menu, you launch into the Media Center interface—complete with built-in TV tuner. Learn more at www.dell.com.

You can also find machines like this from Gateway, HP, and Sony. Pricing ranges from less than $1,000 to more than $2,000, depending on configuration.

FIGURE 5.2

Dell's E510 desktop PC with Windows Media Center Edition loaded—great for a dorm room or small apartment.

There's also a subset of the Media Center desktop PC that you might want to consider for living room use. I'm talking about so-called "silent" PCs that eliminate the fan noise that is part and parcel of a normal desktop PC. For example, Sony's RA-940, shown in

Figure 5.3, is a Media Center PC in a tower design that offers a built-in TV tuner and a 250GB hard drive (upgradeable to 1.2TB) for $1,599. Silent operation comes from water-cooling technology; the PC is cooled by water rather than by the normal noisy fan. (Learn more at www.sony.com.)

FIGURE 5.3

A Sony Media Center PC with silent operation, in a traditional mini-tower cabinet.

Because of the silent operation (and the option of installing multiple large hard disks), this type of PC can be a viable option for the living room—if you don't mind the traditional PC tower design, that is. That said, if you're planning on placing your living room PC inside a closed cabinet or some sort of control room, the unit's form factor might not matter to you. (If you can't see it, what's it matter whether the PC is horizontal or vertical?)

There's also an advantage to going with a vertically oriented PC: This type of tower cabinet is more easily expandable than one in a smaller horizontal cabinet. When you want to install a second hard disk, or change TV tuner cards, or swap out a CD burner for a DVD burner, it's relatively easy to do with a traditional tower PC; upgrading a PC in an audio/video-type cabinet is much more problematic, if not sometimes impossible.

The A/V Component Form Factor Media Center PC

All that said, most consumers who agree to put a PC in the living room will want that PC to look as little like a traditional PC as possible. In many ways, the perfect living room PC is the anti-PC, a device with all the power of a personal computer, but none of its looks or operational quirks.

What we're talking about is a personal computer in a black horizontal cabinet, 3"–4" high and 17" wide—the same size as most other audio/video components, such as DVD players and A/V receivers. This PC should have relatively quiet operation and a full complement of audio/video input/output jacks on the back. (And maybe a FireWire connection on the front so that you can connect your camcorder without mussing about on the back of the unit.) Slide this puppy into your A/V component rack and no one will ever be the wiser.

There are several companies that offer this type of living room Media Center PC. We'll look at some of these offerings in the next section.

note Not all component-like Media Center PCs are 3"–4" tall. Just as some high-end audio components (such as big power amplifiers) raise the height barrier to 8" or more, some Media Center PCs also exceed 8" in height. In particular, the line of Denali PCs from Niveus Media has this type of power amplifier form factor, the better to include a broader assortment of input/output jacks—and to offer a large metal surface for their passive cooling system.

Shopping for a Living Room Media Center PC

When you're shopping for a Media Center PC with an A/V component form factor, you have many models from several different companies to choose from. Depending on the features and performance you want, you can find models priced as low as $1,199—and as high as $6,000 or more. Read on to discover some of the most popular offerings.

note The PCs discussed here were current as of late fall, 2005. Given the rapid rate of change in the personal computer industry, I'd expect you to find different models on sale by the time you read this book. I present this information, then, as representative of what you might expect to find—even though some of the specifics will probably change.

Alienware

Alienware (www.alienware.com) is a boutique company known for its high-performance (and similarly high-priced) gaming PCs. It has also ventured into the Media Center PC market, with a home entertainment unit designed with the gaming enthusiast in mind.

The DHS 5, shown in Figure 5.4, uses a 1.8 GHz AMD Athlon 64 processor. It comes with 1GB RAM, a 160GB hard drive, and a combo CD/DVD burner, and sells for $1,989.

What makes the DHS 5 unique, however, is its capability to play PC games in a plug-and-play fashion, thanks to Discover Console gaming technology. Just load the game disc into the PC drive and the DHS 5 automatically installs and plays the game, just as it would play on an Xbox console.

FIGURE 5.4

Alienware's DHS 5—a Media Center PC for serious gamers.

HP

In my opinion, when it comes to affordable Media Center PCs, Hewlett-Packard (www.hp.com) offers the best bang for your buck. Case in point is HP's z552 Digital Entertainment Center, shown in Figure 5.5.

FIGURE 5.5

HP's z552 Digital Entertainment Center—a low-priced Media Center PC for the mass market.

What you get is a living room PC in an A/V component configuration, running an Intel P4 chip at 3GHz. You get 512MB RAM, a 200GB hard disk drive, a CD/DVD burner, and dual TV tuners (NTSC). The z552 looks just like any other audio/video component, and comes with the expected Media Center remote control and wireless keyboard. The best thing about it, however, is the price; this fully featured Media Center PC costs a relatively measly $1,199.99.

This is a snazzy-looking unit, maybe not the highest-performing Media Center unit out there, but one that's designed for and perfect for the masses.

note HP offers several other Media Center PCs with more advanced feature sets. For example, the z557 comes with three TV tuners (one for HDTV, two for standard-definition broadcasts), 1GB RAM, a 300GB internal hard drive, another 300GB removable hard drive, and a CD/DVD burner, for $2,199.99.

It definitely looks, feels, and acts more like a consumer electronics device than it does a traditional desktop computer.

Niveus Media

With all the great Media Center PCs out there, the one I chose for my personal use was a Denali Edition PC from Niveus Media (www.niveusmedia.com). As you can see in Figure 5.6, the Denali is a big hog, built more like a pro-level audio amplifier than a DVD player. At 8" in height, it towers over the other components—but still has that audio component look. The size is necessary to hold everything that Niveus packs inside, as well as to help cool the unit. That's the thing about this PC; it provides totally silent operation, with no fans at all inside. The cooling comes from the cabinet itself, which is designed like a giant heat sink.

note Keep an eye out for Media Center PCs built around Intel's Viiv technology. Viiv is Intel's new platform for digital entertainment PCs, utilizing a chipset with dual-core microprocessor, 7.1-channel surround sound, and upgraded graphics drivers. Viiv-based PCs also feature access to a variety of Internet-based entertainment services. Most major Media Center PC manufacturers will offer desktop and living room models based on the Viiv platform.

FIGURE 5.6

One of the most feature-packed—and largest—Media Center PCs on the market, Niveus Media's Denali Edition.

Inside the case, Niveus offers a state-of-the-art Media Center PC. You get a 3.2GHz Intel P4 processor, 1MB RAM, two 400GB hard drives (for a total of 800GB storage), a combo CD/DVD burner, Intel high-definition eight-channel audio, a built-in FM tuner, two standard-definition TV tuners, and a third HDTV tuner. With specs like that, there's little that this powerhouse can't do—except be inconspicuous. (It also puts a bit of a dent in your wallet, at a little more than $5,000 as configured.)

Niveus feels your pain, however, and also offers a lower-priced line called the Rainier Edition (seen in Figure 5.7). For just $2,999, you get a lower-profile model with a 2.8GHz

P4 processor, 512MB RAM, 250GB hard drive, and just two TV tuners (both SDTV). It's still not cheap, but it's also not a bare bones machine.

FIGURE 5.7

Niveus Media's more affordable Rainier Edition PC.

Sony

As we discussed earlier in this chapter, Sony makes a line of water-cooled desktop PCs with Windows XP MCE preinstalled, any of which would be a fine living room PC—if you can get around the traditional vertical tower design. Don't fear, however; Sony also makes one very targeted Media Center PC in a horizontal component configuration.

The VAIO VGX-XL1 Digital Living System is more than just a Media Center PC, however. It's a complete digital entertainment system, complete with a Media Center PC system unit, a CD/DVD changer, a built-in Wi-Fi access point with external antenna, and a wireless Media Center keyboard with integrated touch pad.

As you can see in Figure 5.8, the main system unit looks just like any other audio/video component. The front panel of the unit folds down to reveal a media card reader, two FireWire connections, one USB connection, a microphone connection, headphone connection, and audio/video connections. The CD/DVD changer is similarly designed; both components should look right at home in your component rack.

FIGURE 5.8

Sony's VAIO VGX-XL1 Digital Living System—a Media Center PC with accompanying CD/DVD changer.

The PC itself has a 2.8GHz Intel Pentium D dual-core processor, 512MB RAM (expandable to 2GB), and a 200GB hard drive—with room for two additional drives in the case. The system includes a single standard-definition TV tuner, and connects to your TV via HDMI.

The 200-disc changer includes CD/DVD burning capability, so you can use it to play back or burn CDs or DVDs. You can also use the changer as a massive CD ripper; just load it up with 200 of your favorite CDs, and let it rip all those discs to the computer's hard disk automatically, thus freeing you from the chore of inserting and removing all those discs one at a time.

Sony has also done a good job integrating its own proprietary software into the Media Center interface. For example, the CD/DVD changer is operated from a new My Changer menu. DVD burning is accomplished via a Media Center–specific version of Sony's Click to DVD program.

Price for the XL1 is $2,299.99. More information can be found at products.sel.sony.com/xl1/.

Building a Media Center PC from Scratch

For the average consumer, buying a commercially manufactured Media Center PC is the only way to go; taking the PC out of the box and connecting it to your other components is as technical as you want to get. There is another class of consumer, however, who is more technically inclined. These consumers are not only capable of assembling a Media Center PC from its component parts, but get great pleasure out of doing so. If you're one of these high-tech do-it-yourselfers, this next section is for you.

Advantages of Building Your Own Media Center PC

What possible advantage could there be in building your own Media Center PC from scratch? Quite a few, actually.

First, there's the personal factor. That is, you get to construct a PC with just the right components for your own personal needs. Want 2GB of memory and a terabyte of storage? How about four television tuners and a DVD changer? Or a super-silent design with a front-panel display? No problem, all you have to do is build it that way.

When you build your own Media Center PC, you don't have to pick and choose from prebuilt systems that don't quite fit all your needs, or accept components or performance that you don't really want because that's the way the unit comes. With a home-brew Media Center PC, there are no compromises. You get exactly what you want—no more, no less.

And you save money while you're at it. That's the other benefit of building your own Media Center PC: Building it yourself can be (but isn't necessarily) a little cheaper than buying it off the rack. It's not a huge savings (we're talking a few hundred dollars, not thousands), and you probably make up the savings in the time you spend building it, but still. The money you save can be reinvested in a more powerful system.

Finally, you get the intangible benefit of pride of ownership—and the knowledge that you have a truly one-of-a-kind system. All your friends may have Dells and HPs, but you have a custom-built system unlike anything else available. You can't put a price on that.

Necessary Skill Level

How technically inclined do you need to be to build your own PC? The answer is, "very." You have to be comfortable working with motherboards and memory chips and internal disk drives, with screws and cables and card slots, and with BIOS settings and RAID arrays and dip switches. If you don't know a power supply from a serial port, you're probably going to be in over your head.

To build your own PC, you have to know your way around the inside of a computer system unit. You have to know the various types of ports and connectors; you have to know what type of cable runs to which type of component. You also have to know how all these components fit together, and how to make them physically fit together. And you can't be afraid of making mistakes because a lot of home brew computing is all about trial and error.

If you're uncomfortable taking the case off a system unit, you shouldn't try building your own PC. If you rely on professional technical support rather than troubleshooting problems yourself, you shouldn't try building your own PC. If you can't connect a printer without consulting the manual, you shouldn't try building your own PC. You get the picture.

Choosing the Components

If you are comfortable building a computer from scratch, it's time to look at the various components you need to assemble. Obviously, specific makes and models are your individual prerogative, but we can discuss the types of components you should be looking at, in general terms.

note The following sections throw around a lot of techno-speak. There's not space here to go into in-depth explanations of all the technology, but here's a hint: If you don't already know what any of these terms mean, building a PC from scratch is probably something beyond your current expertise!

Case

Choosing a case for your Media Center PC is a crucial decision. Do you want a unit with an A/V component form factor, or a mini-tower design with more expansion room inside? Will the case you choose accept the motherboard you want? What about special features, like an opening for a front-panel display?

These are all important considerations, and should help to guide your case decision. From my experience, you might want to consider the following cases for your personal use:

- Ahanix D5 Media Center Enclosure (www.ahanix.com), a good horizontal component case with front-panel display that can accept full-size ATX motherboards, available in either silver or black, as shown in Figure 5.9.

- Antec Overture II (www.antec.com), a horizontal component case with quiet operating design, in piano black with chrome accents and soft blue illumination.

- nmediapc HTPC BA & S cases (www.nmediapc.com), slightly oversized horizontal component cases with front-panel display and card reader slots, available in either silver or black.

- Silverstone LC11M (www.silverstonetek.com), a slim horizontal component case with front-panel display and hidden front panel FireWire and audio connections, in either silver or black.

FIGURE 5.9

Ahanix D5 Media Center Enclosure—a good choice for your Media Center PC's case.

These cases are designed specifically for Media Center use, and run anywhere from $100 to $300, depending on features.

Power Supply

> **note** Some PC cases come with their own power supplies; others accept power supplies from third-party manufacturers.

When choosing a power supply for your PC, you have two main factors to consider—size (power) and noise. For most Media Center uses, you want at least a 300- or 350-watt power supply, and bigger is better if you're powering additional internal components—multiple hard drives, TV tuners, and the like. For these more demanding systems, going with a 500-watt power supply might make sense.

As to noise, it all comes from the fan. (Save for a little hard disk and CD/DVD drive noise, of course.) Because power supplies tend to get a little warm when generating all that power, they have to be cooled off. The traditional cooling method is to use a fan, which unfortunately creates a level of background noise that might be unacceptable in a living room setting. As an alternative to fan cooling, some manufacturers are offering fanless power supplies. In these power supplies, such as the Antec Phantom (shown in Figure 5.10), cooling is provided by the use of a large metal heat sink surrounding the device.

FIGURE 5.10

The Antec Phantom fanless power supply—it's a big heat sink!

Power supplies are available from Antec (www.antec.com), Aspire (www.aspireusa.net), Cooler Master (www.coolermaster.com), Enermax (www.enermax.com.tw), Silverstone (www.silverstonetek.com), Vantec (www.vantecusa.com), and others. You'll pay between $100 and $200 for an appropriate model.

Motherboard and CPU

Of course, a power supply is just a hunk of useless metal unless it's powering something. And the key thing to power is the motherboard, the big computer circuit that anchors the entire system.

A computer motherboard contains key circuitry to control your entire system, as well as various internal connectors and—most important—the central processing unit, or *CPU*. The CPU is the microprocessor that functions as the brains behind the computer system, and might be the most important component in your entire system.

You can find motherboards from a variety of companies, including Abit (www.abit-usa.com), ASUS (usa.asus.com), Gigabyte (www.giga-byte.com), Intel (developer.intel.com/design/motherbd/), and MSI (www.msicomputer.com). You have to make sure that the motherboard you choose fits in your chosen case, of course, and that it has the proper socket for the CPU you choose. Other than that, consider whether the board has built-in audio or video (and if so, whether it's good enough for Media Center use), how many connectors, controllers, and slots it includes, and so on. Expect to pay $100 to $250 for a decent motherboard.

For example, the Intel D955XBK motherboard, shown in Figure 5.11, is perfect for high-performance Media Center use. It's an ATX board that comes with built-in Intel High Definition Audio. It supports all PCI Express video cards, and includes eight USB ports, one serial port, one parallel port, four serial ATA interfaces with RAID support, and so on. Obviously, it's designed for Intel Pentium 4 chips, including those with hyper-threading technology, and sells for around $250.

FIGURE 5.11

Intel's D955XBK motherboard, with built-in High Definition Audio.

As to CPUs, you can choose from Intel or AMD chips. Intel's Pentium 4 chips, like the one in Figure 5.12, are arguably more popular for Media Center use, but the AMD 64 also has many adherents. If you go the Intel route, you probably want at least a 3.2GHz chip, possibly higher if you're doing a lot of video recording and playback. If you choose an AMD 64, go with the 3200+ or higher series. Expect to pay anywhere from $200 to $400, depending on the precise specifications.

FIGURE 5.12

Intel's Pentium 4 processor.

Memory

You're going to want at least 512MB of memory in your Media Center PC, possibly 1GB or more. You should buy the type of memory modules that your motherboard supports—DDR (double date rate) or DDR2 (double data rate, second generation).

You typically buy memory modules in pairs, so if you want 512MB memory, you should buy two 256MB pairs; if you want 1GB, buy two 512MB pairs. If you go with 512MB total, you'll spend a little under $100; a 1GB kit will cost you between $150–$200; a 2GB kit will run closer to $300. The memory modules, like the one shown in Figure 5.13, plug right into the appropriate slots on the motherboard.

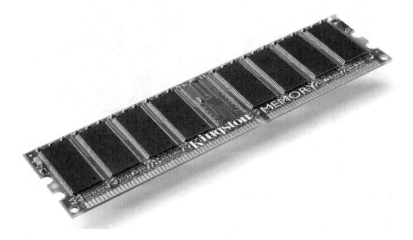

FIGURE 5.13

A DDR memory module from Kingston.

Popular memory manufacturers include Corsair (www.corsairmemory.com), Crucial (www.crucial.com), Kingston (www.kingston.com), and Micron (www.micron.com).

Hard Disk Drives

The amount of hard disk storage you need depends on how you'll be using your Media Center PC. Certainly, many do-it-yourselfers go this route because they can build mega-storage capacity into their systems, more than you typically get with an off-the-shelf Media Center PC. You can get individual hard drives as large as 400–500GB, and install two or more of these monsters in your system unit (depending on the type of system unit you choose). Let's say you go with dual 500GB drives in a RAID array; this gives you 1TB (terabyte) of storage. If you have room for four hard drives, you can get up to 2TB capacity—considerably more than you'll get from any off-the-shelf system.

A basic 200GB hard drive, like the one in Figure 5.14, will cost you a little under $150; a 500GB drive will run closer to $350. Drives are available from Hitachi (www.hitachigst.com), Maxtor (www.maxtor.com), Seagate (www.seagate.com), and Western Digital (www.wdc.com). Look for models designed especially for A/V use; these drives are typically much quieter than standard hard disk drives.

FIGURE 5.14

An internal hard drive from Western Digital.

CD and DVD Drives

Your Media Center PC needs a single CD/DVD drive, like the one in Figure 5.15, capable of playing and burning both types of discs. You don't have to spend a fortune for a decent drive; depending on read/write speed, you can find models priced from $50 to $150. Popular drive manufacturers include LiteOn (www.liteon.com), NEC (www.necsam. com), Plextor (www.plextor.com), Sony (www.sonyburners.com/dvd_burners/), and Toshiba (sdd.toshiba.com).

FIGURE 5.15

An internal CD/DVD drive from NEC.

Video and TV Tuner Cards

If you intend to use your Media Center PC to play and record television programming, you need to install two separate cards in your system unit: a traditional video card and a TV tuner card. In fact, you might want to install *two* tuner cards, one for standard definition NTSC analog broadcasts and a second for high-definition ATSC digital broadcasts.

For the video card, consider the ATI Radeon (www.ati.com) line, as well as any cards that use the NVIDIA GeForce 6 or 7 chips—which includes models from ASUS (usa.asus.com), Gigabyte (www.giga-byte.com), eVGA (www.evga.com), PNY (www.pny.com), and other vendors. You want a high-performance card, like the ATI Radeon X850 shown in Figure 5.16, to handle all the digital video you'll be pumping through your system. You also want a card that includes a component video, DVI, or HDMI output, for best possible picture quality. Expect to spend anywhere from $200 to $1,000, depending on performance and connections.

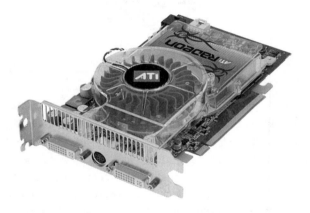

FIGURE 5.16

ATI's Radeon X850 graphics card, with DVI digital video output.

For the NTSC TV tuner card, there are numerous models available from ATI (www.ati.com), AVerMedia (www.avermedia.com), Hauppage (www.hauppage.com), Kworld (www.kworld.com.tw), and Pinnacle (www.pinnaclesys.com), all of which do a decent job. Obviously, you want a card that offers DVR capability; you'll spend anywhere from $50 to $150.

For the ATSC tuner, I really like ATI's HDTV Wonder, shown in Figure 5.17. Similar cards are available from AVerMedia and other companies. Expect to pay $120–$200.

Audio Card

If your motherboard didn't come with built-in digital audio (such as Intel's High Definition Audio), you'll need to buy a separate audio card for your system. You want a card that has digital audio outputs, support for 24-bit/96KHz audio, and full surround-sound decoding for both Dolby Digital and DTS. You're probably looking at one of the Creative Labs Sound Blaster cards, at the upper end of the range. (One particular favorite is the Sound Blaster Audigy 2, shown in Figure 5.18.) Expect to pay anywhere from $100 to $300 for a good quality card.

FIGURE 5.17

ATI's HDTV Wonder ATSC tuner card.

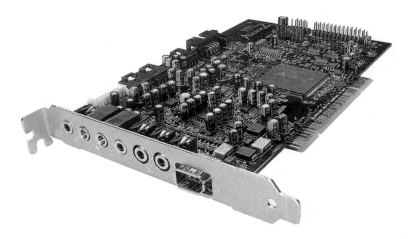

FIGURE 5.18

The Sound Blaster Audigy 2 audio card.

Input Devices

You'll also need to consider how you'll be controlling your system. You'll need three separate devices: a Media Center remote control, a wireless mouse, and a wireless keyboard.

For the remote, you can go with a standard Microsoft Media Center remote, like the one shown in Figure 15.19, which is typically priced around $40. Or you can go with a universal remote that you program for Media Center use, like the Logitech Harmony 880 remote, which sells for around $250.

FIGURE 5.19

The standard Microsoft Media Center remote.

My favorite living room keyboard/mouse combo is the Gyration Media Center Remote & Keyboard, which sells for around $180. You might also want to check out Microsoft's Remote Keyboard for Windows XP Media Center Edition, which combines keyboard/ mouse functionality in a single unit, for around $80.

Windows XP Media Center Edition Software

Last, but certainly not least, is the Windows XP MCE operating system itself. Unfortunately, you can't buy Media Center Edition as a piece of off-the-shelf software. You can, however, purchase an OEM version of the operating system when you buy a piece of major hardware, such as a motherboard or CPU—which you will be doing. Check with your retailer to determine what you have to do to order a copy of MCE. You'll probably pay between $120–$150 for the operating system.

Pricing It Out

How much does it really cost to assemble your own Media Center PC? It all depends on the type and quality of components you buy, and the capacity and speed of the various devices. So, we're talking a range of prices, as detailed in Table 5.1.

TABLE 5.1   Component Prices for a Home-Built Media Center PC

Component	Low-End Price	High-End Price
Case	$100	$300
Power supply	$0 (included with case)	$200
Motherboard	$100	$250
CPU	$200	$400
Memory	$100 (512MB)	$300 (2GB)
Hard disk drive	$150 (200GB)	$700 (500GB × 2)
CD/DVD drive	$50	$150
Video card	$200	$1,000
TV tuner card	$50 (1 NTSC)	$350 (1 NTSC, 1 ATSC)
Audio card	$0 (included with motherboard)	$300
Remote control	$35	$250
Wireless keyboard/mouse	$80	$180
Windows XP MCE operating system	$150	$150
TOTAL PRICE	$1,215	$4,530

As I said, it's a price range—and a rather large one. At the low end, a $1,215 scratchbuilt system is a tad cheaper than a similar off-the-shelf system. On the high end...well, you're paying for performance here, as the $4,530 price tag attests.

Putting It All Together

After you gather all your components, it's time to assemble your new PC. Naturally, you should follow the specific instructions for the individual components, but in general terms, here's how it goes:

1. Install the motherboard into the case.
2. Install the power supply into the case.
3. Insert the front-panel display into the case.
4. Install the hard drive(s) into the case.
5. Install the CD/DVD drive into the case.
6. Insert the CPU into the motherboard, along with any accompanying heat sinks.
7. Insert the memory modules into the motherboard.
8. Install the video card, TV tuner card(s), and audio card.
9. Connect the wireless keyboard and mouse.

10. Connect the system unit to your television set and audio/video receiver.

11. Power up the unit and configure system BIOS and memory.

12. Install Windows XP MCE onto the hard drive.

13. Install and configure the various device drivers.

14. Activate and register Windows XP MCE.

That's it in a nutshell. Obviously, you shouldn't tackle the job yourself unless you're familiar and comfortable with the process. Chances are, the system won't work perfectly the first time out; troubleshooting installation problems is part and parcel of doing it yourself. But if you're technically proficient, it's kind of cool to have a hand-built, one-of-a-kind Media Center PC—and know that you can easily upgrade any individual component at any time in the future.

Build or Buy: Comparing the Options

So, should you buy an off-the-shelf Media Center PC, or build one yourself? For most consumers, especially those who lack the technical interest and proficiency, the off-the-shelf solution is the only solution. If you're a tech wizard, however, you might be able to save a little money—but not a lot—by doing it yourself. More important, the do-it-yourself solution lets you assemble a PC that's exactly what you want, no compromises. In reality, the average custom-built Media Center PC is a higher-end unit, personalized with state-of-the-art video and audio cards, multiple TV tuners, and multiple hard disks. If this is the kind of system you want—and if you possess the technical know-how—then, by all means, investigate this option. Otherwise, buy the best off-the-shelf system you can afford—and learn to love the system you buy.

Setting Up Your Media Center PC

6 Making the Connections

7 Configuring Windows XP Media Center Edition

6

Making the Connections

Whether you buy or build a Media Center PC, you're still faced with the same challenge: how best to connect it to your living home entertainment system. Although different models have different back-panel connections, there remain a plethora of connection choices available to you. For instance, which of the video outputs should you use—HDMI (*high-definition multimedia interface*), DVI (*digital visual interface*), component video, S-Video, or composite video? And the same for audio—optical digital, coaxial digital, or plain old analog right and left RCA jacks?

Although there is no single "correct" way to connect your system, there are some general preferences to which you should adhere. Read on to learn the best ways to connect your Media Center PC—both to your other audio/video components and to your home network.

How Connecting a Media Center PC Is Different from Connecting a Desktop PC

There are many more—and different—things to connect on a living room PC than there are on a desktop model. About the only thing that connects the same way is the network connection;

even the keyboard and mouse connections are likely to be subtly different when you're sitting 10 feet away from the system unit.

You'll first notice the difference between a desktop and living room PC by examining the back panels of the units. Most living room PCs have a back panel that is, in many ways, cleaner than the typical back panel of a desktop PC. The goal, whether achieved or not, is to make the living room PC look and feel like a traditional audio/video component, not like a complicated and confusing personal computer. To that end, the back panel of the living PC is probably simpler, more logically laid out, and better labeled than a comparable desktop unit. (Figure 6.1 shows the back panel layout of a typical living room PC.)

FIGURE 6.1

The back panel of a typical living room PC—nice and clean and orderly.

You'll also notice different connections on the back of your Media Center PC than on your desktop PC. Take, for example, the video output. You probably connect the monitor on your desktop PC via a VGA connection, like the one shown in Figure 6.2. (Some newer monitors connect via DVI, although that's much less common.) But you don't connect your living room PC via VGA because your big-screen television set doesn't have a VGA connection. Most TVs have component video, S-Video, composite video, and, in the case of some newer models, DVI or HDMI connections. So, you have to connect your PC to your TV using the highest-quality type of connection that your TV supports.

Audio connections are also much different on a living room PC. For one thing, you don't connect your living room speakers directly to the PC, as you do with your desktop computer speakers. Instead, your living room speakers connect to an audio/video receiver, which then connects to your PC. Here's why.

All speakers use electricity to produce sound waves. That electricity is fed through a power amplifier, which amplifies the basic signal as directed by the audio input signal. On a typical desktop PC, the speakers you connect contain their own built-in power amplifiers—which is why these are sometimes called *powered speakers*. A built-in amplifier is fine for a smallish computer speaker, but doesn't cut the mustard for a high-fidelity living room audio system. In a larger home entertainment system, the speakers are powered by an external power amplifier—either a freestanding power amp or an amplifier built into an audio or audio/video receiver. It's this external amplifier or receiver that powers your living room speakers—the speakers don't have any amplifiers built in.

FIGURE 6.2

VGA video connectors—common on desktop PCs, seldom used on living room PCs.

This is why you connect your living room PC not to your speakers, but rather to your A/V receiver. (Or, in some high-end systems, to a separate pre-amplifier that is then connected to a power amplifier.) The connection can be via either traditional right/left RCA jacks, or (for surround sound) an optical or coaxial connection. Much different from connecting speakers to a desktop PC.

Then, if your Media Center PC has a built-in TV tuner or two, you have the issue of connecting an antenna, cable box, or satellite receiver. The tuner needs to receive television signals of some sort; those signals typically come via a coaxial cable connected to an over-the-air antenna, cable box, or satellite box. If you have two tuners and one antenna, you have to do some signal splitting. More complications than you have with a typical non-TV desktop installation.

note One important exception to the use of external power is your system's subwoofer. Most subwoofers contain their own built-in amplifiers, making them self-powered—just like your desktop PC speakers. Therefore the typical audio/video receiver contains only five channels of amplification for a 5.1-channel system; the ".1" of the subwoofer is powered outside the receiver, in the subwoofer itself.

note Some newer Media Center PCs come with the infrared (or RF) remote control receiver built into the system unit.

Control of your Media Center PC also dictates some differences in connecting your input devices—your keyboard, mouse, and (this is a new one) Media Center remote control. You can't use a standard corded keyboard or mouse, which means you have to move up to a wireless model—and not just any wireless model. You need a keyboard/mouse combo designed to work from 10 feet away, and a mouse that doesn't require a desktop for rolling. Obviously, you don't connect the cordless keyboard/mouse directly to your PC; you have to connect an infrared receiver to your PC instead (typically via USB), and place that receiver within shooting range of your couch or easy chair. Same thing with the Media Center remote; there's an infrared receiver that has to be connected to the PC itself.

After all this, connecting your Media Center PC to your home network will be comfortingly familiar—if not necessarily simple or easy. You have to decide whether to connect via ethernet or wireless Wi-Fi, and make the necessary connections and configurations. In this aspect, connecting a Media Center PC to your network is no different from connecting any other network PC.

Finally, you have to connect any necessary external peripherals to your PC. There will probably be fewer of these than you have with your desktop PC—at the very least, you probably won't have a printer or scanner in your living room. You might, however, have an external hard disk drive (for backup purposes); this, and any other peripheral, connects in the same fashion as it would to your desktop computer.

> **tip** A quick word on connecting the Media Center PC's power. Unlike other PCs, you leave a Media Center PC on all the time. The power needs to stay on constantly, which means you don't want to connect to a switched power outlet on the back of your A/V receiver or to a wall outlet that is controlled by a switch. Naturally, it's best to connect via a surge suppressor to protect against power surges and the like.

Connecting the Antenna Input

We'll start with the lone input to your Media Center PC: the antenna input. Note that this connection is applicable only if your Media Center contains a built-in television tuner, and if you intend to use the PC for watching and recording television broadcasts.

In almost all instances, your PC's TV tuner has a single coaxial RF input, like the one shown in Figure 6.3. Whatever type of signal you're receiving—over the air television, cable, or satellite—should connect to this coaxial input.

FIGURE 6.3

An coaxial RF antenna connector.

We'll examine all three types of connections in the following sections. But let's note upfront that if you have more than one tuner in your PC, you might have to split the incoming signal. This is easy enough to do, using a coaxial signal splitter, like the one shown in Figure 6.4. Likewise, if you have two signal source (an OTA antenna and a cable box, for example), you can connect each source to a separate RF input.

caution If the original television signal you're splitting is a little weak, the split signal will be even weaker, resulting in a snowy or grainy picture. To alleviate this problem, you might want to insert a signal amplifier into the line ahead of the splitter. You can find low-priced RF amplifiers at your local Radio Shack or another consumer electronics store.

FIGURE 6.4

A coaxial signal splitter.

Connecting to an Over-the-Air Antenna

In many ways, connecting an over-the-air (OTA) antenna is the easiest input connection to make. It doesn't matter whether you're using an indoor or outdoor antenna, the connection is identical. All you have to do is connect the output of the antenna to the antenna input on the back of your PC. Well, that's not quite accurate. If you do this, you don't have a direct antenna connection to your television set, which you probably still want. So, you probably want to split the antenna signal first, running one end to your TV and the other end to your PC, as shown in Figure 6.5.

Connecting to an HDTV Antenna

Surprisingly, connecting an HDTV antenna is no different from connecting a traditional standard definition antenna. Most HDTV signals are broadcast in the UHF band, so you need a high-quality UHF antenna to receive the HDTV signals. Just connect your HDTV antenna to coaxial input on your PC labeled either HDTV or ATSC, as shown in Figure 6.6. (You might also need to split the UHF signal to connect to both your Media Center PC and your television set, as described previously.)

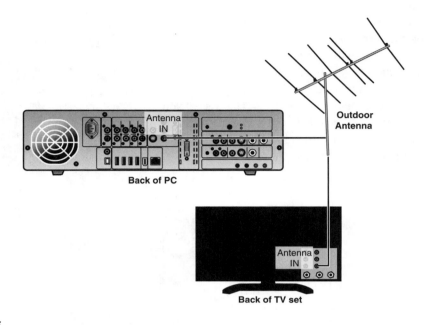

FIGURE 6.5

Connecting an over-the-air antenna to your Media Center PC.

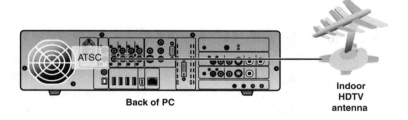

FIGURE 6.6

Connecting a high-definition antenna to your Media Center PC.

Connecting to a Basic Cable Line

More U.S. households receive their television via cable than via any other method. So, it's likely that you'll be connecting your Media Center PC to your cable line.

This is a relatively easy procedure if all you have is basic cable—that is, if you're not using a cable set top box. (If you are using a set top box, read on to the next section for connection instructions.) The tuner in your Media Center PC can receive basic, unscrambled analog cable signals without the need for a set top box. All you have to do is connect the cable signal directly to the antenna input on the back of the PC, as shown in Figure 6.7. (And remember to split the cable signal first, if you want to route a direct signal to your TV.)

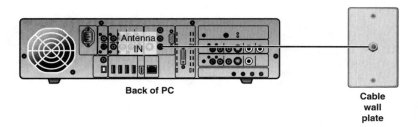

FIGURE 6.7

Connecting an analog cable signal to your Media Center PC.

Connecting to a Digital Cable Box

If you need a set top box to receive your cable signals—typical if you subscribe to digital cable—the connection to your Media Center PC is a tad more complex. The reason? Your PC's tuner can't process direct digital cable signals. The signal first has to be processed via the set top box, with the resulting output fed into the PC's tuner.

This means that your PC receives a single output channel—typically channel 3. You use a coaxial cable to connect the output from the cable box to the antenna input of your PC, as shown in Figure 6.8.

The only exception to this is if the TV tuner in your Media Center PC accepts alternative audio/video inputs. Some tuner cards offer S-Video and RCA audio inputs in addition to the normal RF coaxial input. Going the S-Video route gives you a slightly better picture than you get with the coaxial input; the right/left RCA audio connections let you record high-quality stereo sound.

To connect your set top box in this fashion, run an S-Video cable from the S-Video output on your set top box to the S-Video input on your Media Center PC. Then run a stereo audio cable from the right and left audio outputs on your set top box to the right and left audio inputs on your PC. It should look like the diagram in Figure 6.9.

caution Even though your cable or satellite box probably has higher-quality video and audio outputs—component video and optical digital audio outputs are common—you can't use these outputs to connect to your PC's TV tuner. No tuner currently on the market accepts anything higher quality than S-Video and analog audio inputs.

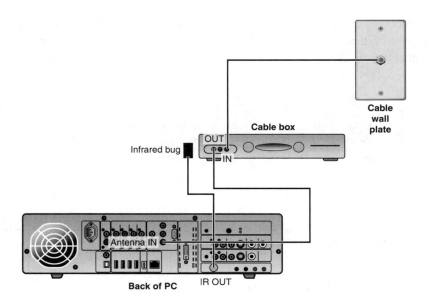

FIGURE 6.8

Connecting a cable box to a Media Center PC via the coaxial connection.

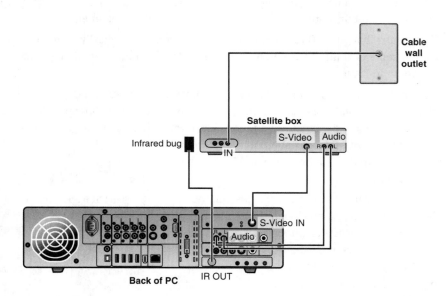

FIGURE 6.9

Connecting a cable box to a Media Center PC via S-Video and stereo audio connections.

Then there's the matter of controlling the cable box—that is, turning it on and off and switching channels to record specific programs in advance. This is accomplished via means of an infrared bug (or *blaster*), like the one shown in Figure 6.10. You connect one end of this bug to the controller output on your PC, and then affix the receiver end of the bug to the front of your cable box, as shown in Figure 6.11. In this fashion your PC sends on/off/channel information through the cable to the bug, which is then beamed directly to the IR input on the cable box. It's an inelegant solution, but a necessary one.

FIGURE 6.10

An infrared bug controller.

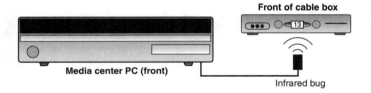

FIGURE 6.11

Connecting an IR bug between the Media Center PC and cable box.

Connecting to a Satellite Receiver

Connecting a digital satellite receiver (for either DirecTV or Dish Network) to your Media Center PC is identical to connecting a digital cable set top box. You run the output from the satellite receiver to the corresponding input on your PC; you can connect via coaxial RF cable (shown in Figure 6.12) or, if your PC's tuner accepts it, S-Video/stereo audio (shown in Figure 6.13). You also have to connect an IR bug controller, of course.

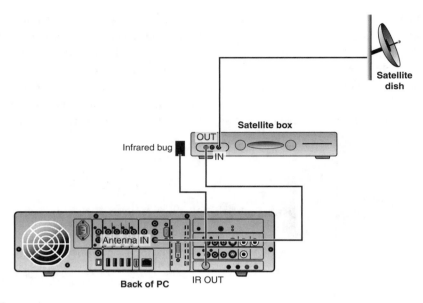

FIGURE 6.12

Connecting a satellite receiver to a Media Center PC via a coaxial connection.

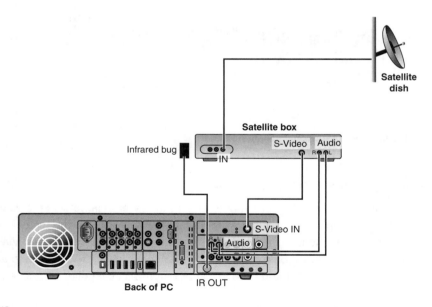

FIGURE 6.13

Connecting a satellite receiver to a Media Center PC via S-Video and stereo audio connections.

Connecting the Video Output

All Media Center PCs have to be connected to a television display (or computer monitor, for desktop systems). This is the case even if you're using your Media Center PC strictly for music, not to play or record television or videos. The reason why is simple: You need to see the Media Center interface to control the Media Center PC, and the interface is displayed on your television set.

The type of video connection you make depends on three factors: the types of video *output* jacks available on the Media Center PC; the types of video *input* jacks available on your TV set; and whether or not you're using your Media Center PC to view DVDs, standard-definition analog television, or high-definition digital television.

The first two items need little explanation; the third item, however, bears discussion. It's like this. If you're not using your Media Center PC to view television or DVDs, you don't need to use a high-quality connection. If you are viewing TVs or DVDs, you need a high-quality connection. And if you're viewing high-definition television, you need the highest-quality connection possible.

We'll discuss all the possible types of video connections next. But first, see Table 6.1 for a quick take on what types of connections to use for which purposes.

note Not all PCs have HDMI connections, nor do all TVs have either HDMI or DVI connections. Most PCs and TVs have all the other three connections (component video, S-Video, and composite video).

TABLE 6.1   Preferred Video Connections

Video Connection	HDTV (1080p, 1080i, 720p)	DVD (480p Progressive Scan)	DVD (480i Interlaced Scan)	SDTV (480i)	Media Center Display
HDMI	Yes	Yes	Yes	Yes	Yes
DVI	Yes	Yes	Yes	Yes	Yes
Component video	Yes	Maybe (may not work with some copy-protected DVDs)	Yes	Yes	Yes
S-Video	No	No	Yes	Yes	Yes
Composite video	No	No	Yes	Yes	Yes

As you can see, HDMI and DVI will handle anything you throw at them. Component video is almost as good, but has some trouble playing some copy-protected DVDs. (More on this in a minute.) S-Video and composite video are poor choices for playing DVDs (they transmit only the standard-definition interlaced signal, not the higher-quality progressive scan signal), and won't transmit HDTV signals at all. You should use S-Video and composite video connections only as a last resort, or if you're using your Media Center PC strictly to listen to music—and thus need to display only the Media Center interface on your TV.

note HDMI stands for *high-definition multimedia interface*. An HDMI cable uses a 19-pin connector that is smaller and sleeker than the older DVI connector.

Connecting via HDMI

The best choice for connecting your Media Center PC to your television display is HDMI. (Figure 6.14 shows an HDMI connector.) HDMI is a pure digital connection that delivers the highest-possible video quality. It is also capable of transmitting both HDTV and progressive-scan DVD signals.

FIGURE 6.14

An HDMI connector.

If your PC has an HDMI output (and not all do), connect this output to the corresponding HDMI input on your television display, as shown in Figure 6.15. Alternately, if your audio/video receiver offers HDMI video switching, you can connect the HDMI output from your PC to the HDMI input on your receiver, and then connect a second HDMI cable between your receiver and your TV, as shown in Figure 6.16.

note Although HDMI can technically carry both digital video and audio signals, the audio capability isn't always implemented in all devices. For this reason, you probably still need to connect a digital audio cable along with the HDMI cable for video.

Connecting via DVI

DVI is similar to HDMI, except that it uses a slightly larger connector and cable (as shown in Figure 6.17), and doesn't carry audio signals. You're more likely to see DVI connectors on a PC than you are on a TV because this type of connector has long been used to connect LCD flat panel computer monitors. DVI is used less often in the consumer electronics industry; in fact, DVI has been supplanted by the newer and more versatile HDMI standard.

note DVI stands for *digital visual interface*. A DVI cable uses a 24-pin connector, with three rows of 8 pins each. (Some variations of the DVI standard use more or fewer pins, but the 24-pin arrangement is the default for home video use.)

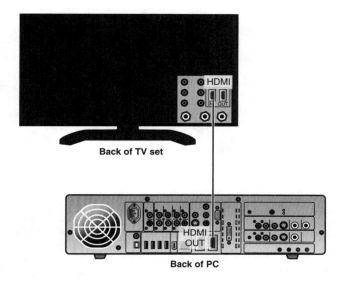

FIGURE 6.15

Connecting a Media Center PC to a TV via HDMI.

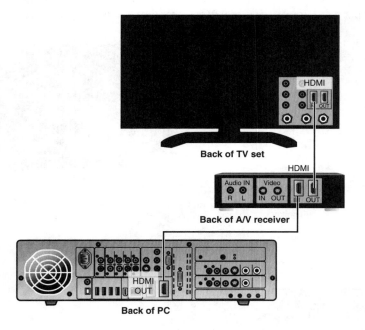

FIGURE 6.16

Connecting a Media Center PC to an A/V receiver via HDMI.

FIGURE 6.17

A DVI connector.

tip It's not uncommon to find that your PC has a DVI output but your widescreen TV has an HDMI input. In this instance, you'll want to use a DVI-to-HDMI adapter to convert the DVI output from your PC to an HDMI input for your TV.

Still and all, the video quality you get with DVI is identical to that produced by an HDMI connection; in a Media Center system, one is as good as the other. Making the connection is simple—just connect the DVI output on your Media Center PC to the DVI input on your television or A/V receiver, as shown in Figure 6.18.

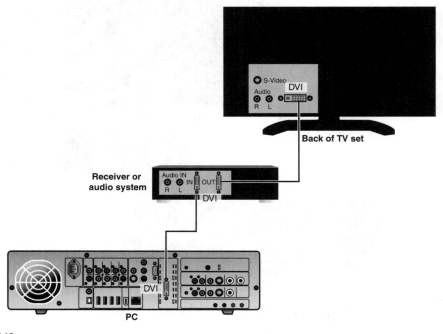

FIGURE 6.18

Connecting a Media Center PC to an A/V receiver via DVI.

Connecting via Component Video

If your PC or TV lacks either an HDMI or DVI connection, the next best choice is to use component video. A component video connection, like the one in Figure 6.19, is an analog connection that uses three coaxial cables with RCA-type jacks on either end. The three cables separate the luminance (Y), red chrominance (Pr), and blue chrominance (Pb) information of the video signal, which produces high-quality picture signals with improved color accuracy and reduced color bleeding (over S-Video and composite video connections).

FIGURE 6.19

Component video connectors.

A component video connection can transmit HDTV signals, as well as progressive-scan DVD signals—with a caveat. The caveat is that the signal from some copy-protected DVDs won't play via a PC's component video outputs. This is because DVD's copy protection thinks that the analog component connections might be used to copy the DVD—running out from the PC to a DVD recorder, for example. Even if this isn't the case, you might run into some commercial DVDs that simply won't play on your Media Center PC when using the component video connections.

The solution to this problem is to switch to a DVI or HDMI output, or to install a third-party universal DVD codec on your system. (This is a piece of software that lets your PC's DVD player play back DVDs encoded for other countries, and that unofficially—and perhaps illegally, if that matters—bypasses the content protection technology.)

That said, component video is the preferred connection for many, especially when you're viewing live and recorded television—both standard and high definition. All you have to do is connect the component video outputs on your Media Center PC to the component video inputs on your TV or A/V receiver, as shown in Figure 6.20.

note Read more about this copy protection issue—and possible solutions—in Chapter 11, "Using Windows XP MCE for DVD Playback and Recording."

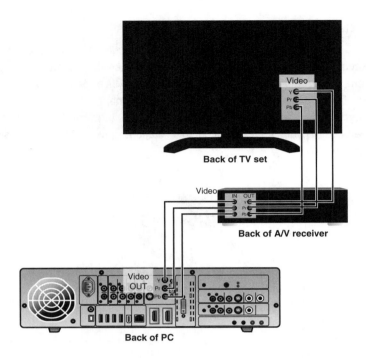

FIGURE 6.20

Connecting a Media Center PC to an A/V receiver via component video.

Connecting via S-Video

Not all PCs have component video connections, nor do all TVs. If you have a lower-priced Media Center PC or an older television, you might be forced to use an S-Video connection instead. An S-Video cable, like the one in Figure 6.21, is a four-pin connector that separates the luminance (brightness) and chrominance (color) in the video signal, thus providing slightly higher quality than a single-cable composite video connection. Aside from having lower picture quality than component video, S-Video cannot be used to transmit HDTV signals, and also cannot transmit progressive-scan DVD signals.

That said, S-Video is more than good enough if all you're doing is displaying the Media Center interface—that is, if you're not watching DVDs or television. The connection is simple: just connect the S-Video output on your Media Center PC to the S-Video input on your TV or A/V receiver, as shown in Figure 6.22.

Connecting via Composite Video

If no other type of video connection is available, you can default to a single-cable composite video connector, like the one shown in Figure 6.23. (This type of connector is typically labeled Video.) The picture quality with composite video is the least sharp of all the connectors we've discussed because it mixes the luminance and chrominance information into a single video signal. Still, it's good enough for displaying the Media Center interface when you're playing music, even if you wouldn't want to use it for much of anything else.

FIGURE 6.21

An S-Video connector.

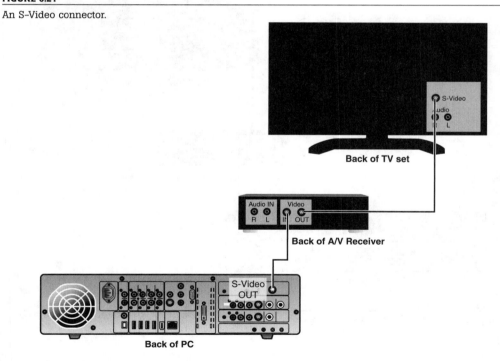

FIGURE 6.22

Connecting a Media Center PC to an A/V receiver via S-Video.

FIGURE 6.23

A composite video connector.

To connect via composite video, connect the video output on your Media Center PC to the video input on your TV or A/V receiver, as shown in Figure 6.24.

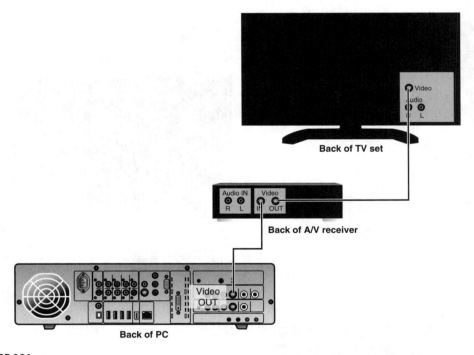

FIGURE 6.24

Connecting a Media Center PC to an A/V receiver via composite video.

Connecting the Audio Output

Connecting the audio output of your Media Center PC is slightly less complicated than connecting the video, simply because there are fewer choices. In fact, you can boil the choices down to two:

- If you're using your Media Center PC to watch TV or DVDs with surround sound, use an optical or coaxial digital connection (either will work fine).

- If you're using your Media Center PC solely to listen to stereo music, use the stereo (right/left) analog audio connection.

You can also, if you want, use a digital connection to listen to stereo audio—but you can't use a stereo connection to listen to surround sound. If in doubt, just use a digital connection, and you'll be good for anything.

Connecting via HDMI

There is one possible exception to the general advice I just offered. If your Media Center PC has an HDMI output, and if your audio/video receiver has an HDMI input, and if both the HDMI connections have the audio option enabled, you can use the same HDMI connection you use for video to transmit your system's stereo and surround sound audio. One connection is simpler than two, and the sound quality is every bit as good as with an optical or coaxial digital connection. Just connect the HDMI output from your Media Center PC to the HDMI input on your receiver, as shown in Figure 6.25.

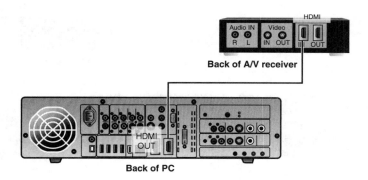

FIGURE 6.25

Connecting digital audio from a Media Center PC to an A/V receiver via HDMI.

Connecting via Optical Digital

That said, the most common type of audio connection these days is via optical digital cable, like the one shown in Figure 6.26. This type of connection transmits the digital audio signal across a fiber optic cable, resulting in the cleanest form of signal transfer currently available. (Just to clarify—both optical and coaxial connections deliver the same

note A digital audio connection (either optical or coaxial) is sometimes called an *S/PDIF connection*, which stands for *Sony/Philips Digital Interface*. (Sony and Philips were co-developers of the digital audio standard.)

quality of digital audio signal—although you get less electrical interference with an optical connection.)

FIGURE 6.26

An optical digital connector.

Optical digital connections transmit multiple channels of digital sound, which makes them ideal—and necessary—for transmitting 5.1-channel and higher surround sound-tracks. Obviously, the digital connection can also carry a stereo audio signal or even a mono television audio signal.

To make an optical digital connection, connect the optical digital output on your Media Center PC to the optical digital input on your audio/video receiver, as shown in Figure 6.27.

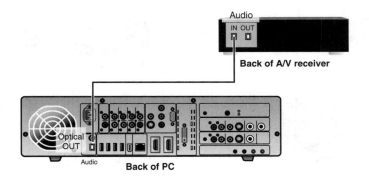

FIGURE 6.27

Connecting a Media Center PC to an A/V receiver via the optical digital connection.

Connecting via Coaxial Digital

The other type of digital audio connection is coaxial digital. As you can see in Figure 6.28, a digital coaxial cable looks like a coaxial cable with RCA connectors on each end. It delivers the same multi-channel digital sound quality as an optical digital connection.

tip

Practically speaking, there's no difference in sound quality between optical and coaxial digital connections; they both transfer the same amount of digital bits. That said, optical cable is probably the better choice for most installations because of the benefits of optical transmission—they're less susceptible to electrical interference and have less signal loss, which makes them better for longer runs.

To make a coaxial digital connection, connect the coaxial digital output on your Media Center PC to the coaxial digital input on your audio/video receiver, as shown in Figure 6.29.

FIGURE 6.28

A coaxial digital connector.

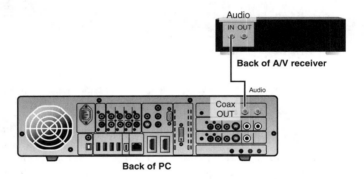

FIGURE 6.29

Connecting a Media Center PC to an A/V receiver via the coaxial digital connection.

Connecting via Right/Left Analog Audio

If you're not using your Media Center PC to watch—and listen to—television programs or DVDs, you don't necessarily need a multichannel digital audio connection. When you're listening to stereo music, an analog stereo connection will do just fine, thank you.

The traditional stereo connection, like the one shown in Figure 6.30, has two RCA jacks: one each for the right and left channels. (Red is typically used for the right channel, white for the left.) To make an analog audio connection, connect the right and left audio outputs on your Media Center PC to the right and left audio inputs on your audio/video receiver, as shown in Figure 6.31.

FIGURE 6.30

An analog stereo audio connector.

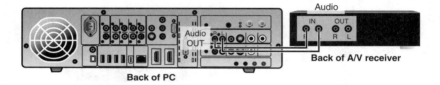

FIGURE 6.31

Connecting a Media Center PC to an A/V receiver via an analog stereo connection.

Connecting to a Stereo Mini-Jack

On the off chance that your Media Center PC has a single stereo mini-jack connector, like the one in Figure 6.32, instead of separate right and left audio connectors, your installation just got slightly more complex—but not overly so. In this instance, what you need is a stereo mini-jack to stereo RCA cable Y adapter cable, like the one shown in Figure 6.33. Connect one end of the Y adapter to the mini-jack connector on your PC, and then connect the other ends of the Y to the R/L stereo audio inputs on your A/V receiver.

Connecting via Multichannel Analog Audio

Some Media Center PCs have multichannel analog audio connections, as shown in Figure 6.34. This is not the type of connection you usually find on PCs; it's more commonly found on freestanding SACD and DVD-Audio players

note True living room PCs are unlikely to have a stereo mini-jack connector. This type of audio connector is more often found on traditional desktop PCs.

note SACD and DVD-Audio players use multichannel analog audio connections instead of single-cable digital audio connections because the SACD and DVD-A formats utilize strict copy-protection schemes. This copy protection blocks digital-to-digital copying by restricting the digital output; by allowing only analog output, bit-perfect digital copies can't be made.

that have built-in surround sound decoders. Most Media Center PCs do not play SACD (*super audio CD*) or DVD-Audio, which is why you probably won't run into this configuration. But if you do, you'll want to connect six (or more) separate shielded RCA audio cables between the multichannel outputs on your PC and the corresponding multichannel inputs on your audio/video receiver.

FIGURE 6.32

A stereo mini-jack connector.

FIGURE 6.33

A mini-jack to stereo Y adapter cable—connect one end to the mini-jack on your PC, and the other end to the stereo cable connected to your receiver.

FIGURE 6.34

A multichannel analog audio output panel.

Connecting to a Network

I can think of only one instance where you wouldn't want to connect your Media Center PC to your home network. (That's if you don't have another PC in your house, and thus run your Internet connection directly to your Media Center PC.) In all other instances, you'll have to connect your Media Center PC to the Internet via your home network. Here's why.

If you're using the PC to listen to music, you'll need to connect to the Internet to download album art and track information. If you're using the PC to watch and record television shows, you'll need to connect to the Internet to download the electronic program guide. I suppose that if all you're doing is viewing photo slideshows you could get by without a network connection, but even then you might want to include pictures stored on your main desktop PC. In other words, making a network connection is essential.

You can connect your Media Center PC to your network via ethernet or Wi-Fi—that is, either wired or wireless. A wireless connection is, in almost all instances, physically easier to accomplish because you don't have any cables to run. An ethernet connection, however, is faster and more reliable, both of which are desirable qualities if you're viewing video or television programming stored elsewhere on the network. For downloading album art and sharing digital photos, however, a wireless connection works just fine. Make your choice accordingly.

Connecting via Ethernet

Most Media Center PCs come with a built-in ethernet port, like the one shown in Figure 6.35. If your PC doesn't have an ethernet connection, you'll have to purchase and install an ethernet card. It's not a hard thing to do, even though it does involve opening up your PC's case.

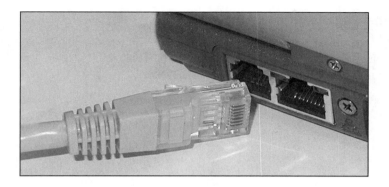

FIGURE 6.35

An ethernet port and connector.

Connecting your PC to your network via ethernet is a relatively simple thing to do. Simply run an ethernet cable from your PC's ethernet port to an open port on your network router, as shown in Figure 6.36. Your router should then be connected to both your main desktop PC and your incoming broadband Internet connection.

note Don't confuse your PC's ethernet connector with the slightly smaller telephone cable connector. They're not the same thing.

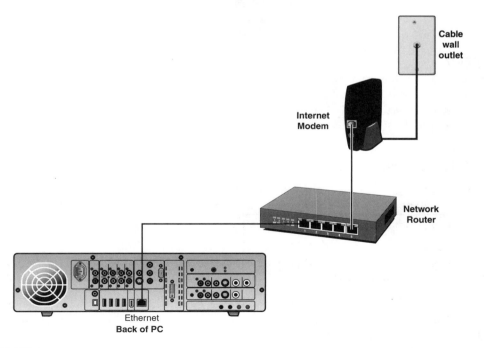

FIGURE 6.36

Connecting your PC to a home network via ethernet.

Connecting via Wi-Fi

Some Media Center PCs come with built-in Wi-Fi. Others don't. If you want to add Wi-Fi capability, you have to purchase an external Wi-Fi network adapter, like the one shown in Figure 6.37, and connect it to your PC via USB.

FIGURE 6.37

The Linksys WUSB54G Wi-Fi wireless network adapter.

When selecting a Wi-Fi adapter, you can choose from three different Wi-Fi standards, as detailed in Table 6.2.

TABLE 6.2   Current Wi-Fi Standards

Standard	Data Rate (Speed in Megabytes per Second)	Frequency Band
802.11b	11Mbps	2.4GHz
802.11g	54Mbps	2.4GHz
802.11a	54Mbps	5.0GHz

Chances are your existing home network uses either 802.11b (if it's an older one) or 802.11g (if it's a newer one). Of these two types of wireless networks, 802.11g is the route to go. However, if you have any problems with interference from other 2.4GHz devices, you might have to upgrade your entire system to the higher-quality 802.11a standard—a more expensive proposition, but sometimes necessary if you're transmitting a lot of video data.

To connect your Media Center PC to your network via Wi-Fi, simply activate the built-in Wi-Fi capability or install an external Wi-Fi wireless access point. Doing so connects your PC to your wireless router, which should then be connected to both your main desktop PC and your incoming broadband Internet connection, as shown in Figure 6.38.

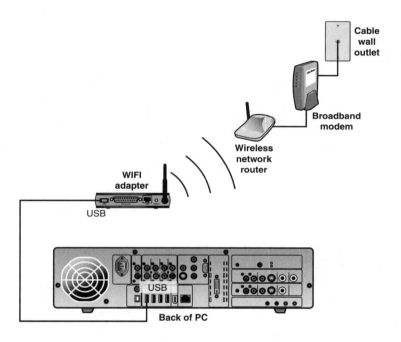

FIGURE 6.38

Connecting your PC to a home network via Wi-Fi.

Connecting the Keyboard, Mouse, and Remote Control

Connecting a wireless keyboard, mouse, and Media Center remote control is a relatively simple procedure. Assuming that your keyboard and mouse come from the same manufacturer, you'll have to connect a single infrared receiver to your PC, typically via USB. Your Media Center remote control probably has its own infrared receiver that also connects to your PC via USB—although some newer

note Most manufacturers, such as Gyration, offer keyboard/mouse combo packages that use a single infrared receiver. If your keyboard and mouse use separate IR receivers, you'll have to connect both of them to your PC.

units come with the IR receiver built into the system unit. In any case, after the necessary IR receivers are connected, you have to position all the receivers so that they have line of sight with your couch or easy chair, as shown in Figure 6.39.

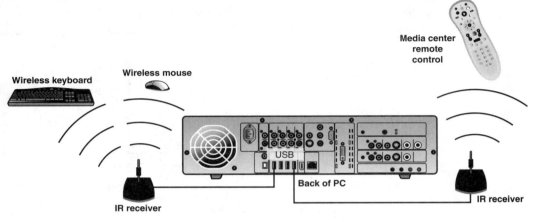

FIGURE 6.39

Connecting and positioning the IR receivers for your keyboard, mouse, and Media Center remote.

Connecting External Peripherals

The last things you'll need to connect to your Media Center PC are any external peripherals you might have, such as an external hard drive (for backup). Most peripherals these days connect via USB, as shown in Figure 6.40, although some high-capacity external drives connect via FireWire. You'll also use FireWire to connect your video camcorder, if you have one. (Most Media Center PCs have front-panel FireWire connections for just this purpose, which is much easier than connecting your camcorder to the *back* of your PC.)

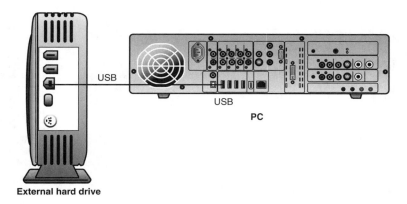

USB

USB

PC

External hard drive

FIGURE 6.40

Connecting an external hard disk drive via USB.

After you make these final connections, you're ready to turn on your PC and start using Windows XP Media Center Edition—which is exactly what you'll learn how to do in the next chapter. So turn the page, and get ready to rock and roll!

7

Configuring Windows XP Media Center Edition

In the preceding chapter you learned how to connect your Media Center PC to your home entertainment system. After everything is connected, you can power up your PC and start using Windows XP Media Center Edition.

Well, sort of. Before you start using Media Center, you have to configure the Media Center interface. That's what this chapter is all about—determining what settings you need to set and what configurations you need to configure. Read on to get properly set up.

Dealing with Windows XP

Before we get into the Media Center configuration, it's time I told you the truth. Media Center Edition is not a freestanding operating system. It's just an interface that sits on top of a real operating system—in this case, Windows XP. So, even though your TV screen displays the Media Center interface, it's Windows XP that's lurking in the background and making everything run.

Because Windows XP is relatively well hidden by the Media Center interface, you don't normally have to deal with it much. (That's not entirely true, either, as you'll learn in various places throughout this book—but for now, let's pretend that it's the case.) Where you most definitely will see Windows XP, however, is when you start up and shut down your PC. That's because Windows starts first, and then loads Media Center, so you see the typical Windows startup screens before the Media Center Start page is displayed. Same thing when you're shutting down; the Media Center interface closes first, and then you see the final stages of the standard Windows shutdown. It's just the way it is.

note Because this is a book about Media Center Edition and not one about Windows XP proper, I won't go into all the gory details on how to configure the Windows operating system. For that, consult my companion book, *Windows XP for Home Users, Service Pack 2 Edition* (Michael Miller, Peachpit Press, 2005).

I mention all of this here because when you first power on a brand new Media Center PC, you might be confronted with the Windows XP setup process. (It all depends on how much work the computer's manufacturer did at the factory, and how much it left for you to do.) This process typically involves waiting for the computer to recognize all the attached devices, configure the screen resolution, set up the network/Internet connection, and then ask you to activate and register your copy of Windows XP. Just follow the onscreen instructions and you'll be fine.

Setting Up MCE for the First Time

After you get past all the standard Windows XP setup screens, Windows launches the Media Center interface. (Or maybe not; if Media Center doesn't launch automatically, go to the Windows Start menu and start Media Center yourself.) Windows normally does a good job of guessing at some important display settings, but there is still a bit of configuration that you might have to do before you can start using Media Center.

Running the Setup Wizard

The first time you start Media Center, Windows launches the Setup Wizard. This wizard walks you through the basic Media Center setup to help you configure the Internet connection, television signal, and electronic program guide. Here's what you'll encounter:

tip You can rerun the Setup Wizard at any time by going to the Media Center Start page and selecting **Settings > Media Center Setup > Run Media Center Setup Again**.

1. The Getting Started screen, shown in Figure 7.1, welcomes you to the Setup Wizard.

2. The next screen, shown in Figure 7.2, tells you a little more about the setup. Click **Next** to keep going.

FIGURE 7.1

Welcome to the Setup Wizard!

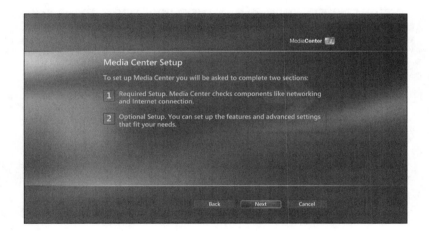

FIGURE 7.2

Getting ready to begin the configuration process.

3. The Media Center Privacy Policy screen, shown in Figure 7.3, lets you read Microsoft's privacy policy, if you're interested. (Click the **Media Center Privacy Policy** button to read the whole thing.)

4. The Help Improve Media Center screen, shown in Figure 7.4, gives you the option of your PC sending anonymous reports to Microsoft, to help improve future versions of Media Center. Click **Yes, I'd Like to Join** to participate, or **No Thank You** to not.

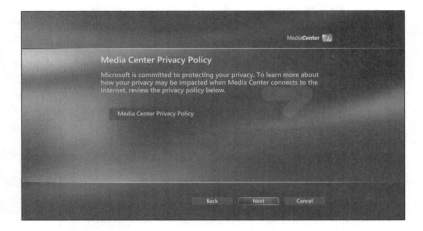

FIGURE 7.3

Get serious—nobody reads the privacy policy, do they?

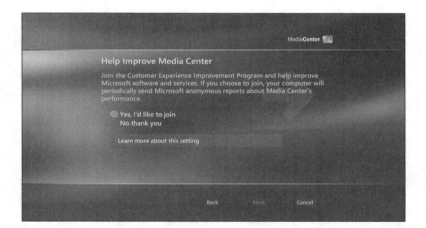

FIGURE 7.4

Opt in to Microsoft's Customer Experience Improvement Program.

5. The Get the Most from Media Center screen, shown in Figure 7.5, lets you configure Media Center to automatically access the Internet for various information. (Select **Yes**.)

6. The Internet Connection screen, shown in Figure 7.6, asks whether you have an always-on Internet connection. Select **Yes** if you have a cable, DSL, or satellite Internet connection, or if you connect to the Internet via a home or corporate network. Select **No** if you have no Internet connection (bad!), or if you connect via an old-fashioned dial-up service. (If you selected No, you have to provide further information; just follow the onscreen instructions.)

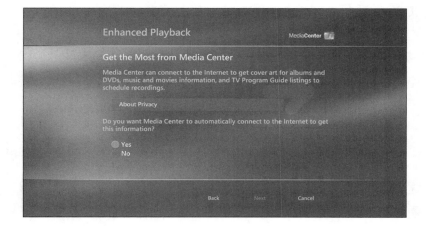

FIGURE 7.5

Internet access is important to get the most out of Media Center.

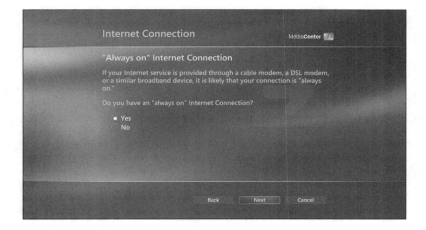

FIGURE 7.6

Configuring Media Center for an always-on Internet connection.

7. You're now prompted to test your Internet connection, as shown in Figure 7.7. Click the **Test** button to perform the test, or click **Next** to proceed without testing.

8. As you can see in Figure 7.8, Media Center now informs you that you've set up all your required components—but you're not done yet. Click **Next** to continue.

9. The Optional Setup screen, shown in Figure 7.9, lets you perform further configuration operations—you can configure your TV tuners, signal, and electronic program guide; optimize how Media Center looks on your television display; and set up your speakers. Click the first of the options to continue the setup process, or click **I Am Finished** to close the Setup Wizard and display the Media Center Start page.

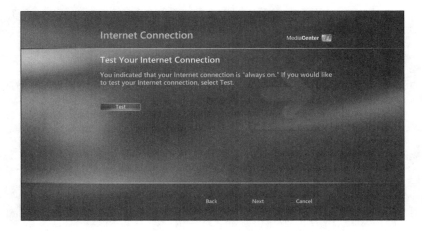

FIGURE 7.7

Testing your Internet connection.

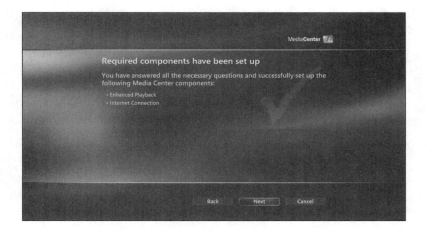

FIGURE 7.8

You've set up the required components—but you're not done yet.

We'll talk about the other configuration options later in this chapter. You can access these settings by continuing with the Setup Wizard, or by accessing them separately from the **Settings** screen.

note Learn more about navigating Media Center from the Start page in Chapter 8, "Getting to Know Windows XP Media Center Edition."

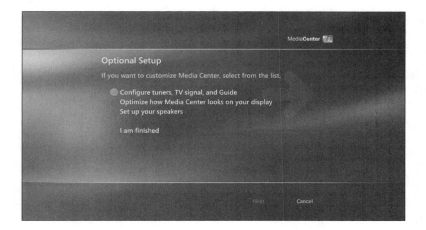

FIGURE 7.9

The gateway to additional configuration settings.

Setting Up the Television Signal and Program Guide

Media Center can receive both analog and (if your PC is equipped with an ATSC tuner) digital television signals. Which type of tuner you have connected should be detected automatically by Media Center during the setup process. This is typically done when you run the Setup Wizard, as previously described, although you can also access these settings separately, as we'll discuss here. Just follow these steps:

note These instructions for setting up your television signal apply specifically to North American PC users with an NTSC or ATSC tuner. The setup is slightly different in countries that use other television standards.

1. Make sure that your television signal (either over the air, cable, or satellite) is connected to the tuner input on your Media Center PC.

2. From the Media Center Start page, select **Settings > TV > Set Up TV Signal**.

3. When the Confirm Your Region screen appears, as shown in Figure 7.10, click **Yes** if the region (country) is correct, or **No** to select a different region, and then click **Next**.

4. When the Automatic TV Signal Setup page appears, as shown in Figure 7.11, you have a choice to make. You can choose to have Media Center detect and set up your signal automatically, or do it yourself manually. I recommend the automatic option; select **Configure My TV Signal Automatically**, and then click **Next**.

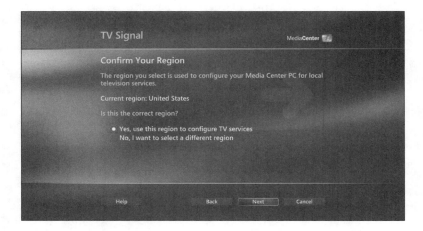

FIGURE 7.10

Does Media Center have your country right?

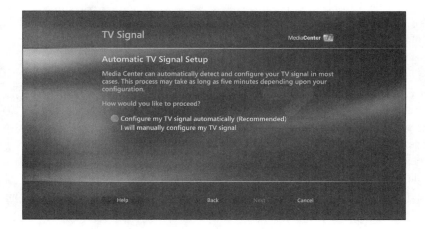

FIGURE 7.11

Getting ready to set up Media Center for your television signals.

5. Media Center now scans for live television signals, as shown in Figure 7.12.

6. The results of the signal scan are displayed on the TV Signal Configuration Result page, shown in Figure 7.13. This page displays the type of signal (antenna, cable, or satellite) and the number of tuners connected. Assuming that the results are correct, select **Yes** and then click **Next**.

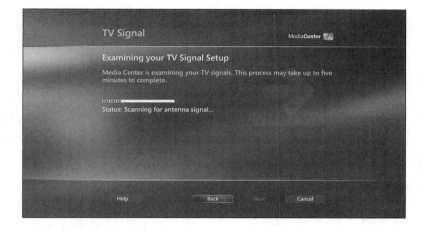

FIGURE 7.12

Scanning for television signals.

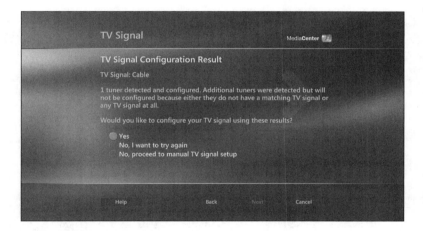

FIGURE 7.13

The results of the television signal scan.

7. If you have a digital (HDTV/ATSC) tuner active, Media Center tells you to connect your digital TV antenna, as shown in Figure 7.14. Click **Yes**, and then click **Next**. (And make sure that antenna is connected!)

8. You're now prompted to set up the Program Guide, as shown in Figure 7.15. This is an onscreen listing of all the channels your PC is set up to receive, along with a two-week listing of upcoming television programs for each channel. To use the guide, you first have to tell Media Center where you are and how you're receiving

your television stations (over the air, cable, or satellite) so that it knows the right Program Guide to use. Click **Yes** to use the Guide.

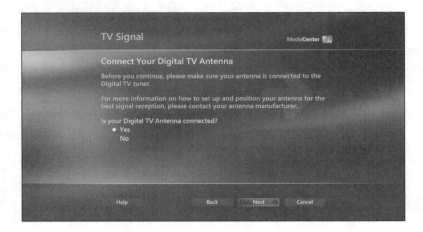

FIGURE 7.14

Connect your digital TV antenna!

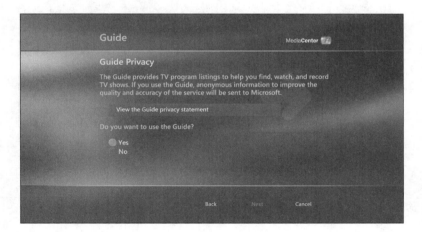

FIGURE 7.15

Click **Yes** to use the electronic Program Guide.

9. Now comes the biggest waste of time in the entire setup process—reading the Guide Terms of Service, as shown in Figure 7.16. Although you could scroll through and read all 57 pages of this document, you could also just click **I Agree** and be done with it.

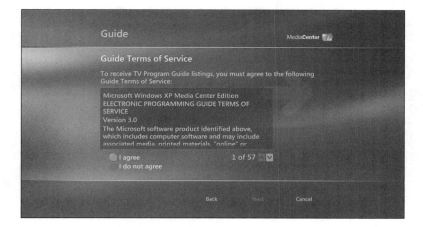

FIGURE 7.16

Who reads a 57-page terms of service?

10. That out of the way, the next screen (shown in Figure 7.17) is where you enter your ZIP code—so that Media Center knows what specific Guide listings to use.

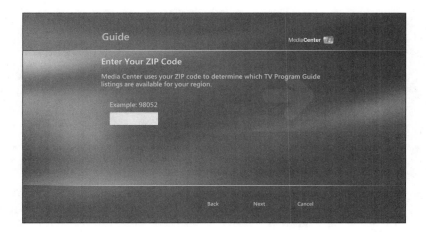

FIGURE 7.17

Telling Media Center where you live.

11. Media Center now downloads information about your television programming provider, as shown in Figure 7.18. Click **Next** when the download is complete.

tip You can return to the Set Up Guide Listings screen at any time by going to the Media Center Start page and selecting **Settings > TV > Guide > Set Up Guide Listings**.

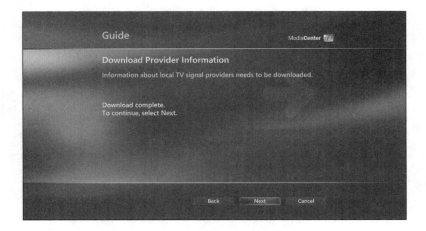

FIGURE 7.18

Downloading information about your local television stations, cable service, or satellite service.

    12. On the Select TV Signal Provider page, shown in Figure 7.19, select your television service provider from the list, and then click **Next**.

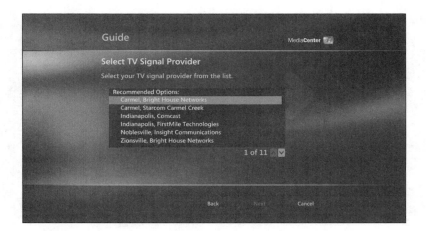

FIGURE 7.19

Selecting your specific television provider.

    13. Media Center now downloads the current TV listings for the Guide. (This might take several minutes.) When the download is complete, as shown in Figure 7.20, click **Next** to continue.

> **note** You'll need to be connected to the Internet to download the Guide listings. The faster your Internet connection, the faster the Guide listings will download.

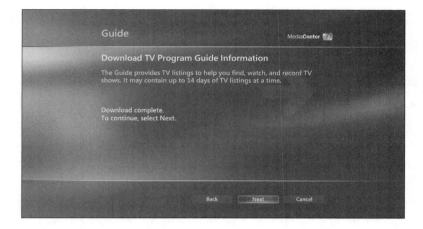

FIGURE 7.20

Completing the Guide download process.

14. If you have an ATSC (HDTV) digital tuner in your PC, Media Center now prompts you to adjust the digital TV antenna for the best signal strength, as shown in Figure 7.21.

FIGURE 7.21

If you have an HDTV tuner in your Media Center PC, you see this screen next.

15. Media Center now displays the Adjust Digital TV Antenna and Choose Channels page, as shown in Figure 7.22. When this screen is displayed, Media Center scans through all the possible digital channels in your area, and displays the signal strength for each. Obviously, the higher the signal strength (the more green bars), the better. (This is a good opportunity to adjust your HDTV antenna for the best possible reception of these channels.)

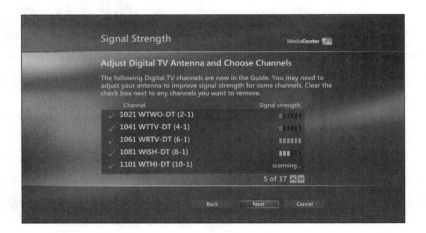

FIGURE 7.22
Detecting the signal strength of nearby HDTV stations.

16. For any channels that have no signal or too weak a signal (red or yellow bars instead of green ones), uncheck those channels in the list.

17. When the entire list has been scanned, Media Center repeats the scan at the top of the list— and keeps repeating it. After you have all the active digital channels selected, click **Next** to finish the wizard.

> **tip** You can return to the Adjust Digital TV Antenna and Choose Channels screen at any time by going to the Media Center Start page and selecting **Settings > TV > Digital TV Antenna Signal Strength**.

Configuring the Display

If you're lucky, Media Center correctly determined the size and resolution of your television display, and configured itself accordingly. If you're not lucky, Media Center is displayed in a little box in the middle of your television screen—or, even worse, you see only part of the screen. If this happens to you, you need to reconfigure Media Center for your particular display.

You can also, if you want, use Media Center to fine-tune your television display. These aren't adjustments within Media Center itself, but rather a series of patterns and tests that you can reference when adjusting the picture controls on your television set.

This display configuration is part of the Setup Wizard, or you can access it separately, as we'll discuss here. Just follow these steps:

1. From the Media Center Start page, select **Settings > TV > Configure Your TV or Monitor**.

2. When the Display Configuration page appears, as shown in Figure 7.23, click the **Watch Video** button. This displays a short video that explains how to configure your television display. If you don't want to watch the entire demonstration video, click the Stop or Back button on your Media Center remote.

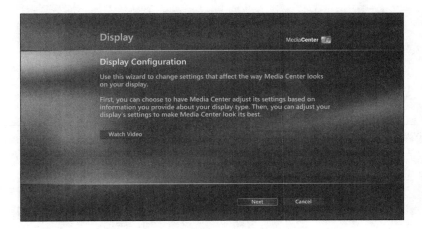

FIGURE 7.23

Getting ready to configure the display settings.

3. When the video is done playing, click **Next** to start the Display Configuration Wizard.

4. On the Identify Your Display Type page, shown in Figure 7.24, select the type of television display you have—traditional CRT TV/monitor, built-in display, flat panel (such as LCD or plasma), rear projection, or front projection. Click **Next** when done.

5. On the Connection Type page, shown in Figure 7.25, select the type of video connection you're using—composite or S-Video connection; DVI, VGA, or HDMI digital connection; or component (three-cable) connection. Click **Next** when done.

note If you're running Media Center in a window on your computer's desktop, the Display Setup dialog box appears and prompts you to display Media Center in full-screen mode. Click Yes to continue.

tip To best display Media Center on a widescreen TV, you might also need to adjust the display size settings for your PC's video card. (For example, my NVIDIA video card lets me fine-tune the video for specific display resolutions.) This means exiting Media Center and adjusting the video display settings from within the standard Windows XP interface, as directed by your video card or computer manufacturer.

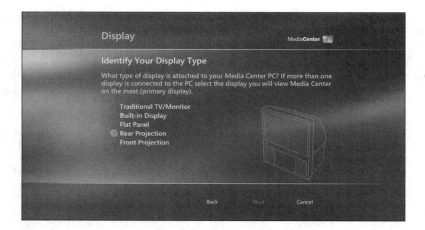

FIGURE 7.24

Select the type of television display you're using.

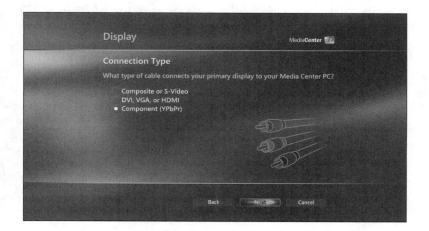

FIGURE 7.25

Select the type of video connection you're using.

6. The Display Width screen asks you whether you have a standard 4:3 display or a widescreen 16:9 display. Make the correct choice, and then click **Next**.

7. The next screen, shown in Figure 7.27, details the current resolution settings for the screen display. If this resolution is correct,

note If you're running a standard definition 480i or enhanced definition 480p display, the screen resolution is 640 × 480 pixels. If you're running a 720p high definition display, the screen resolution is 1280 × 720. If you're running a 1080i or 1080p high resolution display, the screen resolution is 1920 × 1080.

click **Yes**. If not, click **No** and follow the onscreen instructions to change the resolution.

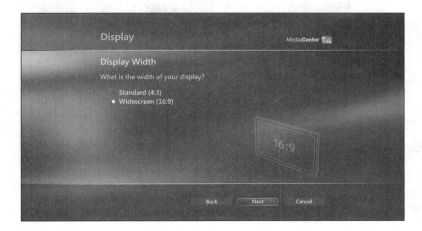

FIGURE 7.26

Choose from standard or widescreen display.

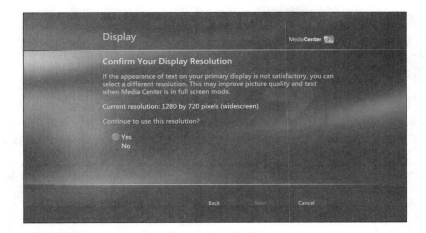

FIGURE 7.27

Confirming the resolution of your television display.

8. When the Adjust the Display Settings page appears, as shown in Figure 7.28, select **Adjust Display Controls** if you want to adjust your television's picture display, and then click **Next**. (If you don't want to adjust your television set, select **Finish This Wizard** instead.)

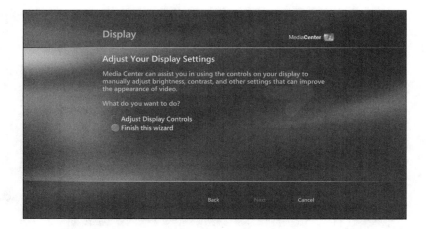

FIGURE 7.28

Getting ready to adjust your television's picture controls.

9. Media Center now displays a series of videos you can use to adjust various settings on your television set. The first display adjustment is for Centering & Sizing. While you're watching this video, adjust the horizontal and vertical size and position controls on your television set until the entire image is displayed and centered on the screen. Click **Next** to continue.

10. The next display adjustment is for Aspect Ratio (Shape). Use this video to configure your television for the proper aspect ratio—typically 16:9 for a widescreen TV, or 4:3 for a traditional TV. Click **Next** to continue.

11. The next display adjustment is for Brightness (Black & Shadow). Use this video to adjust your television's brightness level. Click **Next** to continue.

12. The next display adjustment is for Contrast (White). Use this video to adjust your television's contrast level. Click **Next** to continue.

13. The next display adjustment is for Color. Use this video to adjust your television's color and tint controls so that flesh tones look natural. Click **Next** to continue.

14. The final display adjustment is for Sharpness (Edge Enhancement). Use this video to adjust your television's sharpness control. Click **Next** to continue.

15. When the You Are Done! page appears, click **Finish**.

Configuring Audio Settings

Your Media Center PC has to be configured for the type of sound system you're using—traditional stereo, 5.1-channel surround sound, or 7.1-channel surround sound. It's likely that the factory default settings work just fine for your system, but it's also possible that they don't, and you'll have to adjust them manually. Unfortunately or not, these audio settings are not part of the Setup Wizard, which means you have to access them from the Media Center Settings page.

There are actually two separate settings you need to adjust: one for the type of audio connection you're using, and one for the number of speakers you have. We'll start with the audio connection settings:

1. From the Media Center Start page, select **Settings > DVD > Audio.**

2. The decoder properties page now opens. Because this page is specific to the particular audio decoder installed on your system, it might or might not look exactly like the one shown in Figure 7.29. Click **Configuration** to continue.

FIGURE 7.29

Getting ready to configure your audio connection type.

3. When the Speaker Configuration page box appears, as shown in Figure 7.30, you want to configure the type of output you'll be using with your home entertainment system. (Again, this screen might be different depending on the specific decoder installed on your system.) To do this, click the + or – buttons in the Set Sound Output to Match Your System section until you find the desired configuration.

tip If your system is used strictly for stereo music, select **Analog - 2 Channel**. If your system is also used for surround sound movies or television with an optical or coaxial digital output, select **S/PDIF**. The other options (**Analog - 4 Channel** and **Analog - 5.1 Channel**) are seldom used.

4. If you selected the **Analog - 2 Channel** option, move to the 2 Channel Mode section and select **Stereo**.

5. Click **Save** to save your changes.

FIGURE 7.30

Choosing the proper speaker configuration.

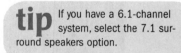

tip If you have a 6.1-channel system, select the 7.1 surround speakers option.

That configured your audio decoder. Now you have to tell Media Center how many speakers you'll be using. Although this is typically done during the Setup Wizard process, you can also access these settings separately. Follow these steps:

1. From the Media Center Start page, select **Settings > General > Media Center Setup > Set Up Your Speakers**.

2. When the welcome screen appears, click **Next**.

3. On the Choose Number of Speakers page, shown in Figure 7.31, select the option that best describes your audio system: 2 speakers, 5.1 surround speakers, or 7.1 surround speakers. Click **Next** to proceed.

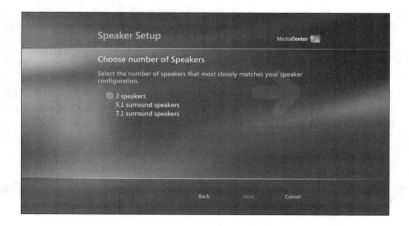

FIGURE 7.31

Configuring Media Center for your specific speaker setup.

4. Media Center now displays a test page, as shown in Figure 7.32. Select **Test to Play an Audio Test File** and make sure that you're receiving sound from each of your speakers. If everything is working properly, check **I Heard Sound from All of My Speakers**, and then click **Next**. (If you don't hear a sound, you need to troubleshoot your audio setup—from the Media Center configuration all the way to the individual speaker connections.)

> **tip**
> You might also need to configure individual settings for your PC's sound card. (For example, I had to access my PC's sound card settings to turn off the digital signal processing mode—I wanted pure stereo, not processed.) You have to do this outside of Media Center, from the standard Windows XP interface; see your manufacturer's manual for instructions.

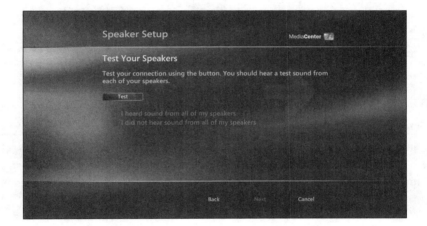

FIGURE 7.32

Testing your audio configuration.

5. Click **Finish** to complete the setup.

Configuring Other Settings

Windows XP Media Center Edition has many more configuration options than the key ones we've just discussed. You probably won't have to adjust any of these settings, but it's always good to know what's where. To that end, Table 7.1 details all the options accessible from the Settings page. (You access the Settings page, of course, by going to the Media Center Start page and selecting **Settings**, as shown in Figure 7.33.)

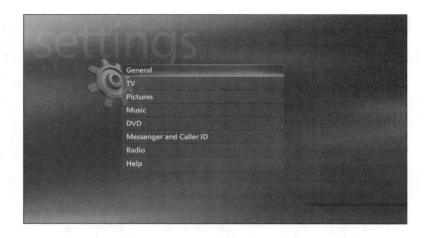

FIGURE 7.33

Available options on the Media Center Settings page.

TABLE 7.1   Windows XP MCE Settings

Setting/Location	Description
Settings > General > Startup and Window Behavior	Determines how Media Center looks and acts—whether it's always "on top" on the desktop, whether it displays a "Not designed for Media Center" message when running non-MCE programs, whether it starts automatically when Windows starts (this is a good setting to check), whether it displays taskbar notifications, and whether it displays TV tips
Settings > General > Visual and Sound Effects	Determines which visual and sound effects are used—whether MCE uses transition animations, whether it plays sounds while you're navigating, and what background color is displayed when you're playing videos
Settings > General > More Programs Options	Determines how applications in the More Programs menu behave—whether they can control the MCE experience or access media information from within MCE
Settings > General > Media Center Setup > Set Up Internet Connection	Sets up the type of Internet connection you're using
Settings > General > Media Center Setup > Set Up TV Signal	Configures MCE for the NTSC and ATSC tuners on your system

Setting/Location	Description
Settings > General > Media Center Setup > Set Up Your Speakers	Enables you to specify how many speakers you're connecting to
Settings > General > Media Center Setup > Configure Your TV or Monitor	Plays videos that help you adjust the picture controls on your television display
Settings > General > Media Center Setup > Set Up Remote Desktop	Configures the ability to control certain MCE functions (such as television recording) from a remote computer
Settings > General > Media Center Setup > Automatic Updates	Configures MCE to receive automatic software updates from Microsoft
Settings > General > Media Center Setup > Join Wireless Network	Configures MCE for wireless networking, if a Wi-Fi adapter is built into the Media Center PC
Settings > General > Media Center Center Setup > Run Media Center Setup Again	Reruns the Setup Wizard
Settings > General > Media Center Setup > Restore Start Page Defaults	Resets the Media Center Start page to its original state
Settings > General > Parental Controls	Activates MCE's parental control features; requires the entry of an access code to view certain types of television programs
Settings > General > Automatic Downloads Options	Configures MCE to download information for CDs, DVDs, and movies from the Internet
Settings > General > Optimization	Activates a utility that optimizes MCE performance by rebooting critical functions once every 24 hours
Settings > General > About Media Center	Displays information about the version of Media Center installed on your PC
Settings > General > Privacy	Displays MCE's various privacy statements
Settings > TV > Recorder	Configures various settings for MCE's DVR function
Settings > TV > Guide	Selects and downloads the electronic program guide for your television provider
Settings > TV > Set Up TV Signal	Configures MCE for the NTSC and ATSC tuners on your system
Settings > TV > Configure Your TV or Monitor	Plays videos that help you adjust the picture controls on your television display

continues

TABLE 7.1   Continued

Setting/Location	Description
Settings > TV > Audio	Selects the type of audio that plays when you're watching television broadcasts—stereo or the separate audio channel (SAP), typically used for foreign languages
Settings > TV > Captions	Configures MCE's closed captioning feature
Settings > Pictures	Determines how digital photo slideshows are displayed
Settings > Music	Selects which graphic visualizations are played when listening to music, and how the visualizations are displayed
Settings > DVD > DVD Language	Selects the preferred language for DVD playback
Settings > DVD > Audio	Configures the audio settings for your system
Settings > DVD > Closed Captioning	Determines how closed captions are displayed in DVD playback
Settings > DVD > Remote Control Options	Configures the DVD-related functions of selected buttons on your Media Center remote control
Settings > Messenger and Caller ID	Activates the receipt of instant messages and notifications for caller ID telephone calls within Media Center
Settings > Help	Accesses Media Center's Help system

And that's how you configure all the settings in Media Center. It's probably worth spending a few minutes investigating all these settings, just to see which ones you might want to edit. Fortunately, after you make the initial configuration, you seldom have to go back to change things. Instead, you can continue forward and start using Media Center—which you'll learn how to do in the next section of this book.

Using Your Media Center PC

8 Getting to Know Windows XP Media Center Edition

9 Using Windows XP MCE for Audio Storage and Playback

10 Using Windows XP MCE for Television Viewing and Recording

11 Using Windows XP MCE for DVD Playback and Recording

12 Using Windows XP MCE for Digital Photos

13 Using Windows XP MCE for Computer Tasks

Getting to Know Windows XP Media Center Edition

You've evaluated different types of Media Center systems. You've shopped for and purchased (or built your own) Media Center PC. You've connected the Media Center PC to your home entertainment system, and configured it appropriately.

Now the fun starts.

Operating a Media Center PC is quite a bit different than operating a traditional desktop PC, for a number of reasons. First, you're operating it from the comfort of your couch or easy chair, from 10 feet or so away, using a handheld remote control unit—no keyboard or mouse. Second, you're doing different things than you do with your desktop PC—watching movies and playing music, instead of surfing the Web and writing memos. Third, and perhaps most important, you're not using the standard Windows XP interface; instead, you're using Windows XP Media Center Edition, which is an entirely different beast, one that requires you to rethink how to accomplish even the most simple tasks.

Given that using Windows XP MCE is key to operating your Media Center PC, let's take a quick tour of the Media Center interface, and learn how you do this and that—and where this and that are located.

Basic Operation

Let's start with the basic operation. Given that you won't be using a keyboard or mouse (at least, not normally), how do you do what you need to do?

Because your Media Center PC is part of your living room entertainment system, it makes sense that you operate it as you do the other components of your home entertainment system—with a handheld remote control. Although different manufacturers supply slightly different versions of the Media Center remote control, they all include pretty much the same buttons and functionality, and look more or less like the unit shown in Figure 8.1.

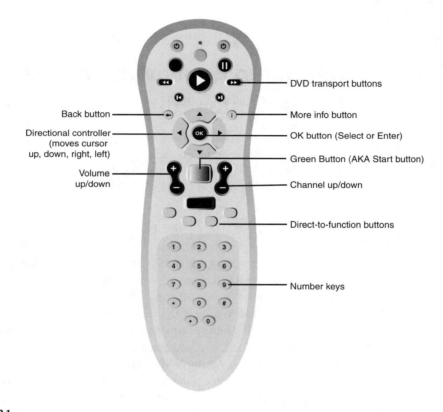

FIGURE 8.1

A typical Media Center remote control.

Probably the most important button on the remote is the big green button in the middle, called—appropriately enough—the Green Button. (The Green Button is sometimes referred to as the *Start button*, for obvious reasons.) When you press the Green Button, you're taken straight to the Media Center Start page. It doesn't matter what you're doing or where you are in the Media Center menu system, the Green Button takes you home.

To get around in Media Center, you use the directional controller, which is a big OK button surrounded by up, down, right, and left arrow buttons. You use the arrow buttons to navigate up and down (or right and left) through the menu system or onscreen items; to select an item, press the OK button.

note Ever wondered where The Green Button website got its name? Now you know!

Also important are the Back and More Info buttons. The Back button simply takes you back a step, returning you to the page previous to the one you're on now. The More Info button displays more information about selected items onscreen, or (in some cases) additional menu options; in many ways, it functions like right-clicking an item with your mouse in Windows.

The Start Page

The first page you see when Media Center launches (or when you press the Green Button) is the Media Center Start page, shown in Figure 8.2. This is a lot different from the main desktop in Windows XP; it's much more streamlined, with only a handful of important options. It's also designed to be seen from clear across the living room, using what is commonly called the *10-foot interface*. That is, everything onscreen is designed to be seen and operated from 10 feet away. Personally, I think Microsoft did a good job in this regard.

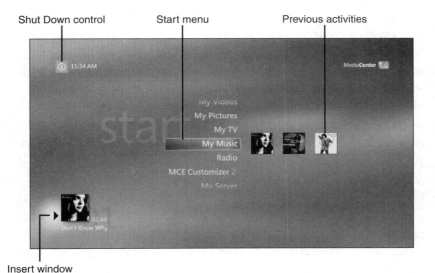

Shut Down control   Start menu   Previous activities

Insert window

FIGURE 8.2

The Media Center Start page.

Examining the Background

A few things about the Start page—and about most Media Center screens, actually. First, note that the name of the screen appears as part of the page background. In the case of the Start page, you see the big word *start* behind the menu options. It's a good way to visually grasp your location within the menu system.

Second, note how the blue background isn't a solid blue. There are lighter areas in the background that seem to move and pulse. Your eyes aren't playing tricks on you; this is just Microsoft's way of adding a little visual interest to what would be an otherwise static background.

Third, note that the background you see is identical to the one shown in this book, and displayed on your neighbor's Media Center PC. Unlike Windows XP proper, which lets you customize your desktop background and color scheme, no such customization is allowed in Media Center. I think this is to ensure a satisfactory experience for all users, but it does take away your ability to personalize the interface. No big deal, unless you really, really hate that shade of electric blue!

The Start Page Menu

Now to the items displayed on the Start page. We'll start in the middle of the page, where you see a scrolling menu. The items on this menu take you directly to different functions within Media Center. Just select an item (using the directional buttons on your remote) and click OK; Media Center will then display the function you selected. For example, when you select My Music, you're taken to the My Music section, which displays all your albums, ready to play.

Next to many of the menu items are the three last things you've done. For example, next to the My Music item are the last three albums you listened to. Instead of going to the menu item itself, you can go directly to one of these previous activities instead.

The menu you see in Figure 8.2 might not look exactly like the menu displayed on your Media Center PC, however. (I know, this goes against the "ensure a satisfactory experience for all users" dictate, but that's Microsoft for you.) There are two reasons for this.

First, your PC's manufacturer might have installed some proprietary software on your Media Center PC, and added that software to the Start page menu. For example, Sony installs its own Click-to-DVD software on its Media Center PCs, and adds it to the Start page menu as a Create DVD option that you don't find on PCs from other manufacturers.

Second, third-party applications that you might at some time install in Media Center sometimes add themselves to the Start page menu. For example, I installed the MCE Customizer utility on my Media Center PC, and now I have an MCE Customizer menu item on my Start page. This isn't necessarily a bad thing.

The Inset Window

When you first launch Media Center, the Start screen is relatively clean—that is, you see the scrolling menu and the Shut Down control (which we'll discuss next). If you've been doing anything in Media Center, however, and return to the Start screen, what you were previously doing now appears in an inset window at the bottom-left corner of the screen.

If you were watching TV (live or recorded), the program appears in the inset window. If you were listening to music, the current album cover appears in the inset window. If you were viewing digital photographs, the last photo you viewed appears in the inset window. And the inset window is *live*—which means the TV program or music continues to play, even though you're now back on the Start screen. To stop playback, you'll need to press the Stop button on your remote.

In fact, this inset window appears on *every* Media Center page. If you're watching TV and decide to edit the configuration in the Settings menu, that little inset window (with the TV program still playing) stays in the lower-left corner of the screen. It's a form of multitasking; you can do whatever you want and still continue doing what you were doing.

The Shut Down Control

Now take a look at the top left corner of the Start page. Many users overlook this little area, called the *Shut Down control,* but it's an essential part of the interface.

First, you see the current time displayed. Not much I can say about that, other than it's yet another clock in your living room. And we all know how much you really needed another clock in your living room.

To the left of the time display is a red I button, called the *Shut Down button.* Click this button (using the directional buttons on your remote) and you display a pop-up menu that lets you exit Media Center and shut down your PC. We'll discuss this procedure in the "Launching and Exiting Media Center" section, later in this chapter, so hang on until we get to that.

Getting Help in Media Center

If you need help using Media Center, you can always access Media Center's Help system. Unfortunately, the Help system is fairly well hidden. You get to it by going to the Media Center Start page and selecting **Settings > Help**. As you see in Figure 8.3, this displays the Media Center Help Center screen.

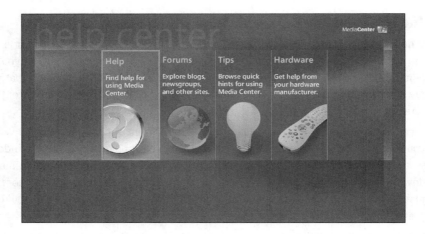

FIGURE 8.3

The Media Center Help Center.

There are four components to the Media Center Help System, as follows:

- **Help**—Displays the standard computer-based Help files, similar to what you're used to in Windows XP
- **Forums**—Takes you online to Internet-based help communities for Media Center
- **Tips**—More computer-based help, in the form of Media Center–specific tips and advice
- **Hardware**—Takes you online to your PC manufacturer's website to better resolve hardware-related problems

Just click an option and follow the onscreen instructions to learn more.

The Menus

The scrolling menu on the Media Center Start page provides direct access to the key areas within Media Center. Click a menu item and you go directly to that area.

Just what are these key areas? Read on to find out!

Play DVD

If you want to play a DVD movie in Media Center, Play DVD is the menu choice to select. Actually, you don't have to click the Play DVD menu option; inserting a DVD automatically takes you to the Play DVD section and initiates playback.

That said, Media Center doesn't include an actual "Play DVD" page. Instead, when a DVD is inserted, it just appears onscreen, in full-screen mode. If you select Play DVD without a

DVD inserted, Media Center displays a message prompting you to insert a DVD. This simplicity is a good thing, especially for consumers accustomed to using a standalone DVD player. No computer-like menus means easier operation.

> **note** Learn more about play-ing—and recording—DVDs in Chapter 11, "Using Windows XP MCE for DVD Playback and Recording."

Online Spotlight

The Online Spotlight section, shown in Figure 8.4, is a repository for a variety of third-party Media Center–compatible programs and services. Many users tend to ignore this section, but you shouldn't; there's some good stuff here that capably extends the basic Media Center functionality. Yeah, there's a lot in this section that you won't care about (or that seem like blatant commercial plugs), but hidden amidst the chaff is some very real wheat, if you follow the metaphor.

FIGURE 8.4

Third-party programs and services in the Online Spotlight.

For example, Online Spotlight is where you'll find some real, honest-to-goodness, actu-ally useful DVD-burning software. It's also where you can gain access to XM Online satellite radio broadcasts and audio programs from National Public Radio. And the good thing is, Microsoft is constantly adding new programs and services to the Online Spotlight; visit regularly to find more new options.

> **note** Learn more about Online Spotlight in Chapter 15, "Exploring the Online Spotlight."

My Videos

My Videos is not, as some might think, where your recorded TV programs are stored. It is also not where you go to play back DVD movies. Instead, My Videos is where you access any and all video files stored on your computer. These might be files you've downloaded from the Internet, or home movies you created with a digital camcorder. In any case, all your video files are listed in My Videos, and can be played back from there.

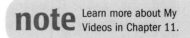

note Learn more about My Videos in Chapter 11.

As you can see in Figure 8.5, most (but not all) video files are displayed with a thumbnail of the first frame of the video. To play back a video, just select it with your remote and click OK. Playback starts automatically.

FIGURE 8.5

Viewing and playing back stored video files in My Video.

My Pictures

Just as My Videos stores all the video files stored on your Media Center PC, My Pictures stores all the digital photographs stored on your system. As you can see in Figure 8.6, each photograph is displayed in a thumbnail state; select a photo and click OK to display the photo full-screen.

My Pictures can also be used to display photo slideshows. You can create slideshows of all your stored photos, or of photos in selected subfolders. In addition, My Pictures lets you do some basic photo editing, including cropping, rotating, adjusting

note Learn more about My Pictures in Chapter 12, "Using Windows XP MCE for Digital Photos."

brightness and contrast, and so on. It's actually a nifty little application, and well worth checking out—high-resolution digital photos look great on a big-screen TV!

FIGURE 8.6

Viewing digital photographs in My Pictures.

My TV

Now we come to My TV. If your Media Center PC includes a television tuner, chances are you're going to be using this function a lot.

As you can see in Figure 8.7, My TV actually encompasses several different functions:

- Select **Live TV**, and you go directly to TV tuner input, with the current channel displayed full-screen, as shown in Figure 8.8.
- Select **Recorded TV**, and you see a list of programs you've recorded and stored on your hard disk, as shown in Figure 8.9; select a program to initiate playback.
- Select **Guide**, and you display the Program Guide, as shown in Figure 8.10, which you can use to select programs to view or record.
- Select **Search**, and you can search for specific shows in the Program Guide, as shown in Figure 8.11.
- Select **Movies**, and you display a filtered version of the Program Guide, shown in Figure 8.12, that lists only broadcast movies—and in a very visually appealing fashion. You can choose to list movies that are on now or due to start soon, movies by genre, top rated, actors/directors, and so on. You can even search for particular movies by title.

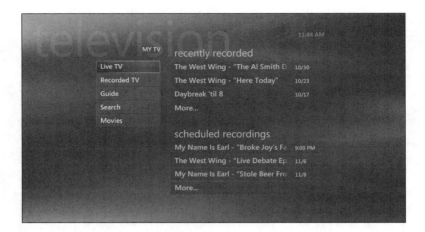

FIGURE 8.7

The many functions available in My TV.

FIGURE 8.8

Viewing live television with My TV.

FIGURE 8.9

A list of recorded programs in My TV.

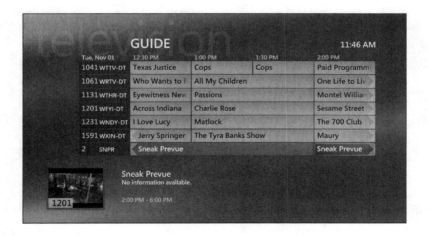

FIGURE 8.10

Selecting programs to view or record with the Program Guide.

FIGURE 8.11

Searching for specific programs—or actors.

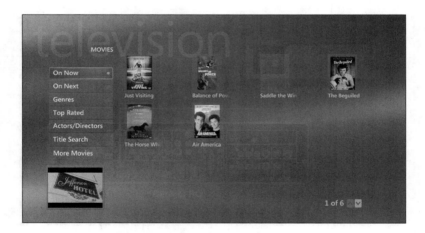

FIGURE 8.12

Displaying movies only in the Program Guide.

Media Center's TV-related functions are fairly versatile. You get most of the functionality of a freestanding device, such as a TiVo, with the added ability to store more programs (depending on the size of your hard disk) and record those stored programs to DVD or share them with other PCs or Media Center Extenders over your home network. Personally, I find Media Center's Program Guide to be every bit as useful, if not more so, as TiVo's similar EPG—and the MCE Program Guide is free!

note Learn more about My TV in Chapter 10, "Using Windows XP MCE for Television Viewing and Recording."

My Music

Here's another section that will see a lot of visits. My Music is where all the music you've ripped from CD to hard disk is stored and accessed. As you can see in Figure 8.13, your music is displayed, by

note Learn more about My Music in Chapter 9, "Using Windows XP MCE for Audio Storage and Playback."

default, as a series of album covers; this list can be alphabetized by album or by artist. You can also display your music as a list of artists, songs, or genres. It's also possible to search for specific songs or to create multisong playlists. And, buried within the submenus of My Music is the ability to burn your own CDs from the playlists you create. To me, My Music is the heart and soul of Media Center, and perhaps the best thought-out and realized functionality of the interface.

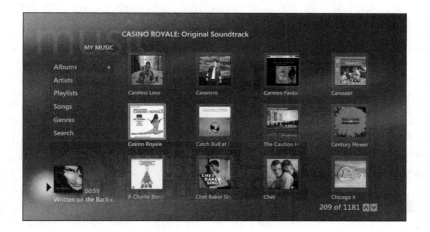

FIGURE 8.13

Playing your music with My Music.

Radio

If your Media Center PC is equipped with a built-in FM radio, or if you've activated Media Center's Internet radio function, you'll find a Radio item on the Start page menu. (If you don't have an FM tuner in your PC or if you haven't activated any Internet radio stations, this menu item does not appear.) Radio lets you play both FM radio and Internet radio stations, as you can see in Figure 8.14.

note Learn more about Media Center's radio functions in Chapter 9.

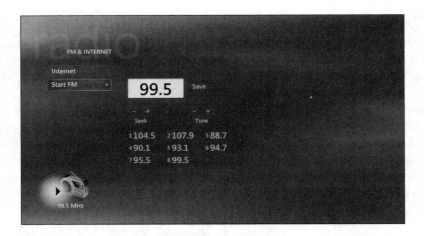

FIGURE 8.14

Playing terrestrial and Internet radio stations with Media Center's Radio function.

More Programs

Then there's the Start page menu item labeled More Programs. This menu item takes you to a list of—wait for it—*more programs.* (At least Microsoft adheres to truth-in-labeling standards!)

As you can see in Figure 8.15, the programs in More Programs are a real mixed bag. Here you can find everything from Media Center's Create CD/DVD function (which can also be accessed from other areas of Media Center) to an MCE-specific version of Windows Messenger instant messaging, and a lot more, besides. The More Programs section really starts to fill up once you start installing third-party add-ons, like the ones we'll discuss in Chapter 16, "Finding and Using Other Media Center Applications." In short, if you want to run an application, an application that you can't find anywhere else in Media Center, chances are it's listed in More Programs.

> **note** Learn more about More Programs in Chapter 13, "Using Windows XP MCE for Computer Tasks."

Settings

Click the Settings item on the Start page menu and you can access all of Media Center's various and sundry configuration settings, as shown in Figure 8.16. Go here when you want to change how Media Center looks and acts.

> **note** Learn more about Media Center's settings in Chapter 7, "Configuring Windows XP Media Center Edition."

FIGURE 8.15

Listing more programs in More Programs.

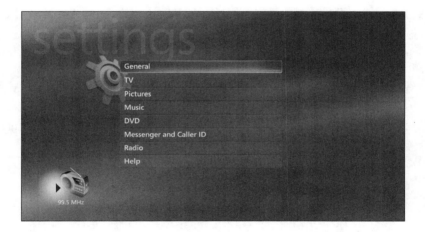

FIGURE 8.16

Accessing all of Media Center's Settings.

Other Menus

Depending on what other Media Center applications that you or your computer manufacturer have installed, you might find a few other items on the Start page menu. For example, Sony includes the Click-to-DVD application on all of its Media Center PCs, which adds a Create DVD item to the Start page menu; other manufacturers add an item for Movielink to the Start page menu. So, if you see a Start menu item on your Media Center PC that isn't discussed here, odds are it's one of these third-party applications.

Launching and Exiting Media Center

On many living room Media Center PCs, Media Center is configured to launch automatically when you turn on your PC, which means you never have to deal with Windows proper. However, you still have to figure out how to close Media Center and shut down your PC—and, in some situations, close Media Center and exit back to Windows.

Starting Media Center from Within Windows XP

If your PC does not load Media Center automatically when it's powered on, you can always launch Media Center manually. This is as simple as clicking the Windows Start button and then selecting **All Programs > Media Center**.

With some systems, you can launch Media Center from within Windows by pressing the Green Button on your Media Center remote. This is definitely the way to go when you're sitting on your living room couch and don't want to haul out the wireless mouse or keyboard.

Starting Media Center Automatically When You Turn On Your PC

You can forget about all the manual launching if you configure Windows to launch Media Center automatically whenever your PC is turned on. You do this configuration from within Media Center, by following these steps:

1. From the Media Center Start page, select **Settings > General > Startup and Window Behavior**.
2. When the Startup and Window Behavior page appears, as shown in Figure 8.17, check the **Start Media Center When Windows Starts** option.
3. Click **Save**.

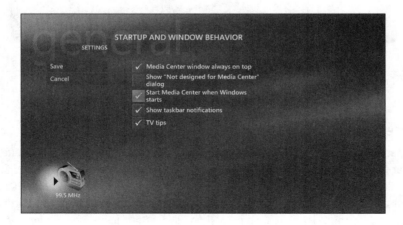

FIGURE 8.17

Configuring Media Center to launch when you first turn on your PC.

Minimizing Media Center to Work in Windows

For some operations (which we'll discuss at various points throughout this book), you need to do what you need to do from within Windows, outside of Media Center. Although you can simply close Media Center to work within Windows proper, you can also perform most operations by *minimizing* Media Center, as you would any other Windows application. With Media Center thus minimized, the Windows XP desktop is displayed full-screen; you can perform all the normal Windows operations using your wireless mouse and keyboard.

caution You have to use your wireless mouse and keyboard to work within the Windows XP desktop. You cannot use your Media Center remote control within Windows.

To minimize Media Center, use your wireless mouse to click anywhere on any Media Center screen. This displays the navigation bar at the top of the screen, as shown in Figure 8.18. Click the Minimize button to minimize Media Center on the Windows desktop.

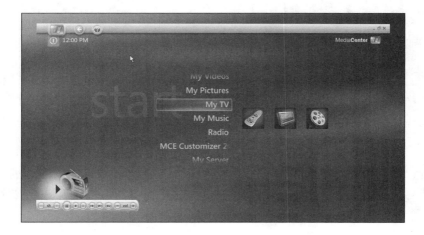

FIGURE 8.18

Displaying the navigation bar on the Media Center screen.

To maximize Media Center back to the normal full-screen mode, you can right-click the Media Center button in the Windows taskbar and select Maximize, or you can simply press the Green Button on the Media Center remote.

Closing Media Center and Returning to Windows

As you've no doubt realized, Media Center is really just another Windows application—one that runs full-screen most of the time, but a Windows application nonetheless. As such, Media Center can be closed just like any other application, which then returns you to the normal Windows XP desktop.

To close Media Center without shutting off your PC—that is, to exit Media Center and return to Windows—follow these steps:

1. From the Media Center Start page, click the Shut Down button in the top-left corner.

2. When the pop-up menu appears, as shown in Figure 8.19, select **Close Media Center**.

FIGURE 8.19

Use the Shut Down control to minimize or close Media Center, or shut down your entire PC.

You can restart Media Center at any time, without needing to restart Windows. Just follow the instructions listed in the "Starting Media Center from Within Windows XP" section, earlier in this chapter.

Exiting Media Center and Turning Off Your PC

On those occasions when you're going to be away from home for an extended period of time—and you don't have any TV recordings scheduled—you might want to shut off your Media Center PC. There are also times when your system gets so gunked up that the only solution is to reboot the PC. (Not an unfamiliar situation for experienced Windows users.)

tip You probably don't want to shut down your Media Center PC, even when you're going to be away from home. You want to leave the PC on *all the time*, so that any scheduled TV recordings can be made.

When you want to turn off or reboot your PC, you don't just press the "off" button on the front of the unit. You have to exit Media Center and shut down the PC properly, which you do by following these steps:

1. From the Media Center Start page, click the Shut Down button in the top-left corner.

2. When the pop-up menu appears, select **Restart** to reboot your PC, or **Shut Down** to completely shut down your system.

caution Windows XP offers a standby mode that might sound attractive to some users. Note, however, that many users have reported severe problems using standby mode with Media Center PCs; see Chapter 18, "Troubleshooting Media Center Problems," for more information.

And that's that. From startup to shutdown, that's how you use Windows XP Media Center Edition. Now it's time to get down to some very specific uses, which we'll do starting in the next chapter.

9

Using Windows XP MCE for Audio Storage and Playback

Whatever else they might do, most Media Center users use their Media Center PCs for listening to music. You might use your Media Center PC to record TV programs and display digital photos, or you might not, but chances are you'll also use it to listen to CDs and digital music files. And, let's face it, a Media Center PC is one heck of a music playback machine.

The great thing about a PC running Windows XP Media Center Edition is that MCE turns the PC into a giant digital music jukebox. Yeah, you can listen to your music collection one CD at a time, but you can also copy all your CDs to the PC's hard disk, and then play all your music digitally. You can even use the Media Center PC to play back digital music files you download from the Internet, or to play music from Internet radio stations. It's as if you turned your living room home entertainment system into a giant iPod, complete with playlists and shuffle mode.

As one would hope, Windows XP MCE has some quite robust digital music management features—if you know where to find them. Read on to learn all there is to know about playing virtually any type of music media on your Media Center PC.

Setting Up Media Center for Audio Use

Before you start with the music listening, you need to do a little configuring of your system. Not a lot of configuring, but a little.

Telling MCE Where to Look for Audio Files

The first thing you need to configure is where Media Center looks for digital audio files to play back. "On my hard disk, of course," I can hear you saying, but that's not good enough. Precisely *where* on your hard disk should MCE look? That's the configuration you need to make.

By default, MCE makes your My Music folder its primary folder for music storage. You can, however, tell MCE to watch other folders for new music files—folders either on your Media Center PC or on another computer on your network. When a folder is watched, its contents automatically appear on the Media Center My Music screen.

Here's how you add new folders to MCE's digital music watch list:

1. From the Media Center Start page, select **My Music**.

2. When the My Music page appears, highlight any of the visible albums and then click the More Info button on your remote control.

3. When the pop-up menu, shown in Figure 9.1, appears, select **Add Music**.

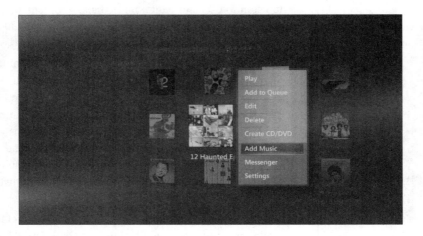

FIGURE 9.1

Starting the add music process.

4. When the Music Discovery screen appears, as shown in Figure 9.2, check **Add Folders** and then click **Next**.

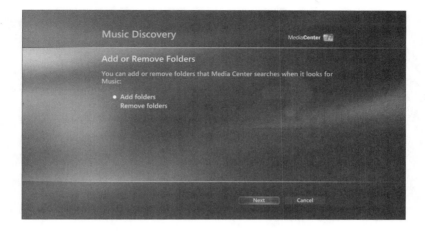

FIGURE 9.2

Choosing to add folders to the watch list.

5. When the next screen appears, as shown in Figure 9.3, select whether you want to add folders on this computer or on another computer (or both), and then click **Next**.

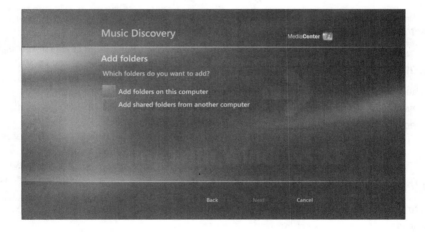

FIGURE 9.3

Telling Media Center on which computer the folders are stored.

6. When the next screen appears, as shown in Figure 9.4, navigate to and select the folder(s) you want to add to the watch list, and then click **Next**.

7. When the final screen appears, click **Finish** to add the selected folders to the watch list.

FIGURE 9.4

Selecting which folders to watch.

Now, whenever you download new digital music files or rip files from a CD, those files are automatically added to Media Center's digital music library, and appropriately displayed on the My Music screen.

Configuring MCE for CD Ripping

The other setting you need to configure concerns how Media Center—or, more accurately, Windows Media Player—saves those files it copies from CDs. You have to choose the file format and the sound quality for these ripped files.

Choosing a File Format

Windows can rip files into several different digital audio file formats. You're probably most familiar with the MP3 format because it's somewhat universally used by portable audio players. MP3 is a compressed format, which means it compresses the size of original files (by sucking out selected bits and bytes) to create smaller files; unfortunately, this process also reduces the sound quality of the file. And what sounds acceptable on a portable audio player typically doesn't sound all that good when played over a high fidelity home audio system.

tip The add music process can be a little time-consuming, especially if you have a very large music collection. That's because when Media Center adds a folder to its watch list, it scans each folder to see what files are already present; the more files in a folder, the longer the add music process takes. Media Center gives you the option of letting the process continue as-is or of running it in the background while you use MCE for other tasks. Selecting the background option increases the amount of time involved by a significant factor; it's much faster to let the process run by itself in the foreground.

note The process of copying music from a CD to a computer hard drive is called *ripping*. The process of copying music from a computer hard drive to a CD is called *burning*. Don't confuse them. Interestingly, ripping is much more processor-intensive than burning is; if you intend to rip a lot of CDs, you might want to invest in a Media Center PC with a high-performance processor.

Microsoft's WMA (*Windows Media Audio*) file format is a tad higher quality than the MP3 format—although it, too, is a compressed format. Files saved in the WMA format sound slightly better than comparable MP3 files, but are still noticeably inferior to the original compact disc.

A better choice when playing your music over a quality home audio system is the WMA Lossless format. Unlike regular WMA or MP3 files, which use "lossy" file compression that affects the resulting sound quality, WMA Lossless uses a "lossless" compression that doesn't have any audible effect. WMA Lossless files are larger than MP3 or WMA files (but still halve the size of the original CD files), but sound identical to the compact disc original. This is the file format I recommend you use when you digitize your CD collection in Media Center.

Choosing the Bit Rate

If you choose to rip in WMA Lossless format, you're ripping at the highest possible audio quality level. If you choose the MP3 or WMA formats, however, you have an additional choice to make, in the form of bit rate. The higher the bit rate (measured in kilobytes per second, or Kbps), the higher the sound quality—and the larger the resulting file size. Choose a lower bit rate and you can create smaller files.

For the WMA format, a bit rate of 160Kbps is probably a decent choice; anything lower will start to sound tinny, even to untrained ears. For MP3 files, similar audio quality requires at least a 192Kbps bit rate. For both formats, higher bit rates are available.

Determining Necessary Hard Disk Space

On one hand, the file format and bit rate you choose should be dictated by the quality of the sound you want to hear; on a good home audio system, most listeners want CD-quality sound. On the other hand, the file format and bit rate you choose are affected by the amount of hard disk space you have; higher-quality audio files take up more disk space, and you might not have enough free disk space to hold your entire collection in this format.

tip MP3 files can be played on virtually any portable audio player. WMA files are compatible with most portable audio players except Apple iPods. Apple uses its own proprietary AAC file format—which is not supported by most Windows Media Center PCs. (Microsoft and Apple don't always play nice together.) If you want full compatibility, go with the MP3 format; if you want better sound quality, go with WMA or WMA Lossless.

note When you copy a digital audio file, you can either copy the file exactly (in noncompressed WAV format) or use some sort of compression to reduce the otherwise huge file size. If you choose a compressed format, you can opt for formats that use either *lossy* or *lossless* compression. Lossy compression (used in the MP3, WMA, and AAC formats) works by sampling the original file and removing those ranges of sounds that the average listener supposedly can't hear; it results in a smaller file that, unfortunately, doesn't sound quite as good as the original. Lossless compression (used in the WMA Lossless format) doesn't affect the original sound quality because it excises bits and bytes that are irrelevant to the recorded audio, essentially squeezing the "air" out of an inflated file. The result is a file that is smaller than the original but larger than a file created with lossy compression—and with sound quality identical to the original.

To that end, Table 9.1 can help you make the best compromise between audio quality and disk space when choosing file format and bit rate.

TABLE 9.1 Disk Space Requirements for Various Audio File Formats

File Format	Bit Rate	Space Required per CD (Typical)	Space Required for 100 CDs (Typical)	Space Required for 500 CDs (Typical)	Space Required for 1,000 CDs (Typical)
WMA Lossless	470–940Kbps (varies)	300MB	30GB	150GB	300GB
MP3	320Kbps	144MB	14.4GB	72GB	144GB
MP3	256Kbps	115MB	11.5GB	57.5GB	115GB
MP3	192Kbps	86MB	8.6GB	43GB	86GB
WMA	192Kbps	86MB	8.6GB	40.3GB	80.6GB
WMA	160Kbps	69MB	6.9GB	34.5GB	69GB
MP3	128Kbps	57MB	5.7GB	28.5GB	57GB
WMA	128Kbps	56MB	5.6GB	28GB	56GB
WMA	96Kbps	42MB	4.2GB	21GB	42GB
WMA	64Kbps	28MB	2.8GB	14GB	28GB

As you can see, the file format and bit rate you choose has a significant bearing on how much disk space you need. If you have a thousand-disc collection, the space you need varies anywhere from 28GB (for the unacceptably low-quality WMA 64Kbps format) to 300GB (for the CD-quality WMA Lossless format). My recommendation is to go with the highest-quality format you have space for—and remember, the prices of both internal and external hard drives have become quite affordable. It might be worth a few hundred bucks to buy a 300GB or 400GB external hard drive solely devoted to digital music storage.

Configuring the Settings

Now we come to the task of setting the file format and bit rate for your ripped audio files. The problem is that this setting is not available from within Media Center. This means that you have to exit Media Center and make the choices in Windows proper—specifically, in Windows Media Player. So, get out your wireless mouse and follow these steps:

1. Minimize or close Windows XP Media Center Edition.

2. From the Windows XP desktop, click the **Start** button and select **Windows Media Player**.

3. When Windows Media Player launches, select **Tools > Options**.

4. When the Options dialog box appears, as shown in Figure 9.5, select the **Rip Music** tab.

FIGURE 9.5

Configuring file type and bit rate in Windows Media Player—outside of the Media Center interface.

5. In the Rip Settings section, pull down the Format list and select the desired file format.

6. If you selected Windows Media Audio or MP3, adjust the Audio Quality slider to the desired bit rate.

7. Click the **OK** button.

8. Close Windows Media Player.

9. Relaunch or maximize Windows XP Media Center Edition.

Fortunately, you need to go through this process only once. The settings you choose will apply to all future CDs you rip—until you decide to change the settings again.

How to Play CDs

Now that you have all that bothersome configuration nonsense out of the way, let's listen to some music. We'll start with the easiest type of medium to listen to, that old standby, the compact disc.

Playing a music CD in Media Center is almost as simple as inserting the disc and then settling back in your easy chair. In fact, it *is* that easy—although there are some playback options you can avail yourself of, if you so choose.

Here's how to play a CD in Media Center:

1. Insert the CD into your PC's CD drive.

2. Sit back and listen to the playback.

That's right, Media Center plays back a CD automatically; all you have to do is insert it. (The only exception is if you're already doing something else in Media Center—listening to another digital album, perhaps, or watching TV—in which case Media Center prompts you to begin playback.)

Easy enough, especially if you want to play the CD straight through from the first track to the last. As you can see in Figure 9.6, Media Center displays the cover art for the CD, with the title and artist info at the top of the screen, and the currently playing track title below the album cover. There's also a menu of playback options along the left side of the screen.

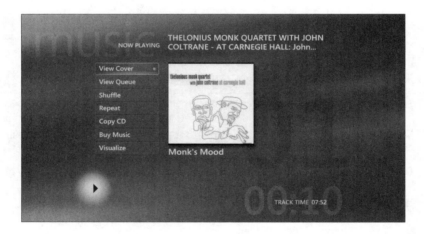

FIGURE 9.6

Playing a CD in My Music—album cover view.

Now let's examine some of the playback choices you can make. (These same choices are available when you're playing back digital audio files from your hard disk.) Here's what you can do:

- To display the entire track listing of the CD, as shown in Figure 9.7, click the **View Queue** option. (You can return to the album cover view by clicking **View Cover** from the menu.)

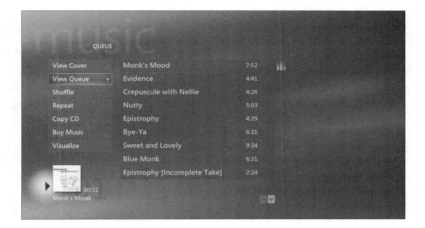

FIGURE 9.7

Playing a CD in My Music—cover view.

- To display a graphic visualization instead of the track listing or cover art (as shown in Figure 9.8), click the **Visualize** option on the My Music menu. Use the direction buttons on your remote to move back and forth through the available visualizations.

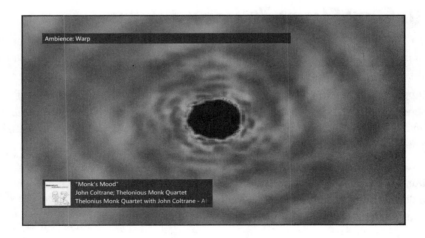

FIGURE 9.8

Viewing a pretty visualization while you listen to a CD.

- To pause playback, press the Pause button on your remote. Press the Play button to resume playback at the same spot in the song.

- To stop playback altogether, press the Stop button on your remote. Now when you press the Play button again, playback starts at the beginning of the current song.

- To fast forward through a song (while still listening to a speeded-up version of the music), press the Fast Forward button on the remote. Press the Fast Forward button again to speed up the playback even more, or press the Rewind button to speed backward through the song.

- To move directly to the next track on the CD, press the right directional button on your remote. To move back to the previous track, press the left direction button on your remote.

- To play tracks out of order, use the up and down directional buttons on your remote control to move up or down the onscreen track list. When you come to the track you want to play, press the Play button on your remote.

- To play the tracks of the CD in random order, click the **Shuffle** option on the left-side menu. Media Center now plays the tracks nonsequentially, starting with the currently selected track.

- To repeat the CD indefinitely, click the **Repeat** option on the My Music.

- To buy this CD (or other music from this artist or similar artists), click the **Buy Music** option on the My Music menu. This takes you online to the MSN Music Store, where you can shop to your heart's content.

How to Copy CDs to Your Hard Drive

When you insert a CD into your Media Center PC, Media Center supposes that you want to play the CD. That's not the only thing you can do, however; whenever you insert a CD, you can also choose to copy (or *rip*) that CD to your PC's hard drive.

Ripping a CD is a fairly simple process. After you insert a CD and the My Music playback screen appears, use your remote to click the **Copy CD** button on the My Music menu. If you're asked whether you really want to copy the CD, as shown in Figure 9.9, click **Yes**. The CD-ripping process now begins.

It takes about 4–5 minutes to rip a typical CD. During this process, playback of the CD continues unless you specifically press the Stop button on your remote. Media Center notifies you when the ripping is complete, and then automatically ejects the CD from the PC. The entire CD is now stored on your hard disk, in the digital audio format you previously selected, and the CD appears in your My Music albums list.

This last point is important—and reinforces why you need to have your Media Center PC connected to an always-on Internet connection. As

caution Nine times out of ten, Media Center guesses correctly and adds the proper artist info, track names, and album art to the downloaded CD listing. That tenth time, however, is a real bear. I'll cover how to edit this downloaded information later in this chapter; for now, know that it pays to check all the information displayed while Media Center is ripping your CDs. It isn't always correct!

Media Center rips your CD, it also connects to the Internet to download the cover art, track list, and artist information for the CD. If you're not connected to the Internet, Media Center can't download this information—or even identify the CD. You have to be connected for proper ripping.

FIGURE 9.9

Ripping a CD to your PC's hard disk.

If, for whatever reason, MCE does not recognize the CD you're ripping, you're prompted to manually enter the album title and artist information. This can sometimes occur with rare or out-of-print CDs, or if you're trying to rip a CD without being connected to the Internet.

How to Download Digital Music to Your PC

As you've just learned, one way to get songs into your digital music library is to rip them from CD. You can also add songs by downloading them from the Internet.

I won't go into all the hows and wheres of downloading digital music because this isn't a book on music downloading. Suffice to say that you can't do your downloading from within Media Center. You have to close or minimize Media Center so that you have access to the regular Windows XP interface. Then you can use your wireless mouse and your web browser to go to your favorite online music store or download site, and from there do the download thing.

There are a few things to watch out for when downloading music for Media Center use, however. First, unless you have an HP Media Center PC, you can't use the iTunes Music Store. That's because iTunes downloads files in Apple's proprietary AAC file format, which neither Windows or Media Center recognizes. (Although the HP Tunes application does, which is one benefit to owning an HP PC.) Download an AAC file from iTunes and you won't be able to play it in Media Center, period. Whichever other sites you use, make sure that you're downloading in either WMA or MP3 format, both of which Media Center fully supports.

Second, know that downloaded WMA and MP3 files are likely to sound subpar when played back on your home audio system. They might sound okay played through typically small computer speakers or on a portable audio player, but when you pump them through a decent receiver/amplifier and large stereo speakers, you'll hear everything that's wrong with compressed digital audio files. Maybe that's okay with you; maybe not. Just know what you're getting before you spend the money to download it.

Third, if sound quality i important to you, consider buying your music downloads from the MusicGiants Network (www.musicgiants.com), shown in Figure 9.10. MusicGiants is unique in that it sells songs in the WMA Lossless format, which provides CD-quality sound. The files are a tad large and take more time to download than files from other services, but what you get is digital music that sounds great when played on your Media Center system.

tip If you have downloaded digital music files stored on another computer on your home network, you can copy those files to the My Music folder on your Media Center PC. Alternatively, you can use Media Center's Add Music function (discussed previously) to watch the music folders on your other PC, over the network.

FIGURE 9.10

High quality WMA Lossless music available for download from the MusicGiants Network.

Finally, remember to download your music files to the My Music folder on your Media Center PC. Because Media Center is always watching this folder, any songs you download are automatically added to the My Music list.

Managing and Playing Digital Audio Files

Okay. You've ripped all your CDs to your Media Center's hard disk, downloaded a couple of hundred other songs, and copied all the other music you'd stored on your desktop PC to Media Center's My Music folder. What you have now is a veritable digital music jukebox. Just what do you do with it?

Displaying Your Digital Music

The first thing you need to learn is how to display all your digital music. My Music provides quite a few options in this regard, all available from the main My Music screen. Just go to the Media Center Start page, select **My Music**, and then do the following:

- To display a visual list of all your albums sorted by album name, as shown in Figure 9.11, click the **Albums** option on the My Music menu.

FIGURE 9.11

Displaying My Music in albums view—sorted alphabetically by album.

- To display a visual list of all your albums sorted by artist, as shown in Figure 9.12, click the **Albums** option then press the More Info button on your remote and select the **Sort by Artist** option from the pop-up menu. (To return to a sort by album, press the More Info button again and select **Sort by Album**.)

> **note** If you have a CD in your PC's CD drive, that disc always shows up at the beginning of the Albums list.

FIGURE 9.12

FIGURE 9.12

Displaying My Music in albums view—sorted alphabetically by artist.

- To display a text listing of all your albums, as shown in Figure 9.13, click the **Albums** option, press the More Info button on your remote, and select the **View by List** option from the pop-up menu.

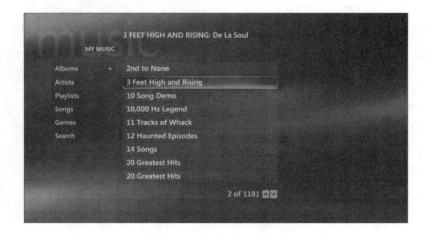

FIGURE 9.13

Viewing My Music in list view.

- To display an alphabetical list of all the artists in your collection, as shown in Figure 9.14, click the **Artists** option. When you select an artist from this list you'll see a list of all the albums or songs (your choice) that this artist appears on, as shown in Figure 9.15.

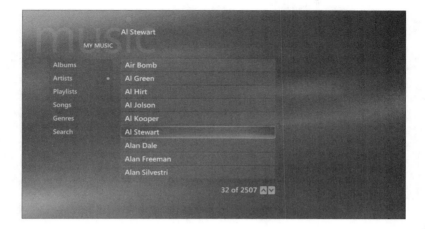

FIGURE 9.14

Viewing all the artists in your My Music collection.

FIGURE 9.15

Viewing all the albums by a selected artist.

- To display an alphabetical list of all the individual songs in your collection, as shown in Figure 9.16, click the **Songs** option.

- To display a list of all the musical genres in your collection (Country, R&B, Rock, and so forth), as shown in Figure 9.17, click the **Genres** option. When you select a genre from the list, all the albums in that genre are displayed, as shown in Figure 9.18.

> **note** Media Center is not the smartest interface around. It alphabetizes all artists by their first name, so that Norah Jones appears alphabetically in the N's, not the J's.

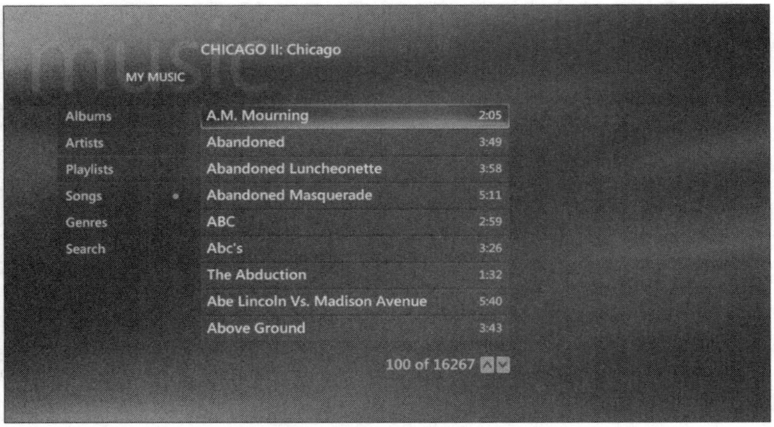

FIGURE 9.16

Viewing all the songs stored in your My Music collection.

FIGURE 9.17

Viewing all the musical genres in your My Music collection.

> **note** Here's an odd Media Center quirk. When you display the main Albums list, words like *A* and *The* are suppressed, so that *The Royal Scam* is listed alphabetically in the R's. But when you display albums in a particular genre, *A* and *The* words are read as part of the title, so that *The Royal Scam* is listed alphabetically in the T's. Go figure!

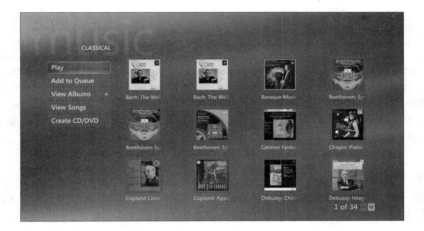

FIGURE 9.18

Viewing all the albums in a particular genre.

Scrolling Through—And To—Your Music

If you have a large music collection, getting from ABBA to ZZ Top takes a bit of effort. (Media Center doesn't let you scroll backward from the A's; the only way to get to the bottom is to scroll there from the top.) Although you can scroll through your list of albums one line at a time, there are two faster ways to get from point A to point Z in your collection.

Normally, you scroll through your selections using the Up and Down navigation keys on your remote control. That's fine, but slow. A faster approach is to scroll through an entire screen at a time, which you can do by using the Channel Up and Down buttons on your remote. In this instance, the Channel buttons function as page buttons, scrolling one page up or down at a time.

An even faster approach is to use the "triple tap" trick. This technique uses the number keys on your remote control much the same way you use the similar keys on your cell phone when text messaging. The "triple tap" refers to the way you tap a number key one, two, or three times to enter a corresponding letter. For example, if you tap the 2 key once, you get the letter A; tap it twice and you get the letter B; tap it three times and you get the letter C.

With this in mind, when you're in the Albums list and you tap a specific letter on the remote, the highlight moves to the first album (or artist, if you're in that view) that starts with that letter. For example, if you tap the 5 button three times, you're

> **tip** You can apply a similar technique when using your wireless computer keyboard to access your music collection. In this instance, you don't have to tap the number keys; just press the appropriate letter key on the keyboard to go to that section of your music collection.

taken automatically to the first album that starts with the letter L. Tap the 8 button once and you're taken to the first album that starts with the letter T.

You can take this technique a step further and immediately tap a second (or third or fourth) letter into what is now essentially a search. For example, to go directly to *Born to Run*, you would tap the 2 button twice (B), followed by the 6 button three times (O), then the 7 button three times (R). The letters you tap are displayed in the bottom-left corner of the screen, so you'll know whether you tapped it correctly. You get the idea. It's a quick way to navigate through hundreds (or thousands) of different albums.

Searching for Music

Another way to manage a large music collection is to use the My Music search function. This lets you search for specific songs, albums, or artists. Here's how it works:

1. From the main My Music screen, click the **Search** option.

2. When the Search screen appears, as shown in Figure 9.19, start to enter the name of the song, artist, or album, one letter at a time. Make sure to pause between entering each letter.

FIGURE 9.19

Searching for music in My Music.

3. Media Center displays matching artists, songs, and albums as you enter your query. The more letters you enter, the more focused the results.

4. Click a specific result to play that item.

Now, to a very important question: How do you enter a query into the search box? You can do it one of two ways.

The first way is to pull out your wireless keyboard and start typing. The second method is to use the "triple tap" technique with the number buttons on your Media Center remote control, as we just discussed. It's awkward when you're performing long searches, but it'll do in a pinch.

Playing Songs and Albums

However you get to a particular song or album, playing it is a snap. In fact, you have several different ways to initiate playback. To play back an entire album, you can

- Highlight the album in the Album list and press Play on your remote control
- Click the album cover to display the track listing, and then click **Play** on the My Music menu
- Highlight the album cover in the Album list, press More Info on your remote control, and then click **Play** from the pop-up menu

To play an individual song, you can

- Navigate to and highlight the song, and then press Play on your remote control
- Navigate to and highlight the song, and then click **Play** on the My Music menu
- Highlight the song in the track list, press play More Info on your remote control, and then click **Play** from the pop-up menu

caution Here's one more thing about large digital music collections: Searching them can be a very time-consuming process. The more files Media Center has to search, the longer the search takes. If you have a thousand or more albums stored, be prepared for some serious lag time when searching.

note Note that the My Music menu changes slightly depending on whether you simply click the album cover (without initiating playback) or if you press Play to begin playback.

tip Media Center can also play all the songs in a given genre, or all the songs by a specific artist. Just navigate to the genre or artist list, highlight the genre or artist you want to play, and then press the Play button on your remote. (When I do this, I like to turn on the Shuffle function so that the tunes play randomly, instead of in album order.)

After you start playback, you can skip songs, move backward and forward through the track list, shuffle the order of playback, and so on just as you do when playing back a CD. Reread the "How to Play CDs" section, earlier in this chapter, to refresh your memory.

Editing Album and Song Information

As I said earlier, nine times out of ten Media Center downloads the correct album title, artist name, track listing, and genre for the albums you rip or download. That tenth time, however....

Fortunately, Media Center makes it relatively easy to edit any of this information, directly from the Media Center interface, no external programs necessary. You do need your wireless keyboard, however—unless you really like entering text from your remote's numeric keypad.

What Kinds of Errors Might You Expect?

Before we get into the editing process, it might help to know what kinds of information errors to look for. In MCE's case (or, more accurately, the case of the online music database that MCE uses),

note The track and artist info associated with each digital audio file is called a *tag*. Each tag can contain a lot more information than MCE displays, including composer, conductor, label, date released, and so on.

there are some very specific types of CDs that are likely to generate the highest probability of error. These include

- Independent or self-distributed CDs (not likely to be in the database at all)
- CDs purchased from Time-Life and other special products labels (oftentimes never listed in the database)
- Out-of-print CDs (oftentimes deleted from the database)
- CDs that have been released with a different track listing than the original (the database often applies the older track listing to the newer CD—or vice versa)
- Double-album, multiple-disc, or boxed sets (sometimes the database recognizes only one of the discs—and applies the same track listing to all)
- Soundtrack CDs (likely to have incorrect or irrelevant artist info for each track)
- Classical music CDs (perhaps the most likely to have incorrect or nonexistent track or artist info)
- Multiple-artist CDs (oftentimes the artist info isn't correct for all tracks)
- Artists with commas in their names (as an example, MCE insisted on displaying *Blood, Sweat & Tears* as *Sweat & Tears Blood* until I edited the info)

In addition, sometimes the info is correct but not consistent with similar info on other CDs in your library. This is a particular issue for the obsessive-compulsives among us, who insist that all Broadway soundtrack albums list the specific performer's name for each track, not the character's name, or who want the Temptations listed as *The* Temptations on every single disc. If this is you, get ready to do a lot of editing!

Where to Edit

In case you didn't know, MCE shares its music library with Windows Media Player (*WMP*). Theoretically, this means that the track and artist info appears the same when you view it in MCE as it does in WMP. It also means—also theoretically—that you can edit the info in WMP and have the changed info appear automatically in MCE.

I say theoretically because there are actually some differences between how MCE and WMP read the same database of information. For example, WMP distinguishes multiple artists on a track by listing them sequentially, separated by a semicolon, like this: **Madonna; Bruce Springsteen; Stevie Wonder**. (Now, wouldn't that be a killer track?)

MCE displays only the first artist in such a list. This means if you want to display multiple artists in MCE, you have to edit the MCE info (not the WMP info) to add the other artists.

In addition, and I don't know why this is, but MCE and WMP don't always synch up in terms of artist and track info. I've had instances—not all the time, mind you, but occasionally—when I've changed the information in WMP but the changes do not appear in MCE. Which doesn't do you any good, of course.

caution There are also several third-party Windows programs that let you perform bulk editing of these audio file tags. I advise against using these editors, however, because their changes are not always picked up by MCE. The most reliable editing method remains doing the editing within Media Center.

The most reliable approach, then, is to make all your edits in MCE, not in WMP. That said, when you're editing a lot of tracks, it's actually easier to do in WMP. But if you make the edits and then they don't show up in MCE, you're out all that work. See the problem? So, my advice stands. When you need to edit track and artist info, do it in MCE.

Editing General Album Info

So, with wireless keyboard in hand (or on your lap, whatever), let's start by editing the general album information, including title, artist, and genre:

1. From the Media Center Start screen, select **My Music**.

2. Use the directional buttons on your remote control to navigate to and highlight the album you want to edit.

3. With the album cover highlighted, press the More Info button on your remote.

4. When the pop-up menu appears, as shown in Figure 9.20, click **Edit**.

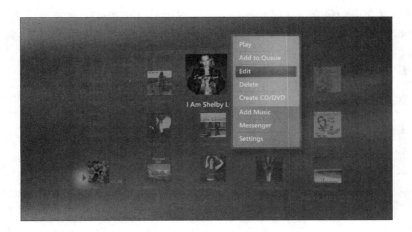

FIGURE 9.20

Getting ready to edit the information for a selected album.

5. When the Edit Album screen appears, as shown in Figure 9.21, use your wireless keyboard to enter a new album title or artist name.

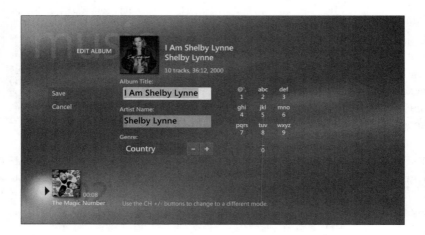

FIGURE 9.21

Editing album title, artist name, and genre.

6. If you want to change the genre of the album, use the up and down arrow buttons on your remote to cycle through the choices in the Genre list.

7. Click **Save** when done.

caution
You can't edit within a field; you can type in only a new title or name. For example, if you want to edit a misspelled name in the Album Title field, you have to highlight the field and re-enter the entire title—you can't just edit a single letter.

Editing Song Name and Info

Editing the title and artist information for an individual track in an album is very similar to editing the entire album info. Follow these steps:

1. From the Media Center Start screen, select **My Music**.

2. Use the directional buttons on your remote control to navigate to the album you want to edit, and then click the OK button on your remote.

3. Navigate to and highlight the individual track you want to edit.

4. Press the More Info button on your remote control.

5. When the pop-up menu appears, as shown in Figure 9.22, click **Edit**.

6. When the Edit Song screen appears, as shown in Figure 9.23, use your wireless keyboard to enter a new song title or artist name.

7. If you want to change your "star" rating of this song, use the up and down arrow buttons on your remote to cycle through the stars in the Rating list.

8. Click **Save** when done.

FIGURE 9.22

Getting ready to edit the information for a selected CD track.

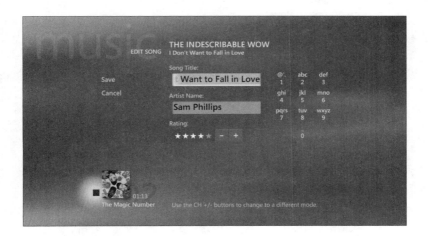

FIGURE 9.23

Editing song title, artist name, and rating.

Fixing Bad Album Art

Sometimes the online database that MCE uses doesn't recognize the CD you're rip-ping. Sometimes it recognizes the CD, but doesn't have any album art stored for that CD. Sometimes it has the wrong album art for the CD. Sometimes the album art is correct, but isn't that great looking—too light, too dark, whatever. Sometimes the album art looks okay, but it's just too low-res to display well on a big-screen TV.

Whatever the reasons, there will be instances when you want to change the album art associated with a CD you've ripped to your hard disk. This can be done, although not within Media Center itself. In fact, there are two different approaches to take—and we'll look at both.

Using Album Art Fixer

My recommended approach to fixing bad or incorrect album art is to use a third-party utility titled, rather appropriately, Album Art Fixer. You can download Album Art Fixer from www.avsoft.nl/ArtFixer/; it's a free download, although you're encouraged to make a donation to the developer if you like it.

The only downside to using Album Art Fixer is that it's not a native MCE application. This means you have to exit or minimize Media Center to use the program from within the standard Windows XP interface. (This also means you have to get out your wireless mouse.)

Album Art Fixer can be used to fix a lot of things, including album title and artist information. For our purposes, however, we're going to focus solely on using it to change album art. Here's how it works:

1. Close or minimize the Media Center interface.

2. In Windows XP, click the **Start** button and select Album Art Fixer.

3. When the Album Art Fixer window opens, as shown in Figure 9.24, pull down the Album list and select the album you want to edit.

FIGURE 9.24

Getting ready to fix some album art with the Album Art Fixer utility.

4. Click the big album cover (or placeholder art) to display the Fix Tags window, as shown in Figure 9.25.

FIGURE 9.25

Searching for new album art.

5. Uncheck the **Fix Album Title** and **Fix Album Artist** options.

6. Check the **Fix Album Art** option.

7. Pull down the Fix Album Art list and select what site you want to use for searching. (I recommend using Google.)

8. Click the **Search** button to begin the search.

9. A list of matching album covers now appears in the window, as shown in Figure 9.26. Navigate to and highlight the cover you want, and then right-click it with your wireless mouse.

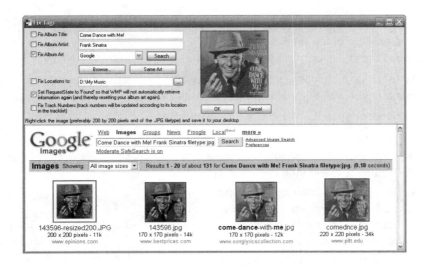

FIGURE 9.26

Selecting replacement album art.

10. When the pop-up menu appears, select the **Save Picture As** option.

11. When prompted, navigate to and save the album art file to your PC's desktop.

12. Click **OK** to replace the existing album art with this new file.

Repeat this process for any other covers you want to change. It's that easy!

One more thing. When you're looking for album art to display on a big-screen TV, look for art at least 200 × 200 pixels in resolution. In fact, I try to find covers that are 300 × 300; anything lower looks pixilated on my 60" TV!

> **tip** If the Google search doesn't find the right album cover, you might have to edit the search parameters. Get out your wireless keyboard and enter a more precise search term in the Google search box. I recommend adding the word **Amazon** to the search query, so that Google knows to search the Amazon.com site; Amazon is a great source of CD cover art.

Replacing Album Art Files Manually

Sometimes even Google can't find a cover image for a really obscure album. In this instance, you might have to use a scanner to scan the original CD cover to a JPG file, and then use that JPG image as the MCE cover art.

Here's a tip on how to make this work. When MCE looks for a cover image for its onscreen display, it looks in the subfolder for that particular album in the My Music folder for a file labeled **folder.jpg**. All you have to do is replace the existing **folder.jpg** file with a new file of the same name, and you've changed the album art.

> **note** The **folder.jpg** file is a system file, which is normally hidden by Windows. To display this file in the My Music folder, you'll first need to configure Windows to show all hidden files. You do this by exiting or minimizing Media Center, opening Windows' Control Panel, and selecting **Folder Options**; when the Folder Options dialog box appears, select the **View** tab and then check the **Show Hidden Files and Folders** option.

Obviously, this all happens within Windows, outside of Media Center. So, get out your wireless mouse and keyboard and follow these steps:

1. Close or minimize the Media Center interface.

2. In Windows XP, click the **Start** button and select **My Music**.

3. Navigate to the subfolder that contains the album you want to change, as shown in Figure 9.27, and then open that folder.

4. Within the selected folder, as shown in Figure 9.28, delete any existing JPG files, including **folder.jpg**, **albumart.jpg**, and **albumartsmall.jpg**.

5. Copy the new JPG file to this folder.

6. Rename the new file to **folder.jpg**.

7. Close the My Music folder and return to Media Center.

> **tip** If MCE insists on displaying the wrong or wrong-sized album art, even after you've added a new **folder.jpg** file, go back and make sure that all the other JPG files in that folder have been deleted—especially **albumartsmall.jpg**.

FIGURE 9.27

Navigating to a specific album folder.

FIGURE 9.28

The contents of an album folder—including the **folder.jpg** file.

How to Work with Playlists

Media Center is great for playing all the songs on an album, or all the songs by an artist, or even all the songs in a particular musical genre. But what makes having a digital jukebox really worthwhile is the ability to create your own playlists, comprised of whatever songs you want to hear. I have playlists for different moods, musical subgenres, combinations of artists, you name it. It's a snap to play back a long playlist and have an entire afternoon's worth of music, shuffled out in random order.

MCE is like WMP in that it offers two different types of playlists: those that it creates automatically, and those that you create manually. An automatic playlist conforms to specific predetermined criteria—artist, composer, genre, year, whatever—and is constantly updated as you add new music to your collection. A manual playlist is created from those songs (or albums or artists) you select, and is constant; it doesn't get updated until you update it manually. Both types of playlists are available from the main My Music screen, and play back in the same fashion within Media Center.

Playing a Playlist

To play an existing playlist, all you have to do is follow these steps:

1. From the Media Center Start screen, select **My Music > Playlists**.

2. When the My Playlists screen appears, as shown in Figure 9.29, your manually created playlists appear at the top of the list (under the heading My Playlists), whereas automatically created playlists appear at the bottom of the list (under the heading Auto Playlists).

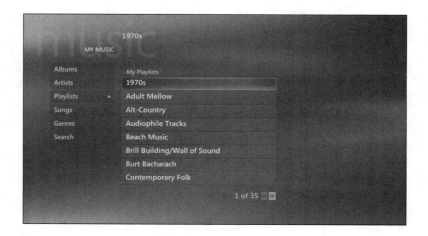

FIGURE 9.29

Viewing all your playlists on the My Playlists screen.

3. Click the playlist you want to listen to.

4. When the next screen appears, as shown in Figure 9.30, click **Play** to begin playback.

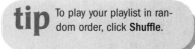 **tip** To play your playlist in random order, click **Shuffle**.

FIGURE 9.30

Playing the selected playlist.

Alternatively, you can simply highlight a playlist on the My Playlists screen and press the Play button on your Media Center remote. This won't turn on the Shuffle mode, however; you have to do that yourself when the next screen appears—and after the first song in the playlist begins to play.

Creating a New Manual Playlist in Media Center

Playing a playlist is as easy as it gets. Creating a playlist is another thing altogether. That's because Media Center presents a horrible interface for creating queues of songs, which is what you need to do to create a playlist. It's a long, laborious process, one that daunts even the most die-hard music lovers. To be honest, I never use Media Center to create my playlists; I prefer the alternative methods, which I'll discuss in the next two sections. But, for completion's sake (and because you might find it less cumbersome than I do), I will present the proper procedure for creating your own playlists in Media Center.

A few things to know in advance. First, you can add not just individual songs, but also entire albums, artists, and genres to your playlist. But you have to start with an empty queue, or else whatever you're currently playing will end up in your new playlist.

Follow these steps:

1. If you're already playing an album or playlist, stop the playback.

2. Click the currently playing album in the inset window.

3. When the Queue screen appears, click **Edit Queue**.

4. When the Edit Queue screen appears, click **Clear All**.

5. When the next screen appears, click **Done**.

6. Use whatever method you like to navigate to and highlight a particular song, album, artist, or genre.

7. Press the More Info button on your remote control.

8. From the pop-up menu, shown in Figure 9.31, select **Add to Queue**. This adds the selection to the Now Playing queue.

FIGURE 9.31

Adding a song to the queue.

9. Repeat steps 6–8 to add more songs to the queue.

10. When you're done adding songs to the queue, click the album in the inset window.

11. This displays the queue you've created, as shown in Figure 9.32.

12. Click **Edit Queue** from the menu.

13. Now you get the queue displayed as an editable list, as shown in Figure 9.33. To move a song higher on the playlist, click the up arrow next to that song. To move a song lower on the playlist, click the down arrow. To remove a song from the playlist, click the X.

14. When your playlist is complete, click **Save As a playlist** from the menu.

FIGURE 9.32

Viewing your queue.

FIGURE 9.33

Editing the current queue.

15. When the Save screen appears, as shown in Figure 9.34, use your wireless keyboard to enter a name for the playlist.

16. Click **Save** to save the new playlist.

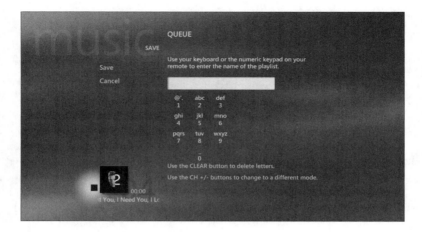

FIGURE 9.34

Saving your new playlist.

Whew! That's a lot of steps—and a lot of clicking back and forth. Fortunately, there are easier ways to create a playlist, which we'll discuss next.

Creating a New Manual Playlist in Playlist Editor

If you think the add-to-queue method of creating a playlist is, at best, counterintuitive, I have a solution for you. Actually, the solution isn't mine; it's a Media Center add-on from Microsoft called, appropriately enough, Playlist Editor.

You can download Playlist Editor from the Microsoft PowerToys page, located at www.microsoft.com/windowsxp/downloads/powertoys/mcepowertoys.mspx. It's a free download, and one I strongly recommend.

After you download and install the file, using Playlist Editor is much, much easier than using Media Center to create playlists. Here's how it works:

1. From the Media Center Start page, select **More Programs > Playlist Editor**. This opens the Playlist Editor screen, shown in Figure 9.35.

2. Click **Create Playlist**.

3. Click the **Albums**, **Artists**, **Songs**, and **Genres** buttons to navigate to the songs, albums, artists, or genres you want to add to your playlist.

4. Click the item(s) you want to add to your playlist, as shown in Figure 9.36, and then click **Add Items**.

5. When you're done adding songs, click **Save Playlist**.

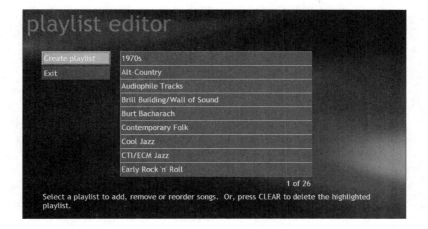

FIGURE 9.35

Using Playlist Editor to create a new playlist.

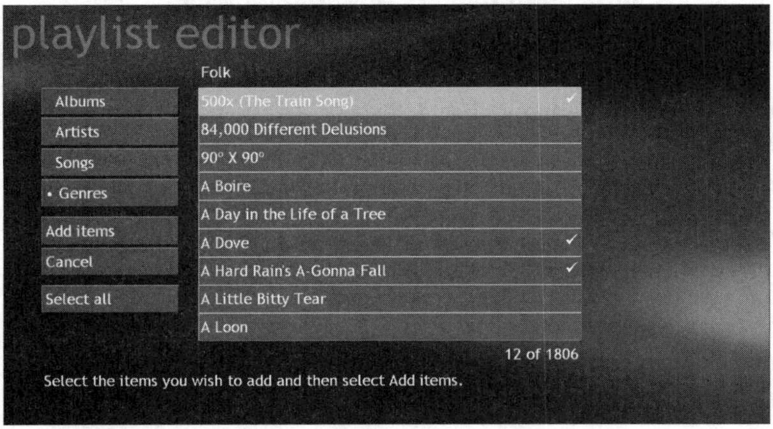

FIGURE 9.36

Adding songs to a playlist.

6. When the next screen appears, as shown in Figure 9.37, enter a name for your new playlist, and then press Enter on your wireless keyboard.

7. Click **Save** to save the playlist.

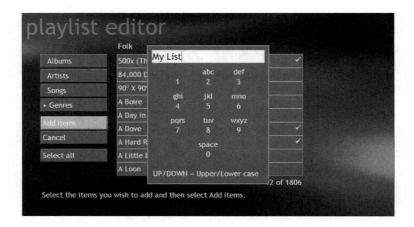

FIGURE 9.37

Saving your new playlist in Playlist Editor.

Creating a New Manual Playlist in Windows Media Player

Another way to create a new playlist is to use Windows Media Player for the task. This means exiting or minimizing the Media Center interface, of course (as well as getting out the old wireless mouse and keyboard), but it's actually a fairly quick way to get the job done.

Here's how to do it:

1. Close or minimize the Media Center interface.

2. In Windows XP, click the **Start** button and select **Windows Media Player**.

3. From within WMP, click the **Library** tab, as shown in Figure 9.38.

FIGURE 9.38

Opening Windows Media Player.

4. Click the **Now Playing List** button (in the upper–right corner) and select **New List > Playlist** from the menu.

5. Use the file/folder tree list on the left side of the main window to navigate to and highlight specific albums.

6. In the Contents pane, highlight the songs you want to add to the playlist.

7. Use your mouse to drag the selected songs or albums from the tree list to the New Playlist pane, on the right side of the window, as shown in Figure 9.39.

FIGURE 9.39

Adding songs to the New Playlist pane.

8. Repeat steps 5–7 to add more songs to your playlist.

9. When you're done adding songs to the playlist, click the **New Playlist** button and select **Save Playlist As**.

10. When the Save As dialog box appears, as shown in Figure 9.40, enter a name for the playlist, and then click **Save**.

11. Close WMP and return to Media Center.

Other than having to exit Media Center, isn't that a whole lot easier than what you have to do from within Media Center to create a playlist? I think so, anyway.

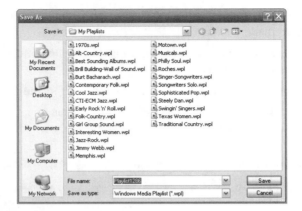

FIGURE 9.40

Saving your new playlist.

Creating a New Automatic Playlist

You can also use WMP to create new automatic playlists. As you recall these are playlists that automatically update themselves when you add new music to your library, based on parameters you specify ahead of time.

> **note** Windows Media Center comes with a number of predesigned automatic playlists—Fresh Tracks, Favorites, and so on. I find these playlists a little too general for my tastes, but others might like them.

To create a new automatic playlist, get out your wireless mouse and keyboard and follow these steps:

1. Close or minimize the Media Center interface.

2. In Windows XP, click the **Start** button and select **Windows Media Player**.

3. From within WMP, click the **Library** tab.

4. Click the **Now Playing List** button (in the upper-right corner) and select **New List > Auto Playlist** from the menu.

5. When the New Auto Playlist dialog box appears, as shown in Figure 9.41, enter a name for the new playlist.

6. Add the first criteria for the playlist by clicking the first green plus sign, and then selecting a field from the list.

7. The first item now contains a subitem for the field you just selected; click **Contains** and select a criteria (Is, Is Not, Contains) from the pull-down list.

8. Now you have to specify what the field is, is not, or contains. Click **Click to Set** to select one or more items from the pull-down list.

FIGURE 9.41

Saving your new playlist.

9. The full criteria now is displayed, as shown in Figure 9.42. To add additional criteria, click the next green plus sign and repeat steps 6–8.

FIGURE 9.42

Saving your new playlist.

10. When you're done fine-tuning the playlist, click **OK**.

Editing Existing Playlists

Need to edit an existing playlist? Again, you have to minimize or exit Media Center and return to Windows Media Player. Follow these steps:

1. Close or minimize the Media Center interface.

2. In Windows XP, click the **Start** button and select **Windows Media Player**.

3. From within WMP, click the **Library** tab.

4. Click the **Now Playing List** button (in the upper-right corner) and select **Edit Playlist** > **Additional Playlists** from the menu.

5. When the Add to Playlist dialog box appears, as shown in Figure 9.43, select the playlist you want to edit, and then click **OK**.

FIGURE 9.43

Selecting a playlist to edit.

6. The contents of the playlist are now displayed in the pane on the right, as shown in Figure 9.44.

FIGURE 9.44

Editing a playlist in Windows Media Player.

7. To remove an item from the playlist, right-click it and select **Remove from List**.

8. To add a new item to the playlist, drag it from the file/folder or contents panes onto the Playlist pane.

9. To change the order of items on the playlist, use your wireless mouse to drag them up or down, as appropriate.

10. When you're done editing, click the **Playlist** button and select **Save Playlist**.

How to Burn Your Own Music CDs

Any music file or files you have stored on your hard disk can be burned to a music CD. All you have to do is create a queue or playlist containing the songs you want to burn, and then use Media Center's Create CD function.

Copying an Entire CD from Your Hard Disk

Perhaps the easiest thing to do is to copy an entire CD from your hard disk to a blank CD. Follow these steps:

1. From the Media Center Start page, select **My Music**.

2. Navigate to and then click the album you want to copy.

3. When the Album Details screen appears, as shown in Figure 9.45, click **Create CD/DVD**.

FIGURE 9.45

Getting ready to copy an album to CD.

4. When prompted, insert a blank CD into your PC's CD drive.

5. Media Center now asks whether you want to create an audio CD or data CD, as you can see in Figure 9.46. Select **Audio CD**, and then click **OK**.

FIGURE 9.46

Choosing to create an audio CD.

6. On the Name This CD screen, shown in Figure 9.47, enter a name for the new CD, and then click OK.

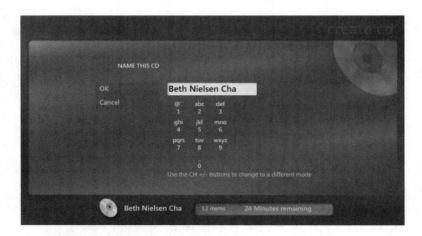

FIGURE 9.47

Naming your new CD.

7. When the next screen appears, as shown in Figure 9.48, click **Create CD**.

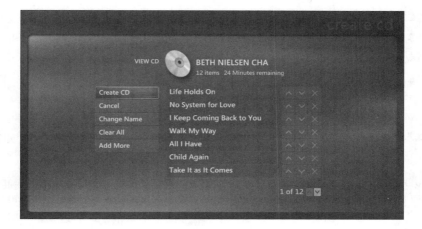

FIGURE 9.48

Creating the new CD.

That's it; a fairly painless process.

Burning a Custom CD from Media Center

You can also burn any music queue or playlist you create to CD. This is the route to take when you want to create a mix tape CD of songs from various artists and albums. Just make sure that the songs you select don't exceed 80 minutes in total, or else they won't all fit on a single CD.

Here's how to do it:

1. If you're already playing an album or playlist, stop the playback.

2. Click the currently playing album in the inset window.

3. When the Queue screen appears, click **Edit Queue**.

4. When the Edit Queue screen appears, click **Clear All**.

5. When the next screen appears, click **Done**.

6. Use whatever method you like to navigate to and highlight a particular song, album, artist, or genre.

7. Press the More Info button on your remote control.

8. From the pop-up menu, select **Add to Queue**. This adds the selection to the Now Playing queue.

9. Repeat steps 6–8 to add more songs to the queue.

10. When you're done adding songs to the queue, click the album in the inset window.

11. This displays the queue you've created; click **Edit Queue** from the menu.

12. Edit your queue to put the songs in the order you want them to appear on the CD.

13. When your playlist is complete, click **Create CD/DVD**.

14. When prompted, insert a blank CD into your PC's CD drive.

15. Media Center now asks whether you want to create an audio CD or data CD. Select **Audio CD**, and then click **OK**.

16. On the Name This CD screen, enter a name for the new CD, and then click OK.

17. When the next screen appears, make any further edits to the song list, and then click **Create CD**.

To burn an existing playlist to CD, simply go to the Media Center Start screen and select **My Music > Playlists**. Click the playlist you want to burn, and then click **Create CD/DVD** and follow the expected steps. Again, make sure that the songs in your playlist don't exceed 80 minutes in total length.

Using Third-Party CD Burning Software

You can also use various third-party Media Center applications to create playlists and then burn those playlists to music CDs. I won't cover these programs here because I will discuss them in Chapter 11, "Using Windows XP MCE for DVD Playback and Recording." (The same programs can burn either CDs or DVDs.) Turn there to learn more.

In addition, you can always exit Media Center and do your CD burning in a regular Windows application, such as Windows Media Player. To be honest, you might find using WMP a bit more convenient than burning from within Media Center; the trade-off, of course, is working from the Windows XP interface instead of the Media Center interface. You have to make up your own mind about this.

note CDs and digital audio files aren't the only types of music you can listen to in Windows Media Center. Most Media Center PCs let you tune into Internet radio stations, and some include FM tuners for listening to local radio broadcasts. Learn more about Media Center's Radio function in Chapter 13, "Using Windows XP MCE for Computer Tasks."

10

Using Windows XP MCE for Television Viewing and Recording

This one surprised me. Who'd have thought that people would put PCs in their living rooms to watch TV?

Well, a living room PC is for a lot more than just simple TV viewing. What we're talking about here is taking control of the television experience, using your Media Center PC to let you watch what you want, when you want, how you want. A Media Center PC can function not just as a television tuner with electronic program guide, but also as a full-fledged digital video recorder (*DVR*). Thanks to the PC's built-in hard disk, you can not only record programs for future viewing, but you can also pause and rewind "live" TV shows, as well as transfer those shows you've recorded to portable media players, burn them to DVD, or stream them to other PCs on your home network. It's kind of like having a TiVo on steroids—and without the monthly subscription fee.

How to Use the Program Guide

The home base for all your television viewing is Media Center's Program Guide. This is an electronic program guide that lists all scheduled programming for the channels in your area (or on your cable or satellite service) for a 14-day period.

You get to the Guide by going to the Media Center Start page and selecting **My TV > Guide**, or by pressing the Guide button on your Media Center remote control.

As you can see in Figure 10.1, the Guide is actually a grid. Available channels are on the left vertical axis, which times (in half-hour intervals) are on the top horizontal axis. At the intersection of each channel and time is the scheduled television program.

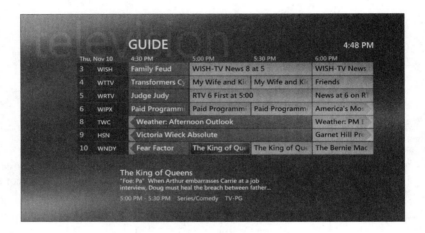

note The programming information for the Guide is supplied by Zap2it, a third-party provider, and downloaded to your PC via the Internet. This is yet another good reason to have your Media Center PC connected to an always-on broadband Internet connection.

FIGURE 10.1

Viewing the Program Guide.

Navigating the Guide

The Guide displays seven channels at a time. You scroll through all the available channels by using the up and down directional buttons on your Media Center remote control; one press of the up or down buttons scrolls the display one channel in that direction. To scroll through a screen of channels at a time, use the Channel up and down buttons on the remote. Alternatively, you can hold down the up or down directional buttons to continuously scroll through the list.

You can also scroll horizontally through the list to view future programming. One push of the right or left directional buttons on the remote moves you a half hour in the selected direction. You can jump back and forth three hours at a time by using the Fast Forward and Rewind buttons on the remote, instead.

When you use the directional buttons to highlight a program, information about that program is displayed below the Guide. You can view even more information, as shown in

Figure 10.2, by pressing the More Info button on your remote, and then selecting Program Info from the pop-up menu.

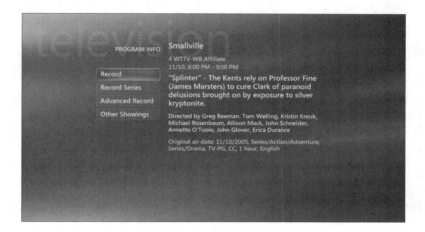

FIGURE 10.2

Displaying more information about a program—with the option of scheduling a recording.

When you click a program that's currently running, that live program is displayed full-screen for you to view. If you click a program that's scheduled at a future date or time, you display the Program Info screen, which you can use to schedule a recording of the show.

Editing the Guide

Back in Chapter 7, "Configuring Windows XP Media Center Edition," you learned how to set up your Media Center PC, including the setup and configuration of the Program Guide. There's no need to repeat that information here, but I will expand on it a little.

Editing Channel Listings

Sometimes the Guide as automatically configured isn't quite right. It might include channels that you don't subscribe to, that are no longer active, or that you don't want to watch (such as preview channels or premium channels to which you're not subscribed), or it might be missing a newer or more obscure channel. Fortunately, there's a way to edit the channels displayed in the Guide, which solves most of these problems.

To edit existing channels in the Guide, follow these steps:

1. From the Media Center Start page, select **Settings > TV > Guide > Edit Channels**.

2. When the Edit Channels screen appears, as shown in Figure 10.3, uncheck any channel you don't want displayed in the Guide.

FIGURE 10.3

Editing the channels displayed in the Guide.

3. To change the number associated with a station, click **Edit Numbers**.

4. The numbers fields on the Edit Channels screen are now highlighted. You can edit each field by entering a new channel number.

5. When you're finished editing, click **Save**.

Adding New Channels

Sometimes the default Guide doesn't display all the available channels in your area. To add new channels to the Guide, follow these steps:

1. From the Media Center Start page, select **Settings > TV > Guide > Add Missing Channels**.

2. When the Add Missing Channels screen appears, as shown in Figure 10.4, click **Add Channel**.

3. When the next screen appears, as shown in Figure 10.5, enter the name of the missing channel, and then click **Next**.

4. On the next screen, shown in Figure 10.6, enter the channel number for the missing channel, and then click **Add.**

5. Click **Add Channel** again to add another channel, or click **Done** to finish the operation.

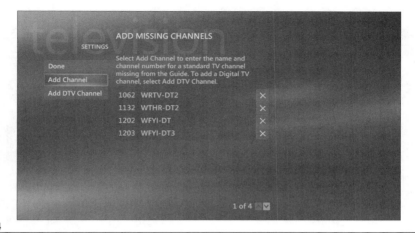

FIGURE 10.4

Getting ready to add a new channel to the Guide.

FIGURE 10.5

Entering the name for the new channel.

FIGURE 10.6

Entering the channel number.

Filtering the Guide

The default Guide display is pretty handy, but there are ways to filter the Guide to display only selected types of programming—which is sometimes easier than scrolling through a hundred or so cable or satellite channels to find the one you want.

For example, if you want to display only movies in the Guide, go to the My TV page and select **Movies**. From there you can filter the movie display by start time (On Now or On Next), Genres, Top Rated, Actors/Directors, and more. As you can see in Figure 10.7, Media Center displays these movies as a series of movie thumbnails, which is a bit more visual than what you get with the standard Guide.

FIGURE 10.7

Displaying upcoming movies.

If you click the Top Rated option, you get a few more options, as you can see in Figure 10.8. You can now sort by star rating, release year, movie title, or start time.

FIGURE 10.8

Movies sorted by release year, newest first.

Here's another way to filter the Guide. If you want to view all the upcoming shows on a given channel, as shown in Figure 10.9, click the channel number/name on the left side of the Guide. Press the Back button on your remote to return to the main Guide.

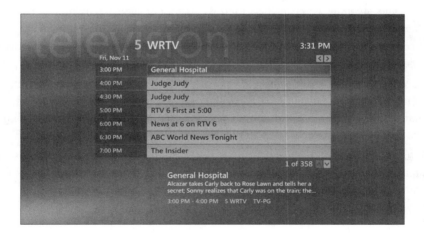

FIGURE 10.9

Displaying all upcoming programs for a single channel.

But if you really want to customize the Guide listings, you have to use the Guide's search function—which we'll discuss next.

Searching the Guide Listings

You access the Guide's search function by going to the My TV page and selecting **Search**. This displays the main Search page, shown in Figure 10.10. From here you have a few different options.

FIGURE 10.10

Getting ready to search for specific programs.

Click **Categories** and you see a list of program categories. Some categories have even more subcategories you can click. Click a category or subcategory and Media Center displays a list of upcoming programs in that category, as shown in Figure 10.11. You can choose to sort this list by date or name; click a program to display more information—and schedule a recording, if you like.

Back on the main Search screen, if you click **Title**, you see the screen shown in Figure 10.12. This lets you search for a particular program by the program's title. Start entering your search query, one letter at a time, and Media Center displays all upcoming programs that match your search.

Return to the main Search screen again and this time click **Keyword**. This displays a similar search screen to the one shown in Figure 10.12. The difference is that this searches for actor, actress, and director, in addition to movie or program title.

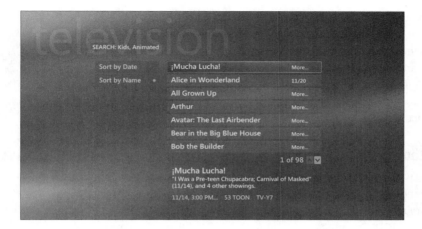

FIGURE 10.11

Searching for programs in a particular category.

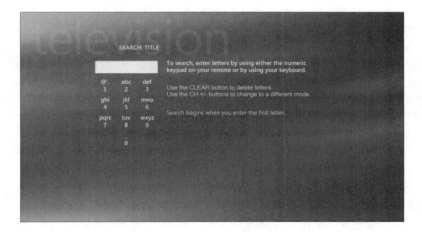

FIGURE 10.12

Search for programs by title.

How to Watch Live Television

Now let's put the Guide to use, to watch live television programming. Of course, you don't have to use the Guide to watch TV; you can also use Media Center the same way you use a normal television set, to tune up and down through the channels and to go to specific channels directly. But I'd be lying if I didn't say the Guide is the easiest way to navigate through the available channels.

First things first, though. Before you can watch TV, you have to switch to Media Center's live TV function. You get there by going to the Media Center Start page and selecting **My TV > Live TV**. This displays the currently selected channel in full-screen mode—no menus or displays to disturb the picture.

note Watching high-definition television on your Media Center PC is really no different from watching standard-definition television; HDTV channels display in the Guide alongside SDTV channels, but with a little HD logo beside the channel number. You do have to configure your Media Center PC for digital TV viewing, however—refer to Chapter 7 for more details.

Zooming the Picture

How the picture is displayed in full-screen mode depends on the aspect ratio of both your TV and the program you're watching. For example, if you're watching a widescreen (16:9 aspect ratio) HDTV program on a widescreen HDTV display, the picture fills the entire screen, as shown in Figure 10.13. If, on the other hand, you're watching a standard 4:3 aspect ratio program on a widescreen display, the picture fills only the middle of the screen, as shown in Figure 10.14; you get black "windowpane" bars on either side of the picture. And if you're watching a widescreen program on a standard 4:3 aspect ratio TV, you get a letterboxed picture, like that shown in Figure 10.15.

Windowpaned or letterboxed pictures preserve the original aspect ratio of the program, without distorting the picture or cropping it in any way. That said, some viewers don't like the black bars, especially when viewing 4:3 programming on a new widescreen display. The solution is to either zoom in on the picture to crop out the bars, or stretch the picture lengthwise to fill the entire 16:9 display. You can do this on your television set, or you can use Media Center's zoom controls.

FIGURE 10.13

A 16:9 program fills an entire 16:9 screen.

FIGURE 10.14

A 4:3 program displayed in windowpane mode on a 16:9 screen.

FIGURE 10.15

A 16:9 program displayed in letterbox mode on a 4:3 screen.

To zoom from within Media Center, press the More Info button while watching a TV program, and then select Zoom from the pop-up menu. Media Center offers four distinct zoom modes, which you select sequentially by continuing to click the Zoom button:

- Zoom 1 isn't a zoom mode at all; it's the standard nonstretched, nonzoomed picture as shown in Figure 10.16.

FIGURE 10.16

A 4:3 ratio program displayed in Zoom 1 mode—standard, nondistorted dimensions.

- Zoom 2, shown in Figure 10.17, enlarges the picture without distorting it; the picture now fills the entire horizontal screen, but the top and bottom of the original picture are chopped off.

tip Zoom 2 is the preferred mode to use when you're watching a widescreen program shown on a 4:3 aspect ratio channel on widescreen TV. (Got all that?) This mode zooms the program to fill an entire 16:9 television screen.

FIGURE 10.17

A 4:3 ratio program displayed in Zoom 2 mode.

- Zoom 3, shown in Figure 10.18, doesn't zoom the picture; instead, it stretches it to fill the entire horizontal frame.

FIGURE 10.18

A 4:3 ratio program displayed in Zoom 3 mode.

- Zoom 4, shown in Figure 10.19, is a combination zoom and stretch mode; it zooms in slightly and also applies a bit of stretch, and is perhaps the most palatable of the zoom/stretch options.

FIGURE 10.19

A 4:3 ratio program displayed in Zoom 4 mode.

Changing Channels

I'm an inveterate channel changer. I can't watch a single channel for more than five minutes without flipping, especially when the commercials start. When you're watching TV on your Media Center PC, there are several different ways you can change the channel. These include

- To scan through the channels one channel at a time, use the Channel Up/Down buttons on your Media Center remote.
- To tune directly to a channel, use the numeric buttons on the Media Center remote to enter the channel number.
- To view all currently showing programs and then tune direct to a channel, press the Guide button on your remote to use the Program Guide.

Displaying Program Info

One of the nice things about having the Program Guide on your PC is that it contains a short synopsis of almost every current and upcoming television program. You can display this information in the Guide, of course, but you can also display it when you're viewing live television, without having to access the Guide.

All you have to do is press the More Info button on your remote while you're watching a program, and then select Program Info from the pop-up menu. This displays the Program Info screen, which I showed you back in Figure 10.2. Press the Back button on your remote to return to full-screen viewing.

Playing in the Inset Window

Here's something else neat about watching TV with Media Center. Whenever you switch to some other operation while you're watching TV, the program you're watching continues to play in the inset window in the lower-left corner of the screen, as shown in Figure 10.20. You can return to full-screen viewing mode by simply clicking on the inset window.

Pausing "Live" Television

Having a hard disk in your Media Center PC not only enables you to record television programs, as we'll discuss in the next section, but it also lets you pause and rewind "live" programs that you're watching. Note that the word *live* is in quotation marks; this is because you really can't pause reality as it happens. What you can do, however, is pause a television program that was recorded a millisecond earlier.

Let me explain.

The way this function works is deceptively simple. Unbeknownst to you, the program you're watching is not transferred directly from your Media Center PC's tuner to your television screen. Instead, the program is automatically written to your PC's hard disk by the disk's magnetic *write head*. Then, a millisecond after the information is written to the hard disk, the disk's magnetic *read head* reads the just-recorded information, and sends that information to your television screen. So, although it appears that you're watching live TV, you're actually watching a recording of the live program. The playback happens so soon after the recording, it's as good as live.

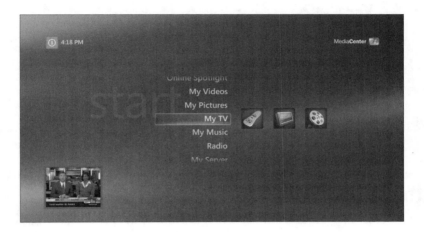

FIGURE 10.20

The current TV program displayed in the inset window.

Because you're watching a recording of the live program, you can pause and rewind that recording as you like, just as you can any recorded program. It might look as if you're pausing the action during a live broadcast, but you're merely pausing the read head on the hard disk; the write head continues to record the real live program as it continues in real-time.

This process, of course, is virtually transparent to you, the viewer. All you know and care about is that you can use the Pause, Rewind, and Fast Forward buttons to manipulate the playback of the program you're watching. When you press one of these transport buttons, Media Center displays a progress bar (called the *seek bar*) at the bottom of the screen, as shown in Figure 10.21. The green part of the seek bar shows how much of the program has been recorded; you can rewind to the beginning of the green bar, or fast forward to the end of the green bar—which corresponds to the current point in the live program.

tip

Instead of fast forwarding to the end of the green bar, you can go directly to the current "live" position by pressing the Live TV button on your Media Center remote.

FIGURE 10.21

Pausing a "live" TV program—and viewing where you're at on the seek bar.

How to Record Television Programs

The real reason you want to watch TV on a Media Center PC, of course, has very little to do with watching live programming. Nope, the main reason you want a PC in your living room is so that you can *record* a television program—and play it back at a more convenient time. If you have two tuners in your PC you can watch one program while you record another, or even record two different programs at the same time. It's all a matter of configuring the recording quality, using the Program Guide to schedule the recording, and then using your PC's playback controls to view the recorded program.

Configuring the Recorder

First things first. Before you start recording, you have to tell Media Center exactly how you want to record—specifically, the recording quality you want, and whether you want to record any buffer before or after programs are supposed to start and end.

Configuring Recording Quality and Storage

There are a couple of different places in Media Center where you can configure the recording quality, but the one I like is the Recorder Storage screen, shown in Figure 10.22. You get there by going to the Media Center Start screen and selecting **Settings > TV > Recorder > Recorder Storage**.

> **tip** Many users assign a dedicated external hard drive to store all their recorded TV programs. This way they can transfer this drive to another PC to watch their archived recordings—or replace a full drive with a new one when they run out of storage space.

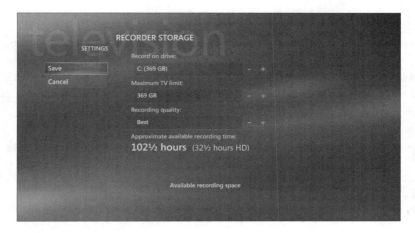

FIGURE 10.22

Configuring recording quality and storage requirements.

Here are the settings you can control from this screen:

- **Record on drive**: If you have more than one hard disk in your system, select which drive you want to use to store your television recordings.

- **Maximum TV limit**: Select how much hard disk space you want to devote to recorded TV programs.

- **Recording quality**: Choose a higher level for best picture quality (uses more hard disk space); choose a lower level to fit more programs on your hard drive.

Below these settings is a visual representation of how much recording space is still available, and how that translates to available recording time. Of course, the recording time is a function of recording quality; the higher the quality, the more hard disk space is required. If you're a discerning viewer, nothing but the Best settings will do. But if you're a tad less discerning, or if your eyes are getting a little weak, or if you're watching on a smaller TV or an older one, you might be able to get by with one of the lower quality settings. It's all up to you, and what kind of compromise you want to make between picture quality and hard disk space.

To help you make this decision, Table 10.1 details how much hard disk space is used for each recording level.

TABLE 10.1   Recording Quality and Storage Requirements

Recording Quality	Space Required for 1 Hour of Recording	Space Required for 11 Hours of Recording (One Full Season of Half-Hour Shows)	Space Required for 22 Hours of Recording Recording (One Full Season of 1-Hour Shows)
Best	3GB	33GB	66GB
Better	2.5GB	27.5GB	55GB
Good	2GB	22GB	44GB
Fair	1GB	11GB	22GB

You see how it adds up. If you record (and keep) a full season of *Lost* at the Best quality level, you need 66GB of storage. Add a full season of *Desperate Housewives* to the list and you need 132GB. Or maybe you're a *CSI* fan; record all the episodes of all three versions of the show (Las Vegas, New York, and Miami) and you need a whopping 198GB of dedicated storage. On the other hand, if you don't mind watching *CSI* at the Good setting, you can reduce that disk space requirement to 132GB. It's your choice.

Configuring Other Recording Settings

Other recording settings are available on the Recording Defaults screen, shown in Figure 10.23. You get there by going to the Media Center Start screen and selecting **Settings > TV > Recorder > Recording Defaults**.

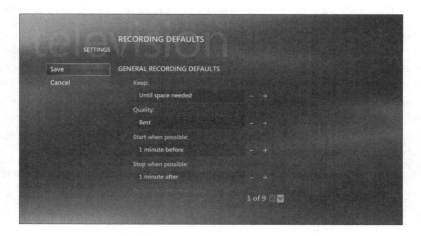

FIGURE 10.23

Configuring the default settings for new recordings.

The settings available on this screen are as follows:

- **Keep**: Determines how long a recording is stored on your hard disk—Until Space Is Needed, For One Week, Until I Watch, or Until I Delete. Obviously, the longer you keep more programs around, the faster your hard disk fills up.

- **Quality**: The same settings as on the Recorder Storage screen: Best, Better, Good, and Fair.

- **Start When Possible**: This lets you record a short buffer (up to four minutes) before a program's official start time. Given how some networks sometimes start programs a few seconds before the exact hour or half-hour mark, this ensures that you capture the complete recording, no matter what.

- **Stop When Possible**: Just as some programs start early, some end late. (This is a particular problem when watching sporting events that have the annoying habit of going into unexpected overtime.) Adjust this setting to add up to a four-minute buffer to the end of each recording.

- **Preferred Audio Language**: Determines the language recorded, when additional language tracks are broadcast. (English is the default.)

- **Show Type**: When you're recording an entire series, determines whether you record only first-run shows, first runs and reruns, or live shows.

- **Channels**: When you're recording an entire series, determines whether you record shows broadcast on one channel only, or on any channel.

- **Airtime**: When you're recording an entire series, determines whether you record shows broadcast at a specific time, any time, or any time once per day.

- **Keep Up To**: Determines how many shows of a series to keep stored on the hard disk, from 1 to 10 or as many recordings as possible.

> **tip**
> I configure my Media Center PC to start recording one minute before the official start time and to end one minute after the official end time. This way I still capture the entire program if it happens to start a little early or end a little late.

All the settings you make on this screen apply to any new recording you make. You can override these settings for any new recording by selecting Record Settings when you schedule the recording.

Scheduling a Recording from the Guide

The easiest way to record an upcoming television program is to schedule the recording from the Program Guide. It's a fairly straightforward operation, as long as you follow these steps:

1. From within the Program Guide, navigate to and click the program you want to record.

2. When the Program Info screen appears, click **Record**.

3. The Program Guide is now updated with a red "record" icon for that program, as well as a "This program will record" message at the bottom of the screen, as shown in Figure 10.24.

That's it. Your recording is now scheduled to be recorded.

> **tip** You can also click the **Advanced Record** button to reset some of the default settings for this particular recording, such as the frequency, stop time, and keep until setting.

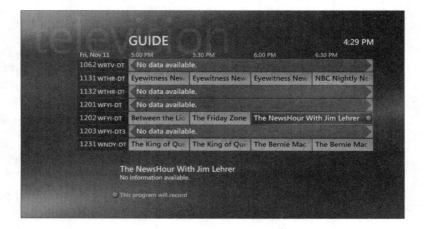

FIGURE 10.24

The Program Guide screen shows that a recording is scheduled.

Recording an Entire Series

The previous routine was for scheduling a single recording of a single instance of a program. But if you're a *Law and Order* junkie, you want to record all the episodes of the series, preferably without scheduling each episode one at a time. There ought to be a way to schedule recording an entire series from a single screen, oughtn't there?

Well, there is. Just follow these steps:

1. From within the Program Guide, navigate to the next episode of the series you want to record, and then click that program.

2. When the Program Info screen appears, click **Record Series**.

3. When you return to the Program Guide, you see the multiple red-dot "record" icon next to that episode, as shown in Figure 10.25.

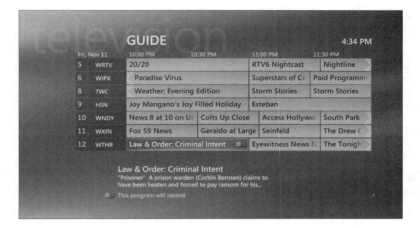

FIGURE 10.25

One episode of a single series scheduled to record.

4. To further configure the recording of the series, click the program again in the Guide.

5. When the Program Info screen appears, click **Advanced Record**.

6. When the Record Settings screen appears, click **Settings for the Entire Series.**

7. The Series Settings screen, shown in Figure 10.26, lets you select just how you want to record the series. Some of these settings (such as Stop and Quality) are familiar; some are specific to series recording. We'll look at the most important of these settings.

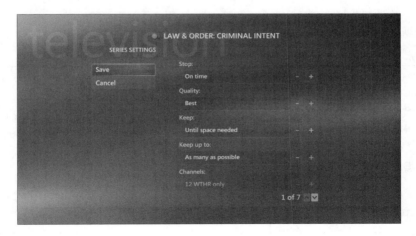

FIGURE 10.26

Setting series recording options.

8. For the **Channels** setting, click the + and − buttons to select whether you want to record episodes only on this channel, or on all channels. (This is helpful in weeding out original network broadcasts from cable channel repeats.)

9. For the **Show Type** setting, click the + and − buttons to select whether you want to record first-run episodes only, first runs and reruns, or live shows.

10. Change any of the other settings on this screen, as necessary.

Searching for Programs to Record

You can also schedule programs to record by using Media Center's search function. Here's how it works:

1. From the Media Center Start page, select **My TV > Recorded TV > Add Recording**.

2. From the Add Recording screen, shown in Figure 10.27, click **Search**.

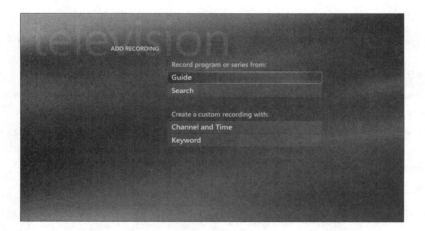

FIGURE 10.27

Different ways to schedule a recording.

3. Enter your search query, one letter at a time.

4. From the list of shows that match your query, click the program you want to record.

5. When the Program Info screen appears, click **Record**.

Scheduling a Manual Recording

As you saw in Figure 10.27, the Add Recording screen offers a few other ways to schedule a recording. One of the most straightforward is to simply supply a channel number and start/end time. This is akin to programming a VCR to record via timer, and it is still a viable method.

Follow these steps:

1. From the Media Center Start page, select **My TV > Recorded TV > Add Recording**.

2. From the Add Recording screen, click **Channel and Time**.

3. When the Manual Record screen appears, as shown in Figure 10.28, enter the channel number into the **Channel** box.

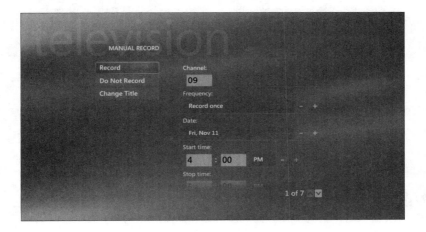

FIGURE 10.28

Entering the start and stop time for a manual recording.

4. In the **Date** field, click the + and − buttons to select the date of the recording.

5. Enter the time for the recording to start into the **Start Time** boxes.

6. Enter the time for the recording to end into the **Stop Time** boxes.

7. When you're done entering information, click **Record**.

> **caution**
>
> Even if you have multiple TV tuners in your Media Center PC, there might still come a time when you've scheduled too many shows to record at the same time. If this happens, Media Center displays an alert to prompt you to change one or more of your scheduled recordings to remove the conflict.

Scheduling a Recording by Keyword

A slightly more complex—but infinitely more powerful—method of scheduling a recording is to schedule a recording by keyword. That is, you enter an actor's name, director's name, movie title, program title, or other keyword, and any programs matching those keywords will automatically be recorded. It's pretty neat, and a great way to record every Humphrey Bogart movie on cable TV, as just one example. Here's what you do:

1. From the Media Center Start page, select **My TV > Recorded TV > Add Recording**.

2. From the Add Recording screen, click **Keyword**.

3. When the Add Keyword screen appears, as shown in Figure 10.29, click the type of keyword search you want to perform—by actor name, director name, movie title, program title, or generic keyword.

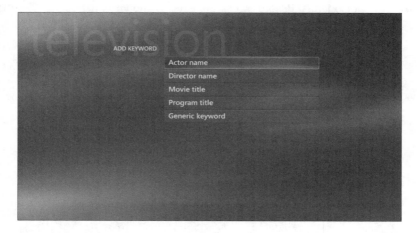

FIGURE 10.29

Determine the type of keyword search you want to perform.

4. When the next screen appears, as shown in Figure 10.30, enter the first few letters of your query.

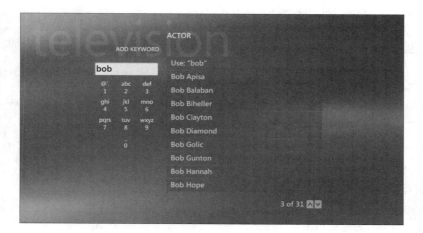

FIGURE 10.30

Enter your search query.

5. From the list of search results, click the name or title that you want to record.

6. Media Center now displays the Keyword Record screen shown in Figure 10.31. Click the + and – buttons next to the **Show Type** setting to select whether you want to record first-run episodes only, reruns, or both.

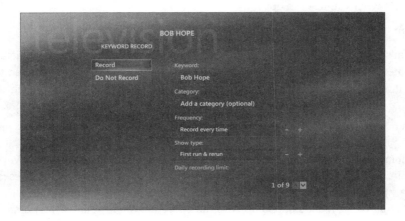

FIGURE 10.31

Fine-tune your keyword recording.

7. Change any other settings on this screen, as necessary.

8. Click **Record**.

9. Media Center now displays a screen, like the one in Figure 10.32, which lists a sample of the types of shows it will record. If the list looks good, click **OK**. If not, click **Change Settings** and edit your previous choices to better fine-tune the list.

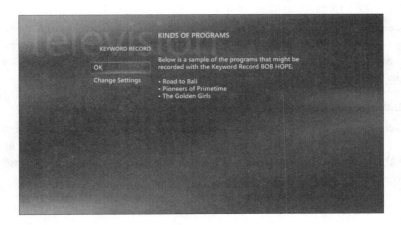

FIGURE 10.32

Sampling the types of shows you're likely to record.

Recording the Program You're Watching

There's another recording method that should be mentioned, although it's intuitive enough that you probably don't need my help. I'm talking about the simple act of recording a program you're currently watching—that is, recording a program in process.

Here's what you need to do:

1. Click the Record button on your Media Center remote.

That's it—there's no step 2. When you press the Record button on your remote, Media Center automatically starts recording the program that you're currently tuned to, and continues recording until the program is over, at which point it automatically stops.

If you just tuned to this channel, the recording starts from this point in time. If you've been watching the channel for awhile, chances are Media Center records some portion of the program prior to when you pressed the Record button. This is because Media Center automatically records a 30-minute buffer whenever you're watching live TV. (This is the buffer that is used for pausing and rewinding "live" television, as we discussed previously.) So, if you tuned into a program from the start but only pressed the Record button 20 minutes in, you'll still end up with the entire program—from the very start—recorded to your hard disk.

Scheduling a Recording from Another Computer—With Remote Record

Stuck at work and need to record the start of this evening's big football game? On vacation and forgot to schedule a recording of *South Park*? Visiting friends and want to make sure that you don't miss this evening's episode of *The Daily Show*?

If you're not home to access your Media Center PC, you need a way to schedule recordings from a remote location. That's where Microsoft's Remote Record Service comes in; it lets you schedule recordings from any PC, over the Internet.

To use Remote Record, you first have to download and install a small add-on to Media Center, and then you have to sign up for the service (it's free). After you're signed up, all you have to do to schedule a recording is access the MSN Entertainment TV website and make your selections.

Installing Remote Record

To activate Remote Record on your Media Center PC, go to the Media Center Start screen and select Online Spotlight. From there, click **TV & Movies** on the menu, and then click the **MSN Remote Record Service**, as shown in Figure 10.33. Follow the onscreen instructions to download and install the applet.

FIGURE 10.33

Remote Record is accessible from the Online Spotlight screen.

Signing Up for the MSN Remote Record Service

As part of the installation process, you'll be asked to sign up for the MSN Remote Record Service. You'll need to enter your ZIP code, choose which type of television service you have (antenna, cable, or satellite), and then select the appropriate cable/satellite provider. This tells MSN which television listings to display when you log on.

To use Remote Record, you must have a valid Microsoft Passport. If you're a Hotmail user, your email address serves as your passport. If you don't have a Hotmail account, you're prompted to sign up for a Passport. It takes only a few minutes to register, and it's free. Just follow the onscreen instructions.

You'll also need to add yourself (and any other family member) as an official user of the MSN Remote Record Service. You do this from your Media Center PC, but outside of Media Center. From the Windows desktop, click the Start menu and select **MSN Remote Record Service**. This launches Internet Explorer and displays the screen shown in Figure 10.34. Click the **Add User** button and follow the onscreen instructions from there.

Scheduling a Remote Recording

You can schedule a remote recording from any PC connected to the Internet. Just use any web browser to go to tv.msn.com/tv/guide/, and sign in with your Microsoft Passport. This displays the TV Listings page, like the one shown in Figure 10.35. This page works pretty much like Media Center's Program Guide; you can scroll down through the available channels and right through future showings.

FIGURE 10.34

Adding a new user to the MSN Remote Record Service.

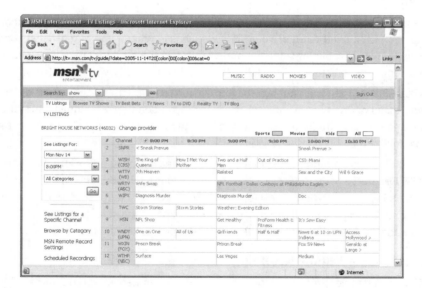

FIGURE 10.35

Use MSN's TV Listings page to schedule a remote recording.

To schedule a program for recording, click that program in the listings. This displays a new Program Details window, like the one shown in Figure 10.36. Click the **Record This Show** button to record this particular showing, or click **Record Series** to record all episodes in the series.

FIGURE 10.36

Click **Record This Show** to schedule a recording.

Your recording request is now routed through the MSN service, over the Internet, to your Media Center PC. After the program is scheduled on your Media Center PC, you'll see the Request Received confirmation, as shown in Figure 10.37. (When you get home, you can verify that the recording is scheduled by following the instructions in the next section.)

note For Remote Record to work, your Media Center PC must be turned on and connected to an always-on Internet connection.

Reviewing Scheduled Recordings

If you want to take a peek at the upcoming programs you've scheduled to record, that's easy enough to do. The main My TV screen, shown in Figure 10.38, lists shows you've recently recorded as well as those shows scheduled for recording. Scroll through the list to view all your scheduled recordings.

FIGURE 10.37

Congratulations—your remote recording is confirmed!

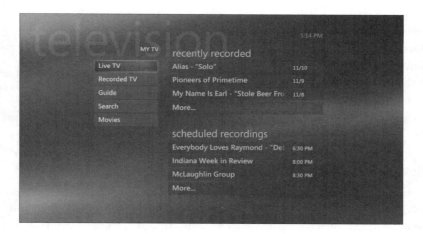

FIGURE 10.38

Viewing scheduled recordings on the My TV screen.

Alternatively, you can go to the My TV screen and then click **Recorded TV > Scheduled** (a little counterintuitive, I know), to display the Scheduled screen, shown in Figure 10.39. From here you can

> **note** Remember, the Guide only lists programs 14 days in advance—which is also how far in advance scheduled recordings are listed.

sort your scheduled recordings by date or title, or view any or all series you've opted to record.

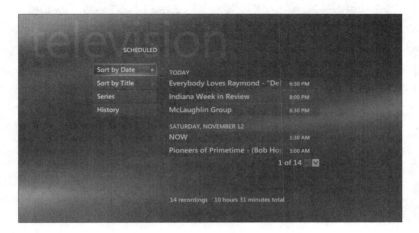

FIGURE 10.39

Viewing the entire list of scheduled recordings.

Canceling a Scheduled Recording

Want to cancel a recording you've scheduled? Just go to the scheduled recording (from **My TV > Recorded TV > Scheduled**, or from the Program Guide) and click the program listing to display the Program Info screen. From here, click **Do Not Record** on the menu; Media Center will dutifully cancel the recording.

How to View Programs You've Recorded

As just noted, the most recent programs you've recorded are listed on the main My TV screen. A more complete list of recorded programs can be had by going to the My TV screen and clicking the **Recorded TV** button. This displays the Recorded TV screen, shown in Figure 10.40; all the programs you have stored on your hard drive are listed here.

Playing Back a Recorded Program

Playing back a recorded program is easy as pie. Just go to the My TV or Recorded TV screens and click the program you want to view. Playback starts immediately.

Of course, you have total control over the playback of your recorded program. Just use the transport controls on your Media Center remote to pause, fast forward, rewind, or stop playback. Whenever you use a transport control, a seek bar appears at the bottom of the screen, just as it does when using the same controls when viewing "live" programs.

FIGURE 10.40

A full list of recorded programs.

Skipping Commercials

One of the joys of watching a recorded television program versus a live one is the ability to skip over those annoying commercials. Media Center doesn't have a commercial skip feature per se, but it does have a convenient 29-second skip instead. Press the Skip button on your remote and the program skips ahead 29 seconds—one second less than the length of an average commercial. If you skip too far ahead and get into the program itself, press the Replay button to jump back 7 seconds.

Saving and Deleting Recorded Programs

When you're done watching a recorded program, Media Center displays a Finished screen, like the one in Figure 10.41. If you want to watch the program again, click **Restart**. If you want to delete the recording, click **Delete**. If you want to continue to store the program on your hard disk, click **Keep**.

You can also delete a recording while you're watching it. (Great for when you discover you recorded a real stinker.) Just press the More Info button on your remote to display the pop-up menu shown in Figure 10.42, and then select **Delete**. Poof! The program is gone.

FIGURE 10.41

When you're finished watching a program, you can delete it—or continue to keep it around.

FIGURE 10.42

Deleting a recorded program while you're watching it.

Another way to delete programs is from the Recorded TV list. Just go to the Recorded TV screen and click the program you want to delete. When the Program Info page appears, as shown in Figure 10.43, click **Delete**. The program is now deleted.

FIGURE 10.43

Deleting a recorded program from the Program Info page.

Transferring a Recorded Program to a Portable Device

If you have a portable media player (sometimes called a *portable digital video player*), you can transfer your recorded TV programs directly to the portable device, for viewing on the go. There are a couple of ways to do this.

If the portable media player is running Microsoft's Portable Media Center operating system, you can use the Sync to Device function on your Media Center PC to transfer the files. You access this utility by going to the Media Center Start screen and selecting **More Programs > Sync to Device**.

You get a little more versatility if you use a third-party Media Center add-on program called MyTV ToGo, shown in Figure 10.44. This program, which runs from within Media Center, lets you copy recorded programs to any Pocket PC, smartphone, or other device that uses standard-issue flash memory cards. MyTV ToGo lets you select from four different quality settings, and can fit up to 16 hours of programming on a 1GB memory card. (It even supports copying of HDTV programs!) What I really like is that the program is totally free; download it from www.mytvtogo.com.

caution Not all programs you record can be transferred to a portable device or burned to DVD. Some programs (typically from premium channels, such as HBO and Showtime) are copy protected and cannot be transferred or copied—they can only be played back on the same PC on which they were recorded.

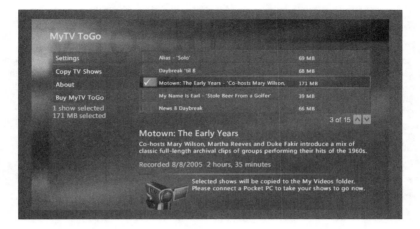

FIGURE 10.44
FIGURE 10.44
Another way to copy TV programs—via the MyTV ToGo program.

Copying a Recorded Program to DVD

It's also possible to burn a permanent copy of any recorded program to DVD. You can use
Media Center's built-in Copy DVD function (which isn't all that great, to be honest), or
one of several third-party DVD burning Media Center add-on programs. I recommend
using one of the third-party programs; I'll tell you more about this in Chapter 11, "Using
Windows XP MCE for DVD Playback and Recording."

11

Using Windows XP MCE for DVD Playback and Recording

If all you do is use your Media Center PC to play DVDs, you've bought yourself a very expensive DVD player. No, I'm assuming you're also using your PC to do something else—record TV programs, function as a digital music jukebox, or whatever. But there's still the issue of playing DVDs, which a Media Center PC is quite good at. And as long as you have the hardware sitting in your living room, you might as well use it for this very popular purpose.

How to Play DVDs

Assuming that your Media Center PC comes with a DVD drive (almost all do), playing a DVD is as simple as inserting it into the drive. Even though there's a Play DVD option on Media Center's Start menu, there's no need to click it; playback starts automatically whenever a movie DVD is inserted.

Actually, it's the DVD's main menu that gets displayed when you insert the DVD, as shown in Figure 11.1. You still have to select the "play movie" option on the DVD menu to initiate playback.

FIGURE 11.1

The DVD's main menu displays when you load the disc in your PC's DVD drive.

After you start playing the movie, you can use the transport buttons on your Media Center remote to control the DVD playback. Which button does what? Table 11.1 describes each button's function(s); not all the functions are intuitive.

TABLE 11.1 DVD Transport Buttons

Button	Function
Play	Plays DVD or resumes normal playback after pause, fast forward, or rewind
Stop	Stops playback
Pause	Pauses the action and displays a freeze-frame picture
Pause+FWD	Frame-by-frame advance
Pause+REW	Frame-by-frame rewind
FWD (press once)	Fast forward 3× speed
FWD (press twice)	Fast forward 40× speed
FWD (press three times)	Fast forward 250× speed
REW (press once)	Rewind 3× speed
REW (press twice)	Rewind 40× speed
REW (press three times)	Rewind 250× speed
Skip	Advances to next chapter
Replay	Returns to previous chapter
DVD Menu	Returns to the DVD's main menu

Whenever you pause, rewind, or fast forward, Media Center displays an onscreen progress bar, called the *seek bar*, like the one in Figure 11.2. To display more information, including the chapter title (as shown in Figure 11.3), press the More Info button on the remote.

FIGURE 11.2

The seek bar is displayed when you press any transport button.

FIGURE 11.3

Press the More Info button to display disc and chapter information.

And that's pretty much all there is to watching DVDs on your Media Center PC. Insert the disc, and then settle back to watch the movie!

How to Record DVDs

If your Media Center PC includes a DVD burner drive, you can use Media Center to burn recorded television programs and other video files to DVD. This is a great way to create a permanent copy of your recorded programs, or to free up valuable hard disk space for future recordings.

caution Most television programs can be burned to DVD, but not all. Some programs are encoded and come with a "no copy" flag; if Media Center encounters such a restricted program, it won't allow copying to DVD. (Fortunately, this "no copy" flag is as yet little used—although this could no doubt change.)

Burning DVDs with Create CD/DVD

Media Center includes a built-in DVD-burning function as part of its Create CD/DVD utility. Unfortunately, Create CD/DVD lets you create only data DVDs, not movie DVDs. This means you can't use this utility to create DVDs that can be played on consumer DVD players—which significantly limits its usability.

note A data DVD stores video files as data files on the DVD, which can be accessed only by a computer's DVD drive. Data DVDs cannot be played in most standalone consumer DVD players.

To burn a data DVD, you follow these steps:

1. From the Media Center Start screen, select **More Programs > Create CD/DVD**.

2. When prompted, insert a blank DVD into your PC's DVD drive.

3. When the Disc Format screen appears, as shown in Figure 11.4, select **Create Data DVD** and click **OK**.

FIGURE 11.4

Choosing to burn a data DVD.

4. On the Name This DVD screen, shown in Figure 11.5, enter a name for the new DVD, and then click **OK**.

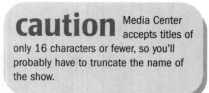

caution Media Center accepts titles of only 16 characters or fewer, so you'll probably have to truncate the name of the show.

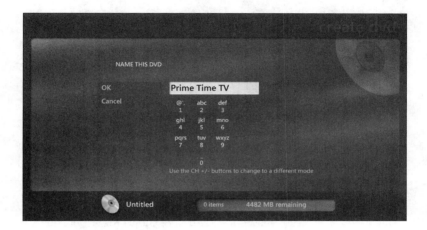

FIGURE 11.5

Naming your new DVD.

5. When the Select Media screen appears, as shown in Figure 11.6, select **Recorded TV**.

FIGURE 11.6

Selecting to copy recorded TV.

6. When the Recorded TV screen appears, as shown in Figure 11.7, check the program(s) you want to copy, and then click **View DVD**.

FIGURE 11.7

Selecting which programs to copy.

7. The View DVD screen, shown in Figure 11.8, shows the list of shows you've selected to copy to DVD. Click **Create DVD** to burn the disc.

FIGURE 11.8

Finalizing the DVD burning process.

One thing to note is that today's recordable DVDs can hold only an hour's worth of programming. That's a one-hour program at the Best quality level. If you recorded the program at a lower quality level, you can fit more time on the DVD—but at the expense of picture quality, of course.

And remember: Any data DVD you burn can be played back only on other personal computers. Data DVDs can't be played back in freestanding consumer DVD players.

Burning DVDs with Third-Party Programs

Okay, so Create CD/DVD isn't that great at burning TV shows to DVD. Fortunately, there are other options, in the form of third-party DVD-burning programs. And, wouldn't you know, Microsoft includes links to two of these programs from the Online Spotlight screen. Just go to the main Media Center Start screen and select **Online Spotlight > Lifestyle**; the two programs you want, Sonic PrimeTime and ArcSoft QuickDVD, are located there. Click either of these two programs to go the company's website and download a free trial version of the program.

note Whichever program you use, know that burning a DVD is very time-consuming. This is primarily because the original DVR-MS format files have to be converted to MPEG format files for inclusion on the DVD. In addition, creating all the menus and chapter stops takes time, as does the physical disc-burning process itself. Don't be surprised if that one-hour program takes more than an hour to burn to DVD.

Sonic PrimeTime

Sonic PrimeTime is the lower-priced of the two DVD burning programs. Clicking on the program in Online Spotlight brings up the product page on the Sonic website; you can download the program for $59.99. (If for some reason the link within MCE doesn't work, just point your web browser to www.sonic.com/products/consumer/primetime/.)

note Sonic also makes a more fully featured version of the PrimeTime program, called PrimeTime Deluxe, which sells for $79.99.

After it's downloaded and installed, PrimeTime is accessible from Media Center's More Programs screen. As you can see in Figure 11.9, it's a fairly easy program to use. Just select the program(s) you want to copy, and then click the **Burn DVD** button. It's pretty much a plain-jane burning program—which isn't necessarily a bad thing. PrimeTime certainly wins my vote for easiest-to-use burning program.

That said, PrimeTime isn't *completely* plain-jane. It creates DVD menus, chapter breaks, and the like, just like you'd find on a commercial DVD. There's nothing you have to do; the program adds the chapter breaks and creates the menu system automatically.

Unlike Media Center's Create CD/DVD, PrimeTime burns DVDs in the standard MPEG DVD video format. We're talking real, honest-to-goodness movie DVDs that can play in any DVD format, not the hockey puck data DVDs that need a computer to play back. PrimeTime is a simple, affordable, and effective solution to the DVD-burning problem.

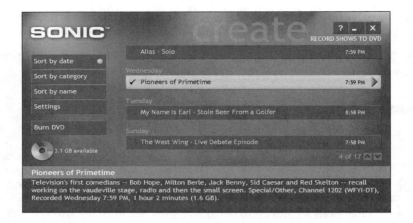

FIGURE 11.9

Selecting programs to burn to DVD with Sonic PrimeTime.

ArcSoft QuickDVD

At $89.95, ArcSoft QuickDVD is a tad pricier than Sonic PrimeTime, but it also does more. When it comes to DVD burning, the "more" includes letting you choose from a variety of menu backgrounds and enter custom DVD titles. And everything's done from your Media Center remote control, using a series of easy-to-use menu screens.

As you can see in Figure 11.10, QuickDVD lets you burn DVDs either from recorded TV shows or from home movies you've recorded on a video camcorder. Just select what type of source material you're using, and then you can choose from a variety of different menu backgrounds, as shown in Figure 11.11. This screen also lets you enter a title for your new DVD.

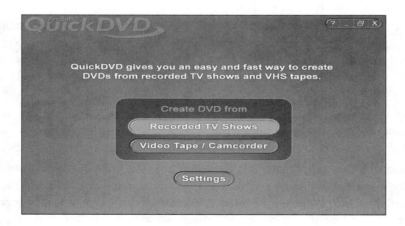

FIGURE 11.10

QuickDVD lets you select what type of video you want to copy to DVD.

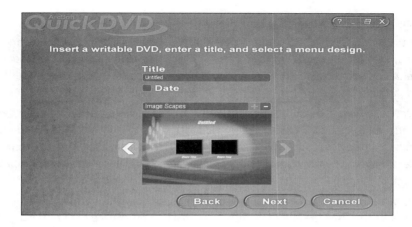

FIGURE 11.11

QuickDVD's selection of menu backgrounds.

Finally, as shown in Figure 11.12, you select which TV programs you want to burn to disc. Select the program(s) and then click the **Burn DVD** button; the rest of the process happens automatically.

You can go to the Online Spotlight page to download a free trial version of the QuickDVD program. If for some reason that doesn't work, just point your web browser to www.arcsoft.com/products/quickdvd/ to download the program from the manufacturer's website.

tip

If you have a Sony Media Center PC, you probably have another DVD program, called Click-to-DVD, preinstalled at no charge. The Media Center version of Click-to-DVD runs within the Media Center interface, and works very much like PrimeTime and QuickDVD.

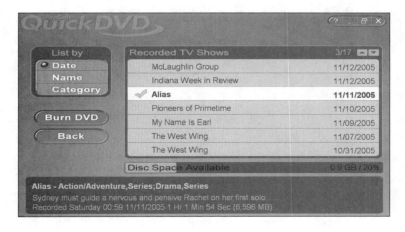

FIGURE 11.12

Selecting what programs to copy in ArcSoft QuickDVD.

Burning DVDs Outside of Media Center

All the Media Center DVD-burning programs are rather simplistic. On one hand, that's good; they're all extremely easy to use. On the other hand, you don't get a lot of customization options, which means that the DVDs you create look a lot like the DVDs your neighbors create.

If you want to create more sophisticated DVDs, you have to exit Media Center and use a Windows-specific DVD creation program, such as Sonic Easy Media Creator or My DVD (www.roxio.com), or Ulead DVD MovieFactory (www.ulead.com). All of these programs offer a lot more menu, background, and animation options, as well as the capability of creating an unlimited number of chapter stops anywhere on the disc.

The challenge you face when copying recorded programs to DVD is the file format that Media Center uses to store these programs. Media Center uses the proprietary DVR-MS format, which isn't readable by consumer DVD players. You have to convert these DVR-MS files to MPEG format before they can be burned to DVD.

Some DVD burner programs (such as Sonic PrimeTime and ArcSoft QuickDVD) do this conversion automatically. Some programs don't. If you need to convert the DVR-MS files before you use a DVD burner program, check out a program called Digital Media Converter. This easy-to-use utility, shown in Figure 11.13, can convert DVR-MS files to any number of formats, including AVI, MPEG-1, MPEG-2, WMV (Windows Media Video), and MOV (QuickTime). It can even covert DVR-MS files to different types of WMV files, including streaming WMVs for playback from a website.

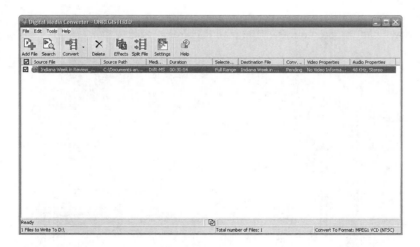

FIGURE 11.13

Converting DVR-MS files to other formats with Digital Media Converter.

One thing I like about Digital Media Converter is that you don't have to convert the entire recorded file. The program lets you split your DVR-MS files and select sections of the file to convert; this is great if you want to copy only a portion of a longer recording.

You can download a 30-day trial version from www.deskshare.com, or purchase the full version for $39.95.

How to Rip DVDs to Your Hard Drive

There's one last DVD-related task we'll discuss here, although I'm the first to admit that it might not be a practical (or legal) task for most users. I'm talking about storing your personal DVD collection on a hard drive so that you can play movies digitally—no DVD player or drive required. It's the video equivalent of ripping, storing, and playing back your CD collection—although it's not nearly as simple an operation.

How Much Space Do You Need?

The first issue you have to deal with concerns disk space. That's because a DVD movie can take up to 8.5GB of storage space—more than twenty times the space required to store a music CD (in WMA Lossless format). At 8.5GB per disc, you'd need 850GB of storage to hold a meager 100-DVD collection. And, as you might be aware, they just don't make hard drives that big.

No, if you go this route, you'll need to purchase multiple hard disks configured in a RAID array. We discussed this some earlier in the book, but what you want is something like LaCie's Bigger Disk Extreme, which uses multiple hard disks in a single housing to deliver up to 2TB of storage. (For what it's worth, 2TB will hold close to 250 DVDs.) If this sounds either too technical or too expensive for you, you might want to consider a DVD changer instead, such as Niveus' Ice Vault 200 (discussed in Chapter 3, "Media Center System #2: The Digital Video Recorder"), or just do like the rest of us and manually insert your DVDs whenever you want to watch a movie.

Ripping DVDs

The technical thing also comes into play when you want to rip a DVD to hard disk. That's because DVD ripping is not a built-in operation in either Media Center or Windows Media Player; in fact, it's an operation that's seriously frowned on by the movie industry. (Some in the industry seem to think that making a copy of a DVD you own is illegal; others believe that it's simply a matter of storing and playing back purchased content in a different medium.) So, when you want to rip a DVD that you've legally purchased, you have to turn to a third-party utility—and these utilities aren't always that intuitive to use.

caution Although the legality of copying your own DVDs is arguable, it is definitely illegal to make copies of rental or borrowed DVDs, or distribute copies of your DVDs to other viewers.

There are several DVD ripper utilities available for download from the Internet. Some of the most popular include

- DVD Decrypter (www.videohelp.com/tools?tool=DVD_Decrypter, freeware), shown in Figure 11.14

- Flash DVD Ripper (www.dvd-ripper.com, $35)

- ImTOO DVD Ripper (www.imtoo.com/dvd-ripper.html, $35)

- Magic DVD Ripper (www.magicdvdripper.com, $35)

- Xilisoft DVD Ripper (www.xilisoft.com/dvd-ripper.html, $35)

> **note** Although very popular and relatively easy to use (and free, of course), DVD Decrypter is no longer officially supported by the developer. It is still available for download for free from many websites, however; do a Google search to find a download site.

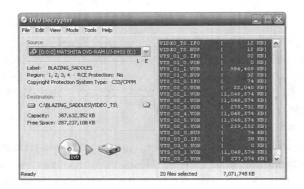

FIGURE 11.14

Ripping a DVD with DVD Decrypter.

Ease of use varies, but I recommend that you have a solid technical grounding before attempting to use any of these programs. The process is much more complicated than what you're used to when ripping CDs. Although the process differs from program to program, here's how it looks, in general terms:

1. Exit or minimize Media Center; all these utilities operate in the Windows environment only.

2. Use My Computer to create a new folder on your hard disk for the DVD you want to rip.

3. Insert the DVD you want to copy in your PC's DVD drive.

4. Launch the DVD ripper program.

5. Select which folder on your hard drive you want to rip the DVD to.

6. Click the "start" button to begin the ripping.

When you start, the ripping process takes about 10–15 minutes. The process creates a dozen or more individual files, representing the different chapters on the DVD, along with audio and other data. (This is why you want to create a separate folder for each DVD you rip.)

After a DVD is ripped to your hard drive, it's another task completely to trick your PC into running it as it would a disc in your DVD drive. The trick is made easier, however, when you activate Media Center's hidden My DVD function—which we'll discuss next.

Changing Play DVD to My DVDs

Back in Chapter 3 we discussed how connecting a DVD changer to your Media Center PC changes the Play DVD function to a My DVDs menu. Well, it's possible to activate the My DVDs function without attaching a DVD changer—and then use this new

note Learn more about Tweak MCE in Chapter 17, "Customizing Windows XP MCE."

screen to manage and play all the DVDs you've ripped to your computer's hard disk.

To change Play DVD to My DVDs, you first have to download and install Microsoft's Tweak MCE PowerToy. The program is distributed free of charge; download it at www.microsoft.com/downloads/.

After you have Tweak MCE installed, it appears as a new option on the More Programs screen. Launch the Tweak MCE program, select **DVD > Enable My DVDs**, check the **Enable My DVDs** option, and then click **Save**. When you return to the Media Center Start screen, you'll see that the Play DVD option has been replaced by the My DVDs option, as shown in Figure 11.15.

FIGURE 11.15

The Media Center Start screen, with Play DVD replaced by My DVDs.

Click **My DVDs** and Media Center displays the main My DVDs screen. As you can see in Figure 11.16, all the DVD movies you've ripped are displayed on this screen. Click a movie to begin playback; from here on out, it's just like you're playing the original DVD, except it's all happening from your hard drive.

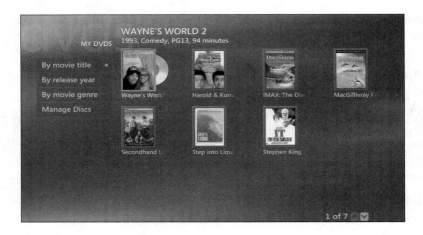

FIGURE 11.16
All your ripped DVDs are displayed on the My DVDs screen.

How to Play Other Video Files

While we're on the topic of playing back DVD files from your hard disk, let's take a minute to discuss playing other video files you might have stored on your Media Center PC. I'm talking about video files downloaded from the Internet, or maybe home movies you transferred from your digital camcorder. All of these video files are accessible from Media Center's My Videos screen, which you get to by going to the Start screen and selecting My Videos.

As you can see in Figure 11.17, the My Videos screen displays all the videos you have stored, with a thumbnail picture representing the first frame of each video. To view more details about any video, highlight the thumbnail, press the More Info button on your remote, and select **Video Details** from the pop-up menu; this displays the Video Details screen, shown in Figure 11.18.

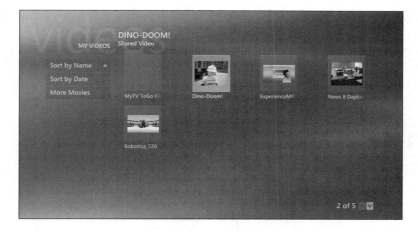

FIGURE 11.17

Viewing stored video files with My Videos.

FIGURE 11.18

Viewing more details about a selected video file.

To play back a video, simply go to the My Videos screen, highlight the video, and press Play or OK on your remote control. The video now plays back in full-screen mode, as shown in Figure 11.19. All the normal transport buttons on your remote control can be used, and the typical progress bar will be displayed onscreen.

FIGURE 11.19

Playing a video in Media Center.

Using Windows XP MCE for Digital Photos

Almost all users know that they can use a Media Center PC to play back CDs and digital music. Most users know they can use a Media Center PC to play back and record DVDs. The majority of users even know they can use a Media Center PC to watch and record television programs. But few users, I've found, know that they can use a Media Center PC to view digital photos.

That is a shame because viewing pictures on a big-screen TV is a real treat—especially if you have a collection of high-resolution digital photos. Any picture shot at anything over one megapixel looks terrific on a 720p HDTV display. (A 720p display has a resolution of 720 × 1280 pixels, which translates to 921,600 total pixels—or .9 megapixels.)

Windows Media Center has a fairly robust digital photo slide-show function built into the interface, which makes viewing digital photos quite enjoyable. Even better, you can view a slideshow while you listen to digital music in the background— a great use of Media Center PC multitasking!

Configuring Your Photo Slideshows

Before we get into how you display a photo slideshow, let's configure Media Center to display slideshows the way you want. You do this configuration from the Pictures Settings screen, shown in Figure 12.1. This screen is accessed by going to the Media Center Start screen and selecting **Settings > Pictures**.

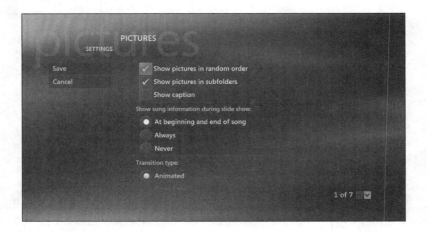

FIGURE 12.1

Configuring Media Center's photo slideshow settings.

Here are the options you can set on the Pictures Settings screen:

- **Show Pictures in Random Order**—Check this option to display your pictures in no set order. Uncheck this option to display your pictures in alphabetical order by filename.

- **Show Pictures in Subfolders**—When you check this option, selecting the My Pictures folder displays all photos stored in that folder and in all subfolders underneath the My Pictures folder. To play only those photos in the selected folder (thus ignoring all the subfolders), uncheck this option.

- **Show Caption**—If a picture has a caption attached, selecting this option displays the caption below the photo onscreen.

- **Show Song Information During Slide Show**—This option is for when you're listening to music and viewing photos at the same time. Select **At Beginning and End of Song** to display the song info only at the beginning and end of each song; the screen is otherwise clean during most of the playback. Select **Always** to display the song info continuously, as shown in Figure 12.2. Select **Never** to never display the song info.

FIGURE 12.2

Displaying song information when viewing a slideshow.

- **Transition Type**—This option makes your slideshows look like a Ken Burns–style documentary. Select **Animated** to make your photos move around and zoom in and out onscreen. Select **Cross Fade** to make your photos fade in and out. Or select **None** to not use any transition effect.

- **Transition Time**—This setting tells Media Center how long to display each picture onscreen before switching to the next photo.

When you're done configuring these settings, click **Save**.

How to View Digital Photos

Media Center lets you view all your photos in a continuous slideshow, or view each picture one at a time. Let's examine the latter task first.

When you go to the Media Center Start screen and select **My Pictures**, you're taken to the My Pictures screen shown in Figure 12.3. As you can see, this screen displays the contents of the My Pictures folder on your PC's hard drive. All photos stored directly in this folder are displayed in thumbnail view. You can use the menu options along the left side of the screen to sort the pictures by name or by date.

Any subfolders within the My Pictures folder are also displayed on this screen. To view the contents of a subfolder, just select the subfolder and click the OK button on your remote. To view any individual picture, just navigate to the picture and click the OK button on your remote. The picture now appears full-screen, as shown in Figure 12.4.

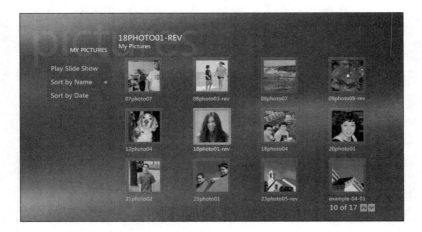

FIGURE 12.3

Viewing picture thumbnails (and subfolders) on the My Pictures screen.

FIGURE 12.4

Viewing a digital photo full-screen.

You can view details about any picture by highlighting the picture, pressing the More Info button on your remote, and selecting Picture Details from the pop-up menu, as shown in Figure 12.5. The Picture Details screen, shown in Figure 12.6, displays the picture's name, resolution, and when it was last modified. You can also use the Picture Details screen to rotate the picture 90° (click the **Rotate** button), print the picture (click the **Print** button), or touch up the picture—which we'll discuss in the "How to Edit Your Digital Photos" section, later in this chapter.

FIGURE 12.5

Press the More Info button to display these options.

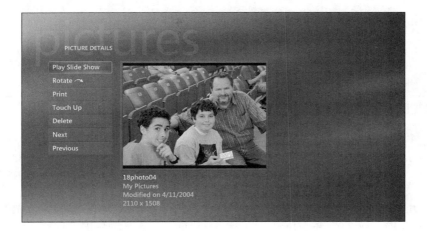

FIGURE 12.6

Viewing details for the selected picture.

How to Manage Your Digital Photos

By default, Media Center watches only the My Pictures folder on your hard drive for photos to display on the My Pictures screen. The easiest way to manage your digital photos is to move outside of Media Center and use the My Documents folder in Windows to move all your photos to this My Pictures folder. (Some things are easier done in Windows than within Media Center.)

Alternatively, you can tell Media Center to watch folders other than My Pictures for photos to display. Just follow these steps:

1. From the My Pictures screen, press the More Info button on your remote.

2. Select **Add Pictures** from the pop-up menu.

3. When the first Picture Discovery screen appears, as shown in Figure 12.7, check **Add Folders** and click **Next**.

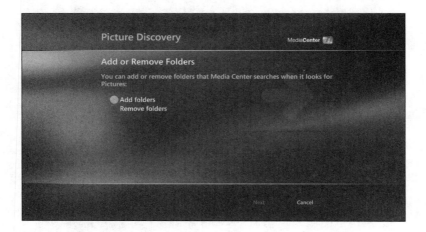

FIGURE 12.7

Getting ready to add folders to My Pictures.

4. When the Add Folders screen appears, as shown in Figure 12.8, check **Add Folders on This Computer** and click **Next**. (Alternatively, to view photos stored on another computer on your home network, check the **Add Shared Folders from Another Computer** option.)

5. When the next screen appears, as shown in Figure 12.9, select those folders that you want to watch, and then click **Next**.

6. When the next screen appears, as shown in Figure 12.10, confirm that these are the folders you want to watch, and then click **Finish**.

tip
To delete a picture from the My Photos folder, highlight the photo, click the More Info button on your remote, and then select **Delete** from the pop-up menu. It's that easy.

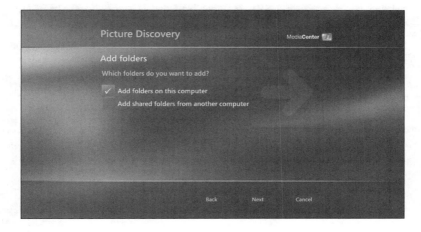

FIGURE 12.8

Choosing where to add the folders from.

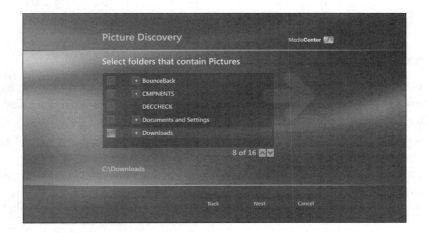

FIGURE 12.9

Selecting which folders you want to watch.

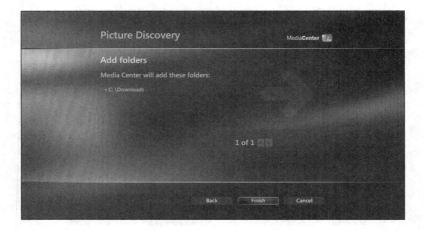

FIGURE 12.10

Confirming the picture discovery process.

Media Center now watches the folders you've selected, and displays pictures stored there on the My Pictures screen.

How to Edit Your Digital Photos

I won't kid you. Media Center is not a great environment for digital photo editing. If you have serious photo-editing chores, exit Media Center and use a Windows-based editing program, such as Adobe Photoshop Elements or Paint Shop Pro. It's the only way to go.

However, if all you need to do is make some quick and easy touchups, you might be able to do what you need to do from within Media Center. That's because Media Center, unbeknownst to most users, includes some rudimentary photo-editing functions—red eye correction, cropping, contrast adjustment, and so on. It's not a perfect solution, but it might do the job.

To access Media Center's photo touchup tools, go to the My Pictures page, select the photo you want to edit, press the More Info button on your remote control, and then select **Picture Details** from the pop-up menu. Then, when the Picture Details page appears, click **Touch Up**.

As you can see in Figure 12.11, the Touch Up page includes several rudimentary picture-editing tools on the menu along the left side. Let's look at each of these tools in turn.

tip
You can preview your changes at any time by clicking the **Preview** button on the Touch Up page menu.

FIGURE 12.11

The My Pictures Touch Up page.

Red Eye

Ever take a picture with your camera's built-in flash and end up with a subject that looks like the spawn of a devil? (Figure 12.12 shows a typical picture with bad red eye.) Fix it fast from the Touch Up screen by clicking **Red Eye** on the menu. This automatic tool does a fairly good job of fixing most instances of red eye.

FIGURE 12.12

A baby with bad red eye to be touched up.

Contrast

If a picture is too light or too dark, like the one in Figure 12.13, let Media Center's automatic Contrast tool fix it for you. This is a one-button solution to a fairly common problem.

FIGURE 12.13

A picture that's too dark and needs to be touched up.

Crop

When the subject of your photo isn't big enough, or too far off to one side, or just poorly framed, you need to crop the picture to focus attention on the main subject. Media Center's Crop tool is fairly effective, although not necessarily that easy to use. (Cropping is a task best done by dragging a mouse, not by clicking buttons on a remote control unit.)

That said, when you click the **Crop** button on the Touch Up page, you display the screen shown in Figure 12.14. Your original picture appears in the main window, along with a series of controls beneath. You use these controls to perform the crop.

To crop to a smaller area in your photo, click the **Zoom +** button; this has the effect of zooming in on your subject. Click the **Zoom –** button to zoom back out. (You can click each button multiple times.) Then, when you've zoomed in, click the arrow buttons to move the crop area left, right, up, or down to properly frame your subject. As you can see, the visible area of the picture reflects your cropping decisions.

When you've done cropping, click **Save** to save your changes. When prompted to apply your changes, click **Yes**. (The result of this particular crop is shown in Figure 12.15.)

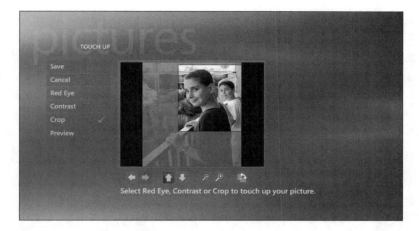

FIGURE 12.14
The cropped area is highlighted in the main window.

FIGURE 12.15
Our original picture, cropped.

How to Burn Your Photos to a CD

If you want to distribute your digital photos to friends and family, the best course of action is to burn the photo files to CD. This is accomplished with Media Center's Create CD/DVD function, which we've discussed several times previously in this book.

Here's how to do it:

1. From the Media Center Start screen, select **More Programs** > **Create CD/DVD**.

2. When prompted, insert a blank CD in your PC's CD drive.

3. On the Disc Format screen, shown in Figure 12.16, check **Data CD** and click **OK**.

FIGURE 12.16

Choosing to burn a data CD.

4. When the Name This CD screen appears, as shown in Figure 12.17, enter a name for this CD and click **OK**.

FIGURE 12.17

Entering a name for your photo CD.

5. When the Select Media screen appears, as shown in Figure 12.18, click **Pictures**.

FIGURE 12.18

Choosing to copy pictures to your data CD.

6. Now you get to select which pictures to burn to CD. When the screen in Figure 12.19 appears, navigate to each picture you want to copy and click it to put a check in the check box.

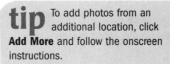

tip   To add photos from an additional location, click **Add More** and follow the onscreen instructions.

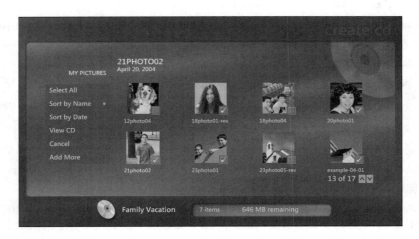

FIGURE 12.19

Selecting which photos to include on the CD.

7. When you're done selecting pictures, click **View CD**.

8. When the View CD screen appears, as shown in Figure 12.20, you have one last chance to edit your list, by unchecking any given picture. If you like your list, click **Create CD** to begin copying the files to CD.

FIGURE 12.20

Starting the copying process.

How to Play a Photo Slideshow

Now we come to the really fun part of My Pictures: displaying a slideshow of your digital photos. It's easy to do; just follow these steps:

1. From the Media Center Start screen, select **My Pictures**.

2. If you want to display all the photos in the My Pictures folder, proceed to step 4.

3. If you want to display only those folders stored in a specific subfolder, navigate to that subfolder and press OK on your remote control.

4. Click **Play Slide Show**.

That's it. The Media Center interface fades away and the entire screen is given over to the slideshow.

Note that photos smaller than your screen are displayed against a black background. For example, Figure 12.21 shows a narrow vertical picture that obviously doesn't fill up the entire widescreen display; it's shown onscreen with black bars on either side.

FIGURE 12.21

Displaying a narrow picture on a wide screen.

While you're playing a slideshow, you can use the directional buttons on your remote control to manually advance to the next or previous photo in the slideshow. To pause the slideshow on the current picture, press the Pause button on your remote. To halt the slideshow and return to the Media Center interface (and the My Pictures screen), press the Stop button on your remote.

How to Listen to Music While Playing a Slideshow

If you thought displaying a slideshow was neat, here's something even neater. Media Center lets you do two things at once by listening to a music album or playlist while viewing a photo slideshow. I gotta tell you, this is a great way to entertain folks at a family gathering; just select some appropriate music, start showing your family and vacation pictures, and the crowd will sit there, mesmerized. It's one of my favorite Media Center features.

Here's how to do it:

1. From the Media Center Start screen, select **My Music > Playlists**.
2. Click the playlist you want to play.
3. Click **Play**, and then click **Shuffle**.
4. Press the Green Button on your remote control to return to the Start screen.
5. Select **My Pictures**.
6. Select the subfolder of pictures you want to view, or proceed directly to step 7.
7. Click Play Slide Show.

Now settle back to view your favorite pictures while listening to the selected music. Way cool!

13

Using Windows XP MCE for Computer Tasks

Let's be upfront about something. A Media Center PC is designed to be an entertainment device, not a workplace tool. Although a Media Center PC can theoretically do anything that a regular desktop PC can do, the fact that you're operating the thing from at least 10 feet away with a handheld remote control means that many operations just aren't practical. For example, sitting on your couch and composing a novel within the Media Center environment would be difficult, if not impossible. The same thing with crunching numbers in a spreadsheet, or even surfing the Web.

As you've learned in the previous chapters, what a Media Center PC does best is play back movies and music. But that doesn't mean you *can't* perform other types of operations. In fact, several traditional computer-oriented applications have been ported to Media Center's 10-foot interface. We'll discuss those applications in this chapter.

Chatting with Other Users via Media Center Messenger

Some people can't go five minutes without checking in with friends and colleagues, which is one of the reasons why instant messaging is so popular. Well, Microsoft figured that if you're one of these folks, you wouldn't want to be out of touch while you're in your living room listening to music or watching movies, and built an instant-messaging application into the Windows Media Center interface.

What you get with Media Center Messenger is a stripped-down version of the regular Windows Messenger program. It's stripped down in that you can't add new contacts to your favorites list; you can only send messages to your established contacts. (If you want to add new contacts, close or minimize Media Center and use the regular Windows Messenger application.)

You can, however, use your wireless keyboard to send instant messages, and receive and read messages onscreen in the Media Center interface. It's actually quite easy to use; just make sure that your Media Center PC is connected to an always-on Internet connection, and you're good to go.

To launch the Media Center Messenger application, go to the Media Center Start page and select **More Programs > Messenger**. This displays the sign-in screen, shown in Figure 13.1. Click **Sign In** and you're ready to start messaging.

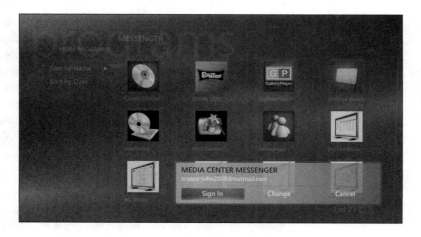

FIGURE 13.1

Signing in to Media Center Messenger.

Media Center now displays a contacts window in the lower-right corner of the screen, as shown in Figure 13.2. When one or more of your contacts are online, you see them listed in this window. To send a message to a contact, just click that person's name.

As you can see in Figure 13.3, you send and receive messages from a separate message window, displayed at the bottom left of your screen. Enter your message in the text box, using your wireless keyboard; press the Enter key to send the message. The conversation itself is displayed below the message box, as shown in Figure 13.4.

FIGURE 13.2

Viewing your contact list on the big screen.

FIGURE 13.3

Sending an instant message with Media Center Messenger.

That's about all there is to it. Media Center Messenger is fairly simple and quite easy to use. It doesn't offer all the bells and whistles of the regular Windows Messenger (you can't send files, use smilies, video conference, or create group chats), but it's a way to send one-to-one messages from the comfort of your living room couch.

FIGURE 13.4

Displaying an entire conversation onscreen, one line at a time.

And here's the secret behind the curtain. If you minimize the Media Center interface, you see that good old Windows Messenger is running behind the scenes, on your Windows XP desktop. As you can see in Figure 13.5, the entire conversation is there, in the background, synched to the Media Center version of Messenger. It might not be invisible, but it gets the job done.

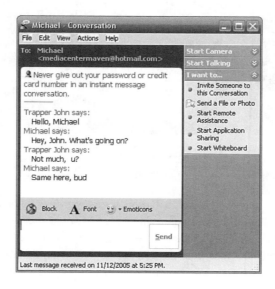

FIGURE 13.5

Behind the scenes: Windows Messenger is running the show.

Checking Your Email with Hotmail Plus Reader

Unfortunately, Media Center doesn't come with a "My Email" function, so if you want to check your email while you're listening to music in your living room, you're out of luck. Oh, you could minimize Media Center and use a Windows-based email reader, but that's a real pain.

The pain is eased somewhat when you install Microsoft's Hotmail Plus Reader for Media Center. This is an optional program that you can download for free from CNET Download.com (www.download.com); it installs directly into the Media Center interface, under the More Programs menu.

What the Hotmail Plus Reader does is let you check and read email messages in your Hotmail or MSN Mail inbox. It's only a reader, so you can't reply to or send new messages; this just reinforces the notion that Media Center is an entertainment-oriented interface, not an application-based one. Still, it's better than nothing.

note Obviously, to use the Hotmail Plus Reader you must first have a valid Hotmail or MSN account. You can't sign for an account from within Media Center; if you need to sign up, you have to use your Windows-based web browser to go to www.hotmail.com and follow the instructions from there.

When you have the Hotmail Plus Reader installed, you can launch it by going to the Media Center Start screen and selecting **More Programs > Hotmail Reader**. This displays the Sign In to Your Account screen, shown in Figure 13.6. Enter your Hotmail email address and password, and then click **Sign In**. (Just to be different, when you go to enter your address and password, the Hotmail Plus Reader displays an onscreen keyboard, shown in Figure 13.7; you can enter your address and password by clicking the onscreen keys, or by using your normal wireless keyboard.)

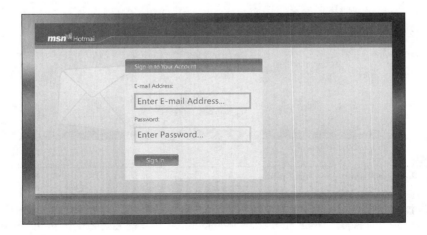

FIGURE 13.6

Signing into your Hotmail or MSN Mail account.

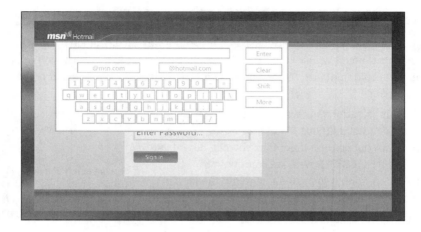

FIGURE 13.7

If you don't want to use your wireless keyboard, you can use this onscreen virtual keyboard instead.

The Hotmail Plus Reader now displays the Inbox screen, shown in Figure 13.8. To check for new messages, click the **Check Mail** button. All messages are listed here; to read a message, click it.

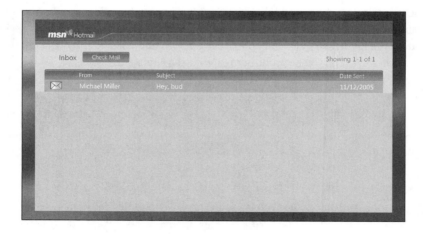

FIGURE 13.8

Viewing all the messages in your email inbox.

Figure 13.9 shows what a typical email message looks like. Notice that there's no "reply" button; this is just an email reader, remember, so there's no replying to the messages you receive. If you want to reply, you need to minimize or close Media Center and use your regular Windows-based email program or web browser. The Hotmail Plus Reader is designed only to keep you up-to-date with any new messages you receive.

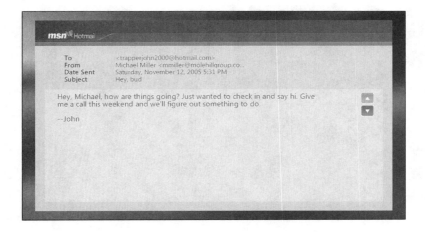

FIGURE 13.9

Reading a new email message.

Managing Your Schedules, Contacts, and Email with MCE Outlook

Microsoft Outlook is one of the most-used scheduling/contact management/email programs both in the corporate workplace and at home. It's not, however, a program designed for use in the living room; not only is it not a Media Center application, it's pretty much impossible to use from 10 feet away.

Media Center itself doesn't offer any scheduling or contact management solutions, but a Dutch developer named SAM-Consult has come up with a Media Center add-on that does the job. MCE Outlook lets you manage your Outlook appointments and contacts from within Media Center, using your Media Center remote control and wireless keyboard. You can also use MCE Outlook to send and receive emails—which makes it a more versatile email solution than Microsoft's own Hotmail Plus Reader.

You can download MCE Outlook from www.mce-software.com. The program is available free of charge, and installs easily within the Media Center interface. After it's installed, it appears as a My Outlook option on the More Programs screen.

As you can see in Figure 13.10, the main My Outlook screen looks a lot like the regular Windows Outlook screen. The different operations—Calendar, Contacts, Inbox, Sent Items, Notes, and Tasks—appear as menu options on the left side of the screen, much like the same options appear as folders on the Windows Outlook screen. Click an option to go to that operation.

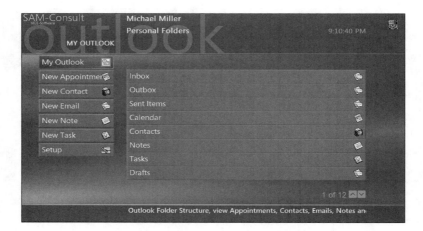

FIGURE 13.10

The main My Outlook screen—just like regular Outlook.

For example, when you click **Calendar**, you see the Calendar screen shown in Figure 13.11. Scheduled appointments are shown on the calendar itself; you can schedule new appointments by clicking on a day in the calendar.

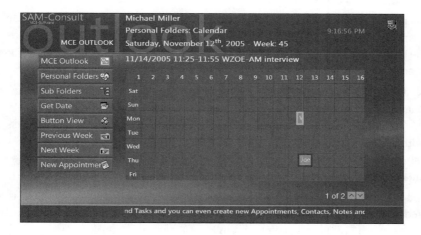

FIGURE 13.11

Viewing appointments on the Calendar screen.

Click **Contacts** on the main screen and you can view all your Outlook contacts, as shown in Figure 13.12. Click any contact to view the complete information, as shown in Figure 13.13.

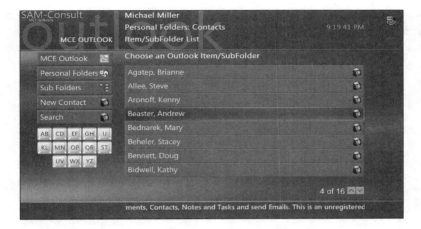

FIGURE 13.12

My Outlook displaying all your Outlook contacts.

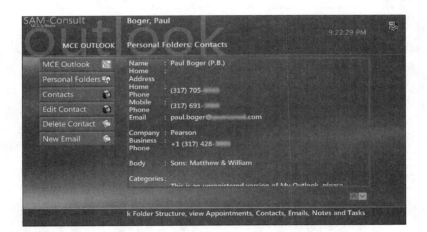

FIGURE 13.13

Viewing the details of a specific contact.

Click **Inbox** on the main screen and you see the Inbox screen, shown in Figure 13.14, with all waiting emails listed. Click any message to read it, as shown in Figure 13.15. You can even create and send new messages, using the onscreen form shown in Figure 13.16. (That's right, unlike Hotmail Plus Reader, MCE Outlook lets you read *and* send email messages!)

Admittedly, performing all these tasks from 10 feet away with a wireless keyboard might be a tad awkward, but MCE Outlook proves that it's doable. Check it out if you want to use your Media Center PC for more than just entertainment.

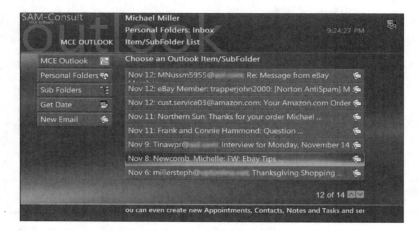

FIGURE 13.14

Viewing a list of new email messages in MCE Outlook.

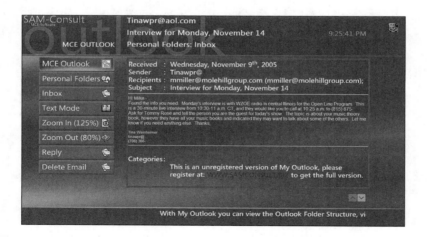

FIGURE 13.15

Reading an email message onscreen.

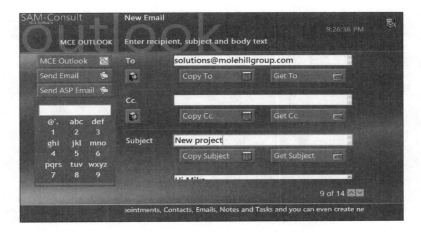

FIGURE 13.16

Creating a new email message.

Managing Your Files with My File Manager

One of the things I dislike about Media Center is that there is no facility for managing files from within the Media Center interface. If I want to copy music or photo files from one location to another, I have to close or minimize Media Center and do the grunt work from Windows proper. It's a pain.

Well, our friends at SAM-Consult have come to the rescue yet again, this time with a Media Center add-in called My File Manager. Like MCE Outlook, My File Manager is available for free; download it from www.mce-software.com.

After it's installed, you access My File Manager from Media Center's More Programs screen. The main My File Manager screen, shown in Figure 13.17, shows a list of all the drives on your computer, much like what you see when you open My Computer from within Windows XP. (Except in the Media Center 10-foot interface, of course.) Click any drive to view that drive's contents.

Figure 13.18 shows a list of folders, subfolders, and files on a typical drive. All available file operations are listed in the menu on the left side of the screen. To perform any given operation, just highlight the file or folder, and then click the menu operation. For example, to delete a file, navigate to and select the file, and then click **Delete File**.

FIGURE 13.17

My File Manager adds basic file management to Windows Media Center.

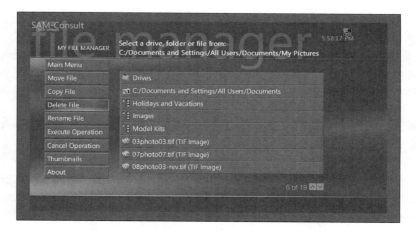

FIGURE 13.18

Viewing folders and files with My File Manager.

For more complex operations, such as copying or moving files, you're taken through a series of screens. You have to select the file to copy, select the drive and/or folder you want to copy to, and then confirm the operation (as shown in Figure 13.19) by clicking the **Execute Operation** button. It's a little time-consuming, but quicker than exiting to Windows and using the My Documents or My Computer function.

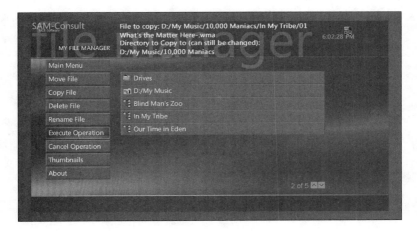

FIGURE 13.19

Executing a complex file operation with My File Manager.

Despite the number of screens you have to use, and the lack of drag-and-drop operation, My File Manager is actually quite intuitive, surprisingly elegant, and easily used with any Media Center remote control. Which begs the question: Why couldn't Microsoft have included this functionality within Media Center proper?

note SAM-Consult offers several other Media Center add-ins, in addition to MCE Outlook and My File Manager. Learn more in Chapter 16, "Finding and Using Other Media Center Applications."

Extending Your Media Center PC

14 Using Your Media Center PC with a Media Center Extender

15 Exploring the Online Spotlight

16 Finding and Using Other Media Center Applications

17 Customizing Windows XP Media Center Edition

18 Troubleshooting Media Center Problems

Using Your Media Center PC with a Media Center Extender

Sometimes one Media Center PC in a household isn't enough. When you want to listen to your digital music throughout your house or watch your recorded television programs on a bedroom TV, you don't have to invest in a second expensive PC system. Instead, you can share the music and programs stored on your main PC over your home network, using a Media Center Extender.

We first talked about Media Center Extenders back in Chapter 4, "Media Center System #3: The Whole House Entertainment System." Now it's time to get down and dirty, and learn how to connect, configure, and use one or more Media Center Extenders.

Connecting a Media Center Extender

As you learned in Chapter 4, there are two primary uses for a Media Center Extender. You can use one or more Extenders to play back, in other rooms of your house, music and programs stored on a living room Media Center PC. Or you can put a Media Center Extender in your living room, in lieu of a Media Center PC, to play back files stored on a desktop Media Center PC elsewhere in your home. Either type of system works on the same principle: Digital files are stored on a primary Media

Center PC, and then beamed over your home network to a Media Center Extender. The Extender, of course, is connected to its own television and (optionally) audio system.

Whichever type of system topography you're using, connecting a Media Center Extender is surprisingly easy. There are two main connections you have to make. First, you have to connect the Extender to your television and (optionally) your audio system. Second, you have to connect the Extender to your home network. That's it.

Connecting Audio and Video

Figure 14.1 shows the back panel on a typical Media Center Extender. As you can see, you have the choice of connecting to your TV via single-cable composite video, S-Video, or three-cable component video. The component video connection delivers the best picture quality, of course, but isn't really necessary if you're primarily using your Media Center Extender to listen to music.

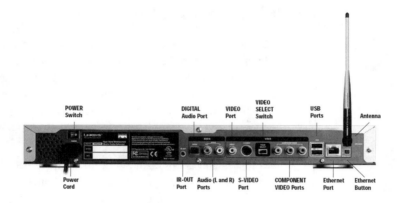

FIGURE 14.1

The back panel connections on the Linksys Media Center Extender.

Audio can be connected via analog right/left RCA audio connections or an optical digital connection. As usual, the digital connection offers superior sound quality, and is necessary if you're connecting your Media Center Extender to a surround sound system. If you're just connecting the Extender to the audio input on a television set, the RCA connections are fine.

Figure 14.2 shows a typical connection between a Media Center Extender and a television set; go this route if you're only sharing television programs and

note You have to connect both the audio and video connections—even if you're interested only in listening to music. That's because you need a television screen to display the Media Center interface, which is where you select the music you want to listen to. So, you need to have some sort of television handy in every room you use a Media Center Extender.

don't have a separate audio system handy. Figure 14.3 shows a typical connection between a Media Center Extender, a television set, and an audio system; go this route if you're interested in sharing music.

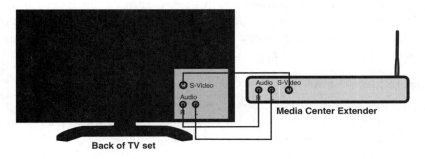

FIGURE 14.2

Connecting a Media Center Extender to a television set.

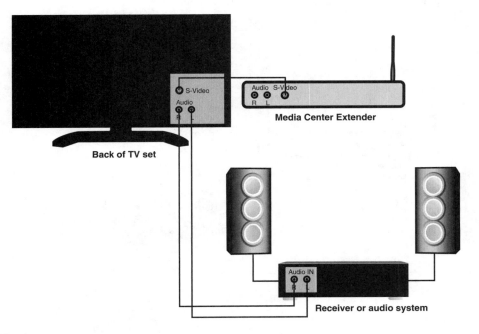

FIGURE 14.3

Connecting a Media Center Extender to an audio system and television set.

Connecting to Your Home Network

For the Media Center Extender to share files with a separate Media Center PC, both the Extender and PC must be connected to your home network. The most common network configuration connects all such devices to a central network router; this router can be wired, wireless, or a combination of both. In most instances, the router is also connected to a broadband Internet connection; this enables all the PCs (and Extenders) on your network to share the Internet connection.

Connecting via Ethernet

If you're connecting to a wired home network, connect a ethernet cable from your network router to the ethernet port on the back of the Extender. Your connection should use the 100Mbps ethernet protocol; the slower 10Mbps ethernet isn't fast enough to transmit streaming video.

> **tip** If you're primarily using your Media Center Extender to play music, you can use either a wireless or wired connection to your network. If you're using your Extender to play video, however, you should use a wired ethernet connection, which is both faster and more stable than a wireless connection.

Figure 14.4 shows an Extender connected via ethernet.

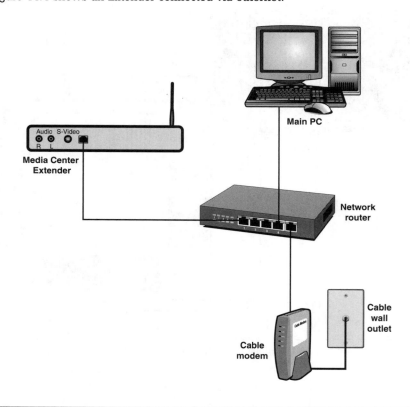

Main PC

Audio S-Video
R L
**Media Center
Extender**

**Network
router**

**Cable
wall
outlet**

**Cable
modem**

FIGURE 14.4

Connecting a Media Center Extender to a wired network.

Connecting via Wi-Fi

If you're connecting to a wireless Wi-Fi home network, there's no physical connection to make—just raise the antenna on the back panel and you're good to go. You can connect via either 802.11a or 802.11g; the newer 802.11a standard operates in the 5GHz band, which makes it more reliable than the older 802.11g connection (which operates in the more cluttered 2.4GHz band).

Know, however, that if you're connecting your Extender wirelessly, you *must* connect your main PC to the router via ethernet. You can't have a wireless-to-wireless connection when using an Extender; the first connection, from the PC to the router, must be wired. Then you can make a wireless connection from the router to the Media Center Extender.

Configuring a Media Center Extender

After your Media Center Extender is physically connected, it's time to make the virtual connection to your home network and main PC. Make sure that you have your television turned on and switched to the appropriate video input, and then power up the Media Center Extender.

The Extender, when first powered on, displays a Setup Key screen, like the one shown in Figure 14.5, along with a setup key number. Write down this number.

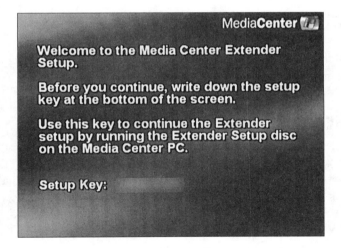

FIGURE 14.5

The Extender's Setup Key screen.

Now go to your main Media Center PC and insert the Windows Media Center Extender Setup CD that came with your Extender. Doing so launches the Media Center Extender

Setup Wizard. Follow the onscreen instructions and when prompted for the setup key, as shown in Figure 14.6, enter the number that was displayed on the Extender's Setup Key screen. Enter any other information as requested, and then finish the wizard.

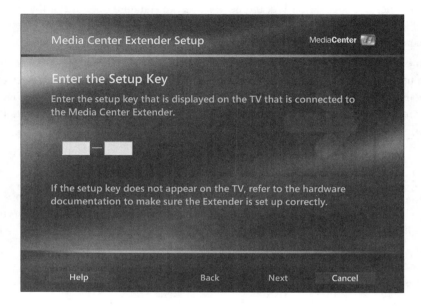

FIGURE 14.6

The Media Center Extender Setup Wizard, displayed on your PC.

That's all there is to it. Your Media Center Extender is now installed and configured on your system, and you're ready to start using it.

Using Your Media Center Extender

Using a Media Center Extender is very similar to using a Media Center PC—so similar, in fact, that you might not even notice the differences. As you can see in Figure 14.7, the Start screen on the Extender looks almost exactly like the regular Media Center interface. So, what's the difference? There's no Play DVD menu option; that's because you can't play DVDs on a Media Center Extender. All the other menu options are the same, although without all the transition animations of the PC–based Media Center Edition.

Given that the Extender screens are pretty much the same as the regular Media Center screens, you'd expect the operation to be equally similar— and you'd be right. Want to play music? Select the **My Music** option. Want to watch live television?

note Media Center Extenders can play back only standard-definition TV programming, not high-definition programming.

Select the **My TV** option. Want to watch a recorded TV program? Select **My TV >
Recorded Programs**. Want to view digital photos? Select **My Pictures**. It's that simple.

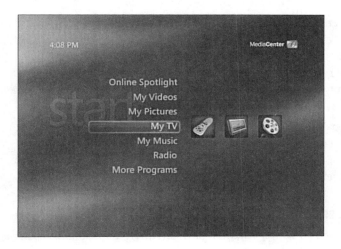

FIGURE 14.7

The Extender's start screen.

Of course, every song, program, or picture you select isn't stored on the Extender itself.
When you select an item, it's actually being played back from your main Media Center
PC, and then beamed over your home network to the Media Center Extender. It all happens so fast you don't notice any latency—although there is some, however slight. It's
not a big deal, though.

You can also configure the Extender the same way you can configure your Media Center
PC: using the Settings screen. The settings you select on the Extender are completely
independent of the settings on your main PC; set one device up one way and the other
another. It's allowed.

And that's pretty much all you need to know about using a Media Center Extender. Other
than playing DVDs, everything you can do on a Media Center PC can also be done on a
Media Center Extender. I'd tell you more if there were more to tell, but this is one
instance where Microsoft has done a good job making the technology do what it is supposed to do—extend the Media Center experience to other rooms in your house, transpar-
ently. What a surprise; it really works!

Tricks for Improving Media Center Extender Performance

Okay, when I said that it really works, I meant that it really works *most of the time*. In
some instances, you might find that you get stuttering or freezing audio or video when

playing through a Media Center Extender. In almost all cases, this is because of poor network performance. To improve the performance of your Media Center Extender, then, you need to improve the stability and performance of your home network.

First off, know that the most reliable network connection you can make is a wired one. I know it's a pain in the rear to install, but an ethernet network is a lot more reliable than a Wi-Fi network when it comes to Media Center Extender performance. In fact, if you're using your Extender to watch television programming (live or recorded), ethernet might be the only way to go. A wireless connection is simply not as fast or as reliable as a wired one; video viewing demands both speed and stability.

If you decide to go the wireless route (it's easy to set up, I know), opt for the more stable 802.11a standard, if you can. That might mean replacing your current wireless router with an 802.11a model (and going with 802.11a access points all around), but the improvement in speed is worth it, especially for video programming.

Troubleshooting Wireless Network Problems

Whether you go with an 802.11a or 802.11g Wi-Fi network, you still might run into occasional connection problems. Let's examine some of the things you can do to alleviate these problems.

Move the Antenna

Got your Extender installed in the back of an audio/video cabinet? There's your problem, pal. The antenna on the Extender needs a fairly clear path to the antenna on your wireless router. Yes, a radio frequency (RF) signal can pass through walls and other obstructions, but every item the signal passes through reduces the strength of the signal. In addition, metal objects can obstruct or deflect the signal.

If you're running into connection problems, the first thing to do is to try repositioning the antenna. Move it from the back of the cabinet to the front, or turn it 90 degrees, or shuffle to the right or the left. Remove any metal objects or electronic components from around the antenna. Even small movements can have a big impact on the resulting signal strength.

Change Channels

A wireless network can use one of several RF channels to transmit data. If one channel isn't working well, it could be due to interference of some sort. Try switching channels on all your wireless devices; another channel might work better than the default one.

Remove Interference

Speaking of interference, 802.11g Wi-Fi networks operate in the 2.4GHz frequency range. Unfortunately, so do many other devices in your home, including cordless phones, microwave ovens, baby monitors, and the like. If you're getting interference from other devices, you might need to replace those devices or curtail their use—or upgrade to an 802.11a network, which operates in the less-crowded 5GHz band.

Upgrade Your Entire Network

If you're running an 802.11b/g network and you have even one older 802.11b device connected, you're slowing down the entire network to 802.11b levels (11Mbps). To get full 54Mbps 802.11g performance for your Media Center Extender, remove or upgrade any 802.11b device currently connected to your network.

Connect the PC via Ethernet

As noted previously, if you're connecting your Extender via Wi-Fi, you can't connect your PC via Wi-Fi, too. You have to connect your PC to your network router via ethernet.

Update Your Firmware

If you're using an older wireless router or access point, you might need to update the software inside the device. (This internal software is called *firmware*.) Some older firmware does not support Media Center Extenders; updating to a newer version of the firmware might be necessary to ensure compatibility.

Record at a Lower Quality Level

If you have performance-based problems with your Extender, consider recording your television programs at a lower quality level. Lower-quality recordings create smaller digital files, and smaller files are more quickly and easily transmitted from the main PC to your Media Center Extender. This won't help the performance of live TV (which is always streamed at its original high quality level), but it might help out with the television programs you record.

Using the Network Performance Tuner

For the more technically inclined, your Media Center PC includes a Network Performance Tuner utility. You open the utility on your main Media Center PC by closing or minimizing the Media Center interface (to return to the main Windows XP screen), and then selecting (on your main Media Center PC) **Start > All Programs > Accessories > Media Center > Media Center Extender Network Performance Tuner**.

The Network Performance Tuner, shown in Figure 14.8, measures the overall bandwidth between your PC and the Media Center Extender, and displays the performance on a graph. You can then make changes to your network configuration, and see the impact in real-time.

note When you install the Media Center Extender software on your PC, you also get another Extender management utility, called Media Center Extender Manager. It's located on the same Windows menu as the Network Performance Tuner, and lets you add, remove, update, and configure all the Extenders connected to your system.

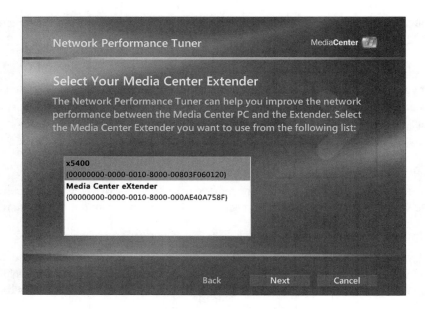

FIGURE 14.8

Fine-tuning Extender performance with the Network Performance Tuner.

If you continue to have connection issues, you might have no other choice but to switch to an ethernet connection. Sorry.

15

Exploring the Online Spotlight

The title of this section of the book is "Extending Your Media Center PC." That can be done literally, by using a Media Center Extender device (as we discussed in the preceding chapter), or it can be done by using Media Center–compatible programs and services. In this chapter we'll talk about the latter way to extend your Media Center experience, focusing specifically on those Media Center services offered in the Online Spotlight.

This chapter offers a preview of all the services and products offered in Media Center's Online Spotlight. I won't get into detailed operational instructions; instead, the focus is on showing you what's available so that you can make an informed choice about which of these Online Spotlight items you want to install and use on your Media Center PC.

Understanding Online Spotlight

What, exactly, is Online Spotlight? When you click the Online Spotlight option on the Start screen menu, you see a list of various services (and a few products) that help you do more with your Media Center PC. Microsoft calls these third-party services *experiences*, and they all are designed to work within the Media Center 10-foot interface.

As you can see in Figure 15.1, the Online Spotlight services are organized into six categories, with a little overlap.

FIGURE 15.1

The main Online Spotlight screen.

- **Showcase** contains those services that are currently featured by Microsoft. Figure that the companies behind these services are paying for the privilege of being listed on this home screen.

- **TV & Movies** contains services that extend your Media Center TV- and movie-viewing experience. This includes downloadable feature films, enhanced program guides, and the like.

- **Music & Radio** contains music-related services, including Internet radio stations, satellite radio feeds, downloadable music, downloadable music videos, and the like.

- **News & Sports** contains a variety of news-related services, including live news feeds, news and sports headlines, RSS (blog) newsreaders, and the like.

- **Games** contains, not surprisingly, a variety of online games.

- **Lifestyle** contains those services that just don't fit anywhere else, including DVD burner programs, picture-sharing services, and so on.

I recommend you skip over the Showcase items and go directly to the category in which you're interested. Most of these services are free, although some require you to register before you can use them. Other services (and most of the downloadable products) are not free, although most offer some sort of free trial you can use to determine whether you like them before you buy them.

> **note** Microsoft is continually adding new services to Online Spotlight, so what you see on your Online Spotlight screen might be different from what I discuss here. In addition, Online Spotlight services differ from country to country; for example, U.K. Media Center users have a BBC News Player option as part of their Online Spotlight.

One more thing. Not every product and service offered via Online Spotlight is entirely Media Center savvy—especially when it comes to downloading, installing, and sometimes even registering. Don't be surprised to see a screen like the one in Figure 15.2, which advises you to either access the Web via Media Center (which requires the use of your wireless mouse) or to save the link as a shortcut on your Windows desktop so that you can access it outside of Media Center using your Windows web browser. I prefer to get out my wireless mouse and do everything all at once; you might prefer to postpone the exit to Windows until a later time. It's your choice.

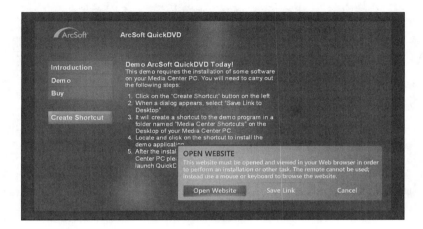

FIGURE 15.2
Some Online Spotlight installations require the use of a traditional web browser.

TV & Movies in the Spotlight

Online Spotlight's TV & Movies category offers a variety of services that have something to do with watching TV and movies. Several of these are movie download services that let you download first- and second-run movies directly to your PC, via the Internet; they're kind of like having a digital Netflix or Blockbuster on your PC. Other services offer on-demand television shows, "enhanced" television shows, and an electronic program guide designed specifically for HDTV channels. Read on to learn more.

Movielink

Movielink is an online movie rental service. Instead of having DVDs mailed to you, a la Netflix, Movielink lets you download the movies you choose over the Internet. (Obviously, you need a fast Internet connection—and sufficient hard disk space—to take full advantage of this service.)

As you can see in Figure 15.3, Movielink offers a mix of first-run and older movies. You can view trailers for the movies online, before you order. Most movies rent for $4.99 apiece. You have up to 30 days to view the movies you download; after it's started, you can watch a movie as many times as you like within a 24-hour period.

FIGURE 15.3

Download movies for rent with Movielink.

CinemaNow

CinemaNow is a Movielink-like service that also offers rental movies for download. As you can see in Figure 15.4, the selection between the two services is similar.

FIGURE 15.4

More movies to download from CinemaNow.

Most films are available on a rental basis (with 24-hour viewing privileges), although some older movies are offered as download-to-own purchases. CinemaNow also offers a subscription service, with unlimited viewing of selected movies.

Akimbo

Akimbo is similar to Movielink and CinemaNow, except with a much larger variety of programs to download. With Akimbo, the focus isn't so much on movies (although some movies are offered); instead, you get television shows, documentaries, kids programs, and the like from a variety of sources—A&E, Discovery Networks, The Travel Channel, Animal Planet, BBC, National Geographic, The History Channel, and so on.

Akimbo organizes its programming into several different categories, such as Foreign Language, Kids, Lifestyle, Music, Sports, and so on. Pick a category (as shown in Figure 15.5), pick a show, and download it to your Media Center PC for viewing.

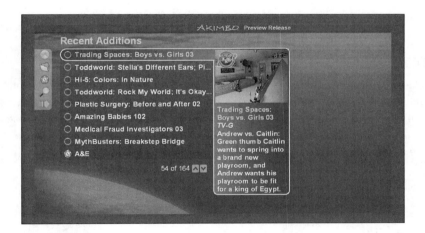

FIGURE 15.5

Some of the vast variety of programming available from the Akimbo service.

What's unique about Akimbo is that you don't pay a per-download rental fee for most programs. Instead, you subscribe to the Akimbo service for $9.99 per month, which gives you access to the bulk of its video library. Additional premium programs are available on a rental or download-to-own basis, with appropriate fees.

TVTonic

I really like TVTonic. It's a free service (free is good) that offers automatic downloads of short news clips, cartoons, music videos, and the like for viewing on your Media Center PC. The clips are downloaded automatically each day, in the background, so they're available whenever you access the TVTonic service. As you can see in Figure 15.6, the clips play in a large window on the TVTonic screen; click a category to see all available clips.

FIGURE 15.6

TVTonic offers automatic downloads of news clips, music videos, cartoons, and such.

Discovery Media Center

Where, you might ask, is the Discovery Media Center option in Online Spotlight? It's hidden behind the American Chopper icon, that's where. Click American Chopper and you get the Discovery Media Center screen, shown in Figure 15.7. From here you can watch or download various Discovery Network programs (including *American Chopper*); the selection is constantly changing.

FIGURE 15.7

View Discovery Network programs in the Discovery Media Center.

ABC Family

The ABC Family service, shown in Figure 15.8, offers streaming videocasts of popular programs shown on the ABC Family cable network. Shows include *Smallville*, *Gilmore Girls*, *Whose Line Is It Anyway?*, and so on.

FIGURE 15.8

View streaming videocasts from the ABC Family service.

ABC Enhanced TV

This one is a little unusual, and not really that impressive (at least to me). From time to time, the ABC network offers "enhanced" versions of some of their popular programs. According to ABC, enhanced television (or *ETV*) is "a LIVE Interactive Television experience on the Internet that allows you, the TV viewer, to interact with the broadcast of some of your favorite shows."

The interactivity varies from program to program, of course. It might include onscreen games, trivia questions, polls, or additional information about the program in process. There's not a lot of this enhanced programming available, however; the mainstay appears to be *Extreme Makeover: Home Edition* (see Figure 15.9) and the occasional *Monday Night Football* or PGA golf game thrown in on the side. Fortunately, this service, as it is, is free.

TitanTV

If you have an HDTV tuner in your Media Center PC, TitanTV is a must-have Online Spotlight service. As you can see in Figure 15.10, TitanTV offers an electronic program guide for all the digital TV channels in your area; you can also use this guide to schedule recordings on your Media Center PC.

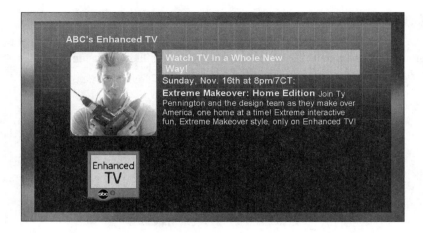

ABC's Enhanced TV—*Extreme Makeover* edition.

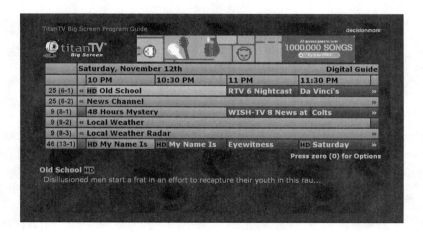

TitanTV—an electronic program guide for HDTV and digital television.

What makes the TitanTV guide so attractive is that it's more comprehensive and more accurate than the normal Media Center Program Guide when it comes to HDTV channels. The Media Center Program Guide typically lists information for only the first digital channel for a given TV station; most stations have two or three different digital channels (broadcasting a variety of programming), and TitanTV has info on them all.

Best of all, the TitanTV service is free (although you do have to subscribe), so it costs you nothing to see what all the fuss is about.

Comedy Central MotherLoad

The funny folks at Comedy Central bring you the MotherLoad, a combination of original Internet programming and excerpts from Comedy Central's television programming. As you can see in Figure 15.11, available programming includes clips from *South Park*, *The Daily Show*, *The Colbert Report*, *Drawn Together*, *Chappelle's Show*, *Reno 911!*, and more.

FIGURE 15.11

Online Spotlight brings the funny with Comedy Central MotherLoad.

InterActual

This is a service that's not really a service. InterActual is an enhanced DVD player that works only with special InterActual-compatible DVDs. These DVDs offer additional interactive features that can be accessed only with the InterActual player. The InterActual item in Online Spotlight is really just a big advertisement for InterActual DVDs—there's nothing to view or download; the InterActual player is included on each InterActual DVD. So you probably can skip this one in the Online Spotlight; there's no *there* there.

Music & Radio in the Spotlight

If you use your Media Center PC to listen to digital music, you'll want to spend some time checking out the Music & Radio offerings in Online Spotlight. There's some good stuff here—although none of it's free.

XM Satellite Radio Online

I'm a big XM radio fan. I have XM radio in my new car, and I listen to it constantly. With its 150+ channels, it offers a little bit of everything; where else can you find channels devoted purely to '60s/'70s soul music, or folk music, or techno music, or comedy routines? That's XM for you, and now you can listen to it on your Media Center PC.

Click the XM Satellite Radio option in Online Spotlight and you're offered a free three-day trial to the XM Online service. If you like what you hear, you can subscribe for $7.99 per month. Better yet, if you're already an XM subscriber, you can listen to XM Online for free.

note XM Online is a subset of the full XM satellite radio service. It offers more than 75 XM music channels (including a half-dozen channels exclusive to the Internet), but none of XM's news or talk channels.

As you can see in Figure 15.12, the Media Center XM Online player lets you scroll through all the available channels. Click a channel to listen, and you'll see information on the currently playing song and artist. It's a great way to add even more music variety to your Media Center system.

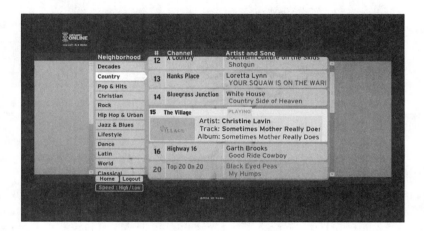

FIGURE 15.12

Listening to XM Online via Media Center.

Live365

Live365 is an Internet radio service designed specifically for the Media Center interface. As you can see in Figure 15.13, Live365 lets you listen to thousands of Internet radio stations, all characterized by genre. Click a genre, find a station you like, and then click it to listen.

If you really like a station, you can add it to Media Center's Radio menu by clicking the Add to My Radio button. After you do this, tuning into your favorite stations is as easy as going to the Media Center Start screen, selecting **Radio**, and then clicking on the station you want to listen to. (Figure 15.14 shows the Media Center Radio screen with several Live365 stations listed.)

FIGURE 15.13

Scrolling through the Internet radio stations offered by Live365.

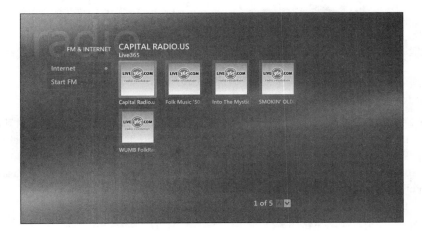

FIGURE 15.14

Media Center's Radio screen with several Live365 radio stations displayed.

Most Live365 stations can be listened to free of charge. Some premium stations, how-ever, require VIP membership, which costs $5.95 per month. (Less if you sign up for a longer-term subscription.) VIP membership also lets you listen without the Live365 com-mercial interruptions, and offers better sound quality than the free service; if you listen to a lot of Internet radio, the VIP membership might be worthwhile.

MSN Music

Another source of Internet radio stations is the MSN Music service. As you can see in Figure 15.15, MSN Music offers a selection of Internet radio stations and digital music for download. As with Live365, most stations can be listened to free of charge, whereas others require Plus membership ($4.99/month or $29.99/year). Most song downloads cost 99 cents.

FIGURE 15.15

Internet radio and digital music downloads at MSN Music.

Napster for Media Center

When you need more songs in your Media Center music collection, check out Napster. As you can see in Figure 15.16, the Media Center version of Napster offers more than one million songs for download at 99 cents per track, or $9.95 per album. In addition, the Napster service offers unlimited access to those same one million tracks for just $9.95 per month, if you don't mind renting your music by the month.

Musicmatch for Media Center

As you can see in Figure 15.17, Musicmatch offers a monthly music service that's similar to what Napster offers, with more than 800,000 songs in their library. You can also purchase songs for 99-cents a download, or $9.95 per album. In addition, you get access to Musicmatch Radio, another Internet radio service with both fee and paid components.

FIGURE 15.16

One million songs for $9.95 per month, via Napster for Media Center.

FIGURE 15.17

Digital music downloads and Internet radio from Musicmatch for Media Center.

AOL Radio/Music on Demand/Pictures

AOL offers a variety of Online Spotlight services. AOL Radio has more than 150 Internet radio stations, plus select XM satellite radio channels; AOL Music on Demand, shown in Figure 15.18, offers streaming music videos, concerts, music news, and interviews; and AOL Pictures offers online photo storage and sharing. You don't have to be an AOL subscriber to partake of any of these services, although you do need to sign up for each service separately—and they're all free.

FIGURE 15.18

Music videos and concerts on your Media Center PC, thanks to AOL Music on Demand—just one of three separate AOL services in the Online Spotlight.

MTV Overdrive

MTV Overdrive is a "broadband video channel" that offers music videos, live performances, music news, artist news, movie trailers, and footage from various MTV programs. As you can see in Figure 15.19, you get a lot of variety with this one, and it's all free.

FIGURE 15.19

More music videos and live performances from MTV Overdrive.

mtvU

Even better than MTV Overdrive, in my opinion, is mtvU, an online music channel targeted at college students. As you can see in Figure 15.20, mtvU offers a live feed from the same mtvU channel you find on today's college campuses, but adds a variety of archived pro-gramming and a huge database of on-demand music videos. It's the database of music videos that I find most valuable; the videos span the alphabet (and the decades) from A Flock of Seagulls to ZZ Top, covering all the top acts from the 1980s, the 1990s, and today.

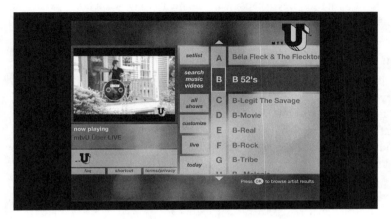

FIGURE 15.20

Live programming and music videos for college students, courtesy of mtvU.

VH1 VSPOT

If you're past college age but still like your music videos, check out VH1 VSPOT. As you can see in Figure 15.21, VH1 VSPOT has the same database of music videos offered by mtvU, this time surrounded by programming excerpts from the VH1 cable channel.

FIGURE 15.21

Music videos and programming excerpts form VH1 VSPOT.

News & Sports in the Spotlight

Media Center isn't just about entertainment; there's a bit of useful information presented, as well. Case in point: the various news and sports services offered via Online Spotlight. (And don't forget the news clips available on TVTonic, which happens to be categorized on the TV & Movies screen.)

MSNTV Today

This is a very rich, very impressive service. As you can see in Figure 15.22, MSNTV Today offers a variety of news and informational video clips, all for free. My only beef is that there's so much here and it's so poorly organized, it's sometimes difficult to find exactly what you want—or even realize all that MSNTV Today has to offer. I suggest you spend some time clicking around the MSNTV screens; you'll be pleasantly surprised by what's available.

FIGURE 15.22

A variety of news and weather videos, courtesy of MSNTV Today.

Reuters

Famed news service Reuters offers an appealing interactive TV news channel via Media Center's Online Spotlight. As you can see in Figure 15.23, the Reuters channel offers video streams of more than 200 news clips a day, organized into key categories: Top News, Business, World, Entertainment, Life!, and Oddly Enough. Each clip is one to five minutes long; the mix includes both fully produced reports and raw video segments.

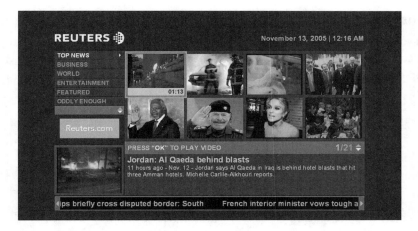

FIGURE 15.23

View hundreds of news clips from Reuters on your Media Center PC.

NewsGator Online

I'm a news junkie, and I especially like the information you can get via the Internet's thousands of bloggers. To that end, I'm a big fan of NewsGator Online, which functions as an online content aggregator and newsreader. Just tell NewsGator which blogs and news feeds you want to monitor, and it displays the latest posts and stories onscreen, as shown in Figure 15.24. Click a headline to read the entire post.

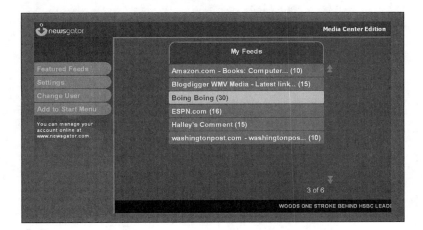

FIGURE 15.24

Monitor your favorite blogs and newsfeeds with NewsGator Online.

Fox Sports for Media Center

If you're a sports fan you'll love the Fox Sports for Media Center service. What you get is a combination of sports news and headlines (shown in Figure 15.25), sports photos, and up-to-the-minute scores (shown in Figure 15.26). All your sporting needs consolidated into one Media Center service—and it's all available free of charge!

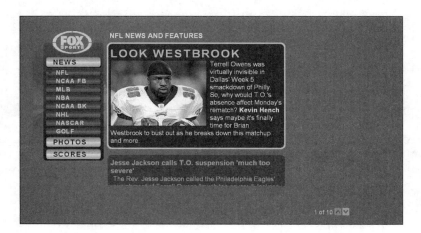

FIGURE 15.25

Sports news via Fox Sports for Media Center.

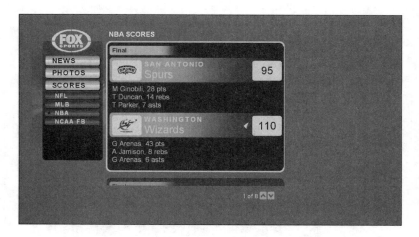

FIGURE 15.26

Detailed scores and game info at Fox Sports.

NPR for Media Center

Online Spotlight's final news services is a classy one. The NPR for Media Center service lets you listen to your favorite National Public Radio programs on your Media Center PC, at your convenience. Just click a show on the Programs menu (shown in Figure 15.27), and sit back to be entertained and informed. All the popular shows are available for online listening, including *Morning Edition, All Things Considered, Day to Day, Talk of the Nation, Fresh Air*, and more.

FIGURE 15.27
Listen to your favorite NPR programs on your Media Center PC.

Games in the Spotlight

It's funny that so little attention has been paid to game playing in the Media Center environment. I would think that a Media Center PC would be a perfect game machine for big-screen living room TVs, but only Alienware seems to have focused on this application of the platform.

That said, a handful of companies are offering downloadable games via Media Center's Online Spotlight. Let's take a look.

Game xStream

Game xStream is an on-demand gaming service, customized for the Media Center interface. As you can see in Figure 15.28, you can purchase games from a variety of leading game developers, including 3D Realms, Eidos Interactive, Encore, Jarhead Games, Merscom, Piranha Games, and Radioactive Clown. Thanks to the use of "intelligent" streaming technology, you can start playing games within minutes of pressing the Buy button; you don't have to wait for the entire game to download.

FIGURE 15.28

Download the latest games from Game xStream.

DISCover My Games

DISCover My Games is another game-streaming download service. As you can see in Figure 15.29, hundreds of games are available for trial or on-demand downloading and purchase.

note The DISCover instant play technology used in My Games is the same technology offered on Alienware Media Center PCs.

FIGURE 15.29

More on-demand game downloads from DISCover My Games.

Lifestyle Options in the Spotlight

The final batch of Online Spotlight offerings falls under the general heading of *lifestyle*. This is kind of a catch-all category, although there is a subtle focus on visual media—in the form of digital photo viewing and DVD movie burning.

Kodak Share

Kodak Share is a service that lets you access digital photos stored on the Kodak EasyShare Gallery (www.kodakgallery.com/) website via your Media Center PC. Upload your photos to the EasyShare Gallery, and then view them in the comfort of your living room on your big-screen TV. As you can see in Figure 15.30, it works similarly to Media Center's My Pictures function; there's no charge to use the application, but you will pay for various Kodak services.

FIGURE 15.30

Viewing photos on the big-screen with Kodak Share.

GalleryPlayer

If your own photos aren't good enough to display, you can always purchase some professional art files to display on your Media Center system. This is where GalleryPlayer comes in; it's a high-definition image display program that accompanies an art download service. As you can see in Figure 15.31, the GalleryPlayer service offers a variety of different types of art for download. You purchase art by the collection, and then display it as high-class wallpaper or screensavers on your system.

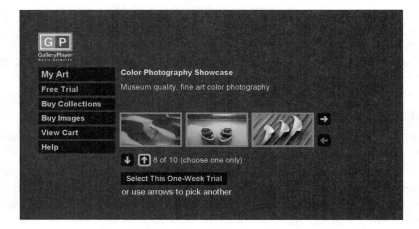

FIGURE 15.31

Download fine art to display with the GalleryPlayer.

10 Foot World

What is 10 Foot World? As you can see in Figure 15.32, it's a series of websites and services designed for use with Media Center's 10-foot interface. A number of services are available, including Horoscope, Current Movie Reviews, Daily Currency Watch, My Recipe, and My 10' Bar (shown in Figure 15.33). As you can see, each of these services looks especially nice on the big Media Center screen; they're all free, and they're all accessible via Online Spotlight.

FIGURE 15.32

10 Foot World offers a variety of onscreen web portals.

FIGURE 15.33

Want to mix the perfect martini? Then follow the instructions offered by My 10' Bar.

KMS Software

This section of Online Spotlight is nothing more than a blatant advertisement for Media Center software offered by KMS Software. It's not bad stuff; as you can see in Figure 15.34, they currently have a Contacts program and a Word Trivia game, each priced at $19.99. Future programs include a Calendar, Home Organizer, and To Do list, all optimized for the Media Center environment.

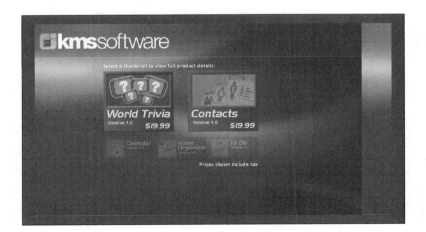

FIGURE 15.34

Media Center applications for sale by KMS Software.

ArcSoft QuickDVD

This is the DVD burning program first discussed in Chapter 11, "Using Windows XP MCE for DVD Playback and Recording." Read more about the program there; click on the icon in Online Spotlight to purchase or download a free trial version.

Sonic PrimeTime

This is the other DVD-burning program we discussed in Chapter 11. As with QuickDVD, you can read more about the program in Chapter 11; click on the icon in Online Spotlight to purchase or download a free trial version.

16

Finding and Using Other Media Center Applications

In the previous chapter we examined various ways to extend your Media Center experience using the various services offered as part of Media Center's Online Spotlight. These aren't the only ways to extend Media Center's functionality, however. Dozens of software developers have developed a number of add-on programs that let you perform all manner of interesting tasks, right from the Media Center interface.

Some of these programs come from small software developers. Some come from large developers. Some come from Microsoft. Some come from individuals working in their spare time.

Some of these Media Center add-ons are free. Some have a free trial period, but then require payment. Some require payment upfront. Most can be downloaded from the Web, so you don't have to get in your car and go shopping for them. Almost all have a similar look and feel to what you're used to with Media Center.

To be completely honest, some of these programs are more useful than others. Some integrate better with Media Center than others. Some just plain work better than others. But they're all interesting, and all worth taking a look at.

And, while I'm being honest, you should know that although most of these programs look and feel like they're part of Media Center, in reality they're not. That's because Microsoft has only recently released a Media Center software developer's kit. Most of the earlier add-on programs were developed using a variety of programming languages (including HTML) to appear as though they're part of Media Center. But if you minimize Media Center, you'll see that the application is still running—within Windows but outside of (and, for all intents and purposes, on top of) Media Center. Not that there's anything wrong with doing it that way; if a Windows application looks and feels and smells like it's working within Media Center, that just means the developer did a good job.

One last thing: Although most of these programs are fully tested and work seamlessly on all machines, some are still in the informal testing stages. Which means that they might or might not function properly on your particular Media Center PC. You pays your money, you takes your chances.

And now, without further ado, let's take a cursory look at the various Media Center add-ons that are available today—so you can have a better idea which programs you might want to install on your Media Center system.

News Programs

Chances are you're accustomed to getting the latest news and sports headlines from the Web, using your desktop PC. Well, because your Media Center PC is also connected to the Web, why can't you use it to access news and sports information?

The answer, of course, is that you can—with the right add-on programs installed. Read on to learn more.

My Portal

My Portal turns your Media Center PC into a full-fledged information portal. My Portal displays news headlines (shown in Figure 16.1), local weather (shown in Figure 16.2), movie times, horoscopes, and more. Information is updated every five minutes when you have an always-on Internet connection. My Portal costs $19.95; download it from mceLabs (www.mcelabs.com/).

MyUK Portal

This add-on is similar to My Portal, but customized for U.K. Media Center users. It features a U.K.-specific electronic program guide, traffic news, Google maps, local cinema listings, and more. Download it for free from MyUK (myuk.aceinternet.co.uk/mce/).

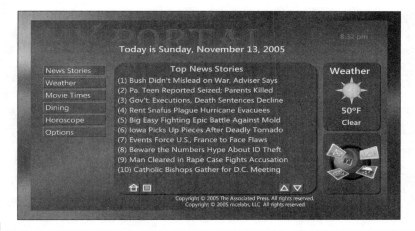

FIGURE 16.1

Turn your Media Center PC into a news and information portal, courtesy of the My Portal add-on.

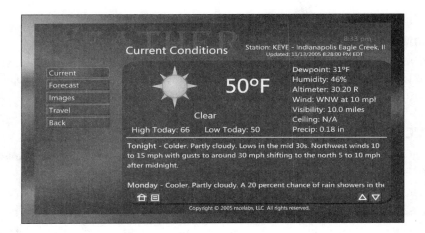

FIGURE 16.2

Get local weather conditions and reports with My Portal.

My Web News

My Web News, shown in Figure 16.3, is a neat little application that downloads and organizes the latest headlines from the RSS feeds offered by most major news websites. You can use the default newsfeeds, or enter your own list of sites to watch. Download it for free from SAM-Consult (www.mce-software.com/).

FIGURE 16.3

Download the latest news headlines with My Web News.

mNewsCenter

If you're into blogs, check out this RSS feed/blog newsreader. Enter the blogs you want to watch, and then read the latest posts on the Media Center screen. Download it for $19.99 from www.embeddedautomation.com/EAHAmNewsCenter.htm.

MCE RSS Reader

This is another Media Center blog/RSS feed newsreader. Download it for free from OABsoftware (www.oabsoftware.nl/).

ReadNews

ReadNews is yet another RSS newsreader, but with a difference. This one lets you browse through the headlines in a pop-up window while you watch TV or DVDs. Download it for free from developer Martin Milmore (www.millmoreweb.com/readnews/).

My NFL Scores for MCE

Get the latest football scores on your Media Center screen, updated instantly over the Web. Download it for free from Double B Computers (www.doublebcomputers.com/mce.htm).

Weather Programs

News isn't the only type of information you can display on your Media Center PC. When you want to see what kind of coat you need to wear today, turn to one of these colorful and informative Media Center weather add-ons.

mceWeather

This is one of my favorite add-on programs. As you can see in Figure 16.4, mceWeather displays a variety of weather information over multiple pages, including current conditions, a five-day forecast, radar maps, and more. Download it for free from Christoph Buenger Software (www.cbuenger.com/).

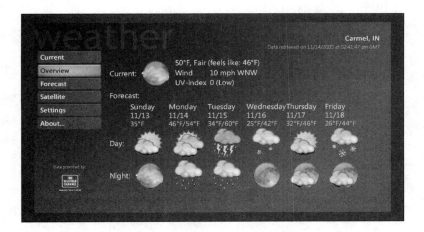

FIGURE 16.4

View comprehensive weather information and forecasts with mceWeather.

Simply Weather

Another live weather add-on, Simply Weather is designed to display the most relevant information on a single screen—current conditions, five-day forecast, and an animated radar map. Simply Weather is freeware; download it from zapgun (www.zapgun.com/).

My Weather

Yet another live weather add-on. My Weather displays both current conditions and forecast screens. Download it for free from unmitigatedrisk.com (www.unmitigatedrisk.com/).

Entertainment Programs

As you already know, a Media Center PC is a perfect music and movie playback device. Now you can add even more functionality to Media Center with these third-party entertainment add-ons.

My Movies

This utility organizes and displays all the DVDs in your collection—stored both on your computer and elsewhere in your house. Just enter the titles of the movies you own, and My Movies downloads and displays cover art, actors, director, running time, and other information, as shown in Figure 16.5. Download it for free from developer Brian Binnerup (www.mymovies.name/).

FIGURE 16.5

Catalog your entire DVD collection with the My Movies add-on.

My Netflix

If you're a Netflix customer, this is a cool way to manage your Netflix account. My Netflix displays all the waiting movies in your Netflix queue, your rental history, and new Netflix releases. Download it for free from unmitigatedrisk.com (www.unmitigatedrisk.com/).

In the Movies for MCE

No, this add-on doesn't play movies on your Media Center PC. Instead, it downloads and displays information about movies currently playing at your local movie theaters—reviews, show times, and so on, as you can see in Figure 16.6. Download it for $15 from Double B Computers (www.doublebcomputers.com/mce.htm).

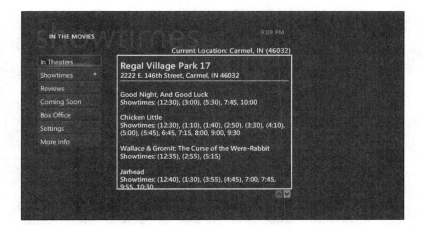

FIGURE 16.6

Find out when your favorite movies are playing with In the Movies for MCE.

My Trailers for MCE

This is a companion program to the In the Movies add-on; it lets you download and view current movie trailers on your Media Center PC. Download it for $15 from Double B Computers (www.doublebcomputers.com/mce.htm).

Playlist Editor

Microsoft's Playlist Editor Power Toy is an essential add-on for creating and editing your digital music playlists. I discussed this add-on in more depth in Chapter 9, "Using Windows XP MCE for Audio Storage and Playback"; as you can see in Figure 16.7, it lets you use the Media Center interface to manage all your playlists. Download it for free from Microsoft (www.microsoft.com/downloads/).

MyWebTV

MyWebTV lets you view hundreds of Internet TV channels and video on demand sites on your Media Center PC. Download it for free from Nicefactory (www.nicefactory.ch/).

Web Media

As you can see in Figure 16.8, Web Media is a plug-in that helps you access and manage Internet radio and TV stations from within Media Center. Download it for free from mcesoft (www.mcesoft.nl/).

FIGURE 16.7

An easier way to create and edit playlists, courtesy of Microsoft's Playlist Editor add-on.

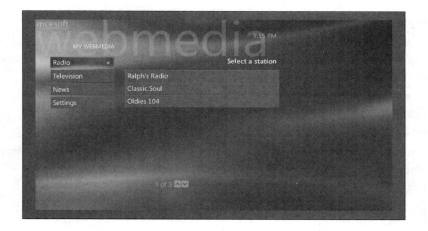

FIGURE 16.8

Manage all your streaming audio and video with the Web Media add-on.

MyTV ToGo

We first discussed MyTV ToGo in Chapter 10, "Using Windows XP MCE for Television Viewing and Recording." It's a useful add-on that lets you copy programs you've recorded on your Media Center PC to any Pocket PC or flash memory card. Download it for $19.95 from CNET Download.com (www.download.com/).

WebGuide3

This utility lets you schedule TV recordings from any computer with an Internet connection. Just install the application on your Media Center PC, and then do your scheduling from any PC with a web browser—or from any web-enabled cellular phone. Download it for free from developer Doug Barrett (www.asciiexpress.com/webguide/).

note WebGuide3 is very similar to Microsoft's MSN Remote Record Service, which was discussed in Chapter 11, "Using Windows XP MCE for DVD Playback and Recording."

Recorded TV

This is a quick and easy little utility that adds a menu item on the Media Center Start page for Recorded TV. Download it for free from The Green Button (www.thegreenbutton.com/).

Share Recorded TV

Use this utility to more easily share recorded TV programs between two or more networked Media Center PCs. Download it for free from The Green Button (www.thegreenbutton.com/).

Power Compress

When disk space is at a premium, check out this utility. Power Compress works within Media Center to compress recorded TV shows; at the highest compression level, you can fit 10 times the normal amount of programming onto your hard drive. Buy it for $29.95 from Market Engines (www.powercompress.com/).

Karatron

Karatron is a MIDI karaoke player that works within the Media Center interface. It boasts automatic melody track detection, animated backgrounds, and more. Download it for $29 from Chronotron (www.chronotron.com/).

Microsoft Media Center Karaoke Plug-In

This is Microsoft's attempt at providing karaoke via Media Center. (Is karaoke really this big a deal?) Download it for free from CNET Download.com (www.download.com/).

DVD-Burning Programs

We discussed several of these programs back in Chapter 11. Simply put, these are programs that go beyond the simple (and mostly unsatisfying) DVD-burning features of Media Center's built-in Create CD/DVD function and let you burn recorded TV programs to regular movie DVDs.

ArcSoft QuickDVD

As you can see in Figure 16.9, QuickDVD is a fairly robust DVD burning program, complete with your choice of menu designs, backgrounds, and animations. Buy it for $89.95 from ArcSoft (www.arcsoft.com/products/quickdvd/).

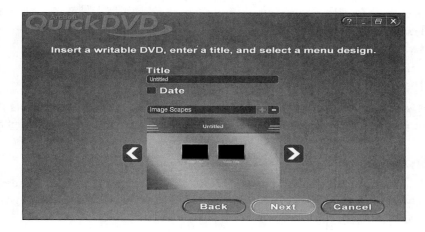

FIGURE 16.9

Burn your own DVDs from within Media Center with QuickDVD.

muvee autoProduce unPlugged

This Media Center DVD burner features automatic scene slicing and chapter assignment, along with your choice of menu and background styles. Download it for $69.96 from muvee (www.muvee.com/).

Sonic PrimeTime

PrimeTime is one of the easiest-to-use Media Center DVD burner programs available, as you can see in Figure 16.10. Buy it for $59.99 from Sonic (www.sonic.com/products/consumer/primetime/).

Sonic PrimeTime Deluxe

A more versatile version of the basic PrimeTime program, with your choice of menu designs and backgrounds. Buy it for $79.99 from Sonic (www.sonic.com/products/consumer/primetime/).

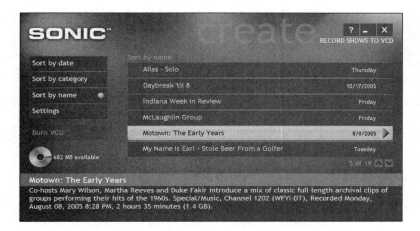

FIGURE 16.10
Copy your recorded TV programs to DVD with Sonic PrimeTime.

Lifestyle Programs

Clever developers can find a way to use Media Center for just about any function imaginable. Read on to discover some of the lifestyle programs designed especially for Windows Media Center.

mceAuction

If you're a heavy eBay buyer or seller, you'll love this add-on. As you can see in Figure 16.11, mceAuction lets you search for items, browse through item categories, bid on and buy items, and monitor all your auction activity from My eBay. Download it for free from Christoph Buenger Software (www.cbuenger.com/).

My Mapquest for MCE

This is a cool little add-on. As you can probably tell from the name, My Mapquest adds MapQuest driving directions to the Media Center interface. Just enter your start and end points, as shown in Figure 16.12, and My Mapquest accesses the MapQuest website and displays the directions (and accompanying maps) onscreen. Download it for free from Double B Computers (www.doublebcomputers.com/mce.htm).

Alarm Clock

Microsoft's Alarm Clock Power Toy turns your Media Center PC into a very large, very expensive clock radio. Download it for free from Microsoft (www.microsoft.com/downloads/); it's in the "What Others Are Downloading" section of the page.

FIGURE 16.11

Manage your eBay auction activity with mceAuction.

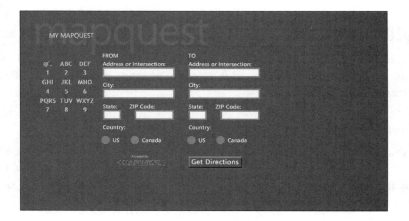

FIGURE 16.12

Get onscreen driving directions from My Mapquest.

My Recipes

Look up your favorite recipes with the My Recipe add-on. Download it for free from unmitigatedrisk.com (www.unmitigatedrisk.com/).

Lottery Results for MCE

If you're into playing the numbers, check out this little add-on, shown in Figure 16.13. You get up-to-the-minute results, updated via the Web. Download it for free from Double B Computers (www.doublebcomputers.com/mce.htm).

FIGURE 16.13
Are you feeling lucky? Find out with the Lottery Results for MCE add-on.

Home Automation Programs

Just as you use your Media Center PC to control your home theater system, you can also use it to control your home automation system. We're talking about dimming the lights, turning on the alarm system, activating the sprinklers, even closing the motorized drapes. (Assuming that you have motorized drapes, of course.) If you already have a home automation system installed, check out these plug-ins that let you control your system via the Media Center interface.

HAI Home Control for Windows Media Center

If you have an HAI Omni home automation system, you can control it with this Media Center add-on. See your HAI dealer for pricing.

HomeSeer MCE Plug-In

This add-on lets you control your HomeSeer home automation system from any Media Center PC. Download it for $59.95 from HomeSeer Technologies (www.homeseer.com/products/software/pi-mce.htm).

mControl

This full-featured utility lets you control all your home automation (lighting, heating/cooling systems, sprinkler systems, and so on) from the comfort of the Media Center screen. Download it for $149.99 from www.embeddedautomation.com/EAHAmControl.htm.

Caller ID Programs

That's right, you can use your expensive Media Center PC to display Caller ID information onscreen. It's a bit of technological overkill, of course, but there's no denying that it's handy if the phone rings while you're watching *Monday Night Football*.

mceTapiRex

This utility displays information about all incoming phone calls on the Media Center screen. It also displays a list of your most recent incoming calls. Download it for free from Christoph Buenger Software (www.cbuenger.com/).

MCE Caller ID

This is another useful program for displaying Caller ID information from incoming calls on your Media Center screen. One nice thing about this program is that your Media Center PC doesn't have to be connected to a phone line; it can access incoming call information from any PC on your home network that's so connected. Download it for free from OABsoftware (www.oabsoftware.nl/).

MCE-YAC

Yet another Caller ID program for your Media Center PC. Download it for free from David Ethan Zoller, the developer (www.byz.org/~ethanz/mce-yac/).

Internet Phone Utilities

Internet phone service is the latest high-tech fad. Any computer connected to the Internet can be used to make and receive phone calls from any other Internet user—or, with the right service, traditional landline and cellular phones. Read on to learn how to turn your Media Center PC into an Internet phone with a really big screen.

mcePhone for Skype

This is a utility that lets you use your Media Center PC for Skype Internet phone service. mcePhone works within the Media Center interface and lets you call any Skype user for free, call any "normal" phone number, accept incoming calls, and so on. Download it for free from Christoph Buenger Software (www.cbuenger.com/).

MCE SIP Phone

This utility lets you make phone calls and video calls from your Media Center PC, over the SIPphone service. Download it for free from OABsoftware (www.oabsoftware.nl/).

note Another popular Media Center phone program is Media Center Communicator, discussed in the "Remote Control Utilities" section, later in this chapter.

Computer Applications

Underneath the Media Center interface, your Media Center PC is a regular Windows computer—which means it can do anything your desktop PC can do. If you want to perform traditional computer operations from within the Media Center interface, however, you need to use these third-party Media Center add-ons. Read on to learn more.

MCE Browser

I wonder why it took so long for some smart developer to come up with a WebTV-like web browser for Media Center? As you can see in Figure 16.14, MCE Browser is just that, a Media Center front end that lets you browse the Web with your Media Center remote control. You can even create your own Favorites list, and zoom in on web pages to see more detail. (You can't enter your own URLs, however, so you have to navigate solely from within your Favorites list; MCE Browser picks up the Favorites you have defined within Internet Explorer.) The program can be downloaded for free from developer Anthony Park (www.anpark.com/)

FIGURE 16.14

Browse the Web from Media Center with MCE Browser.

My File Manager

We first discussed My File Manager in Chapter 13, "Using Windows XP MCE for Computer Tasks." As you can see in Figure 16.15, this add-on lets you manage all your files and folders from within Media Center, without exiting out to Windows. Download it for free from SAM-Consult (www.mce-software.com/).

FIGURE 16.15

Manage all the files on your hard disk with My File Manager.

MCE Outlook

As first presented in Chapter 13, MCE Outlook brings all the functionality of Microsoft Outlook (email, contacts, scheduling, and so forth) to the Media Center environment. Download it for free from SAM-Consult (www.mce-software.com/).

mceContacts

This program displays and manages all your personal and business contacts. You can add new contacts directly from the program, or you can import all your existing contacts from Microsoft Outlook. Download it for free from Christoph Buenger Software (www.cbuenger. com/).

Contacts

Another contact management program for the Media Center interface. Download it for $19.99 from KMS Software (www.mediacenterware.com/).

Hotmail Plus Reader for Media Center

As we first discussed in Chapter 13, this is a Media Center–based email reader for your Hotmail account. As you can see in Figure 16.16, you can read your email on the Media Center screen, even if you can't reply or create new messages. The software was developed by Microsoft; download it for free from CNET Download.com (www.download.com/).

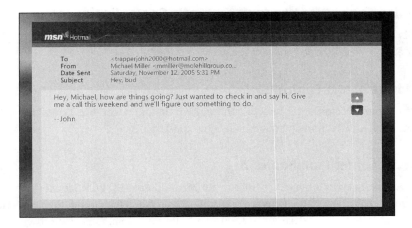

FIGURE 16.16

Read your email onscreen with Hotmail Plus Reader for Media Center.

PhotoConnect

PhotoConnect is an application that extends the functionality of Media Center's My Pictures feature. You can create more sophisticated slideshows (with music), view image EXIF information, send images as email attachments, create custom photo lists, and more. You can purchase PhotoConnect from Mediapoint Technologies (www.webmediapoint. net/) for $29.95; additional monthly charges apply for use of the Web-based PhotoConnect service.

Remote Control Utilities

Did you know that you can use your Media Center remote control as a wireless mouse? Or that your Pocket PC device can be used as a Media Center remote control? You can, really. Read on to learn more.

MyRemoteMouse

Now this is one nifty idea. MyRemoteMouse turns your Media Center remote control into a wireless mouse. You can point and click, drag and drop, and do everything you can with a normal mouse, just by using the buttons on your remote control. Download it for $24.99 from Whittaker Moore Associates (www.whittakermoore.com/MyRemoteMouse.htm).

Niveus Pocket Remote

This nifty little utility turns your Wi-Fi–enabled Pocket PC into a handheld remote control for your Media Center PC. What's really neat is all the useful information displayed on the Pocket PC screen. Download it for $34.95 from Niveus Media (www.niveusmedia.com/).

Rudeo Control for Windows XP Media Center Edition

This is another utility that turns your Pocket PC into a Media Center remote. Download it for $29.95 from Rudeo (www.rudeo.com/).

PadOne Media Controller

Yet another Media Center remote control program for Pocket PCs. Download it for $38 from High-Def Technology (padone.hd-tec.com/).

Media Center Communicator

Add voice recognition and control to your Media Center PC with Media Center Communicator. After the software is installed, you can subscribe to the One Voice VoIP Internet telephone service for $14.95/month. Buy the Communicator software for $149.95 from One Voice (www.onev.com/).

MediaUFO

This is an odd one. MediaUFO lets you control your Media Center PC from your Bluetooth cell phone. Buy it for $29.99 from Flying Saucer PC (www.mediaufo.com/).

Media Center Utilities

Now we come to those Media Center add-ons that really don't fall into any other category. These utilities let you reconfigure Media Center itself; they're a must for any serious tweaker.

Tweak MCE

This is arguable the most important Media Center add-on you can install on your system. As you can see in Figure 16.17, Tweak MCE lets you configure all sorts of hidden Media Center settings; it's so important that I've devoted an entire chapter to discussing Tweak MCE and a similar utility, MCE Customizer. Turn to Chapter 17, "Customizing Windows XP MCE," to learn more. (And, in the meantime, you can download Tweak MCE for free from www.microsoft.com/downloads/.)

MCE Customizer

As you can see in Figure 16.18, MCE Customizer is also extremely useful for fine-tuning your Media Center system—including changing the default Media Center screen background. Read more about it in Chapter 17; you can download it for free from MCEDev.com (www.mcedev.com/).

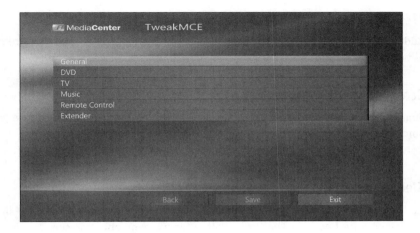

FIGURE 16.17

Use Tweak MCE to configure hidden Media Center settings.

FIGURE 16.18

Another Media Center tweaking program—MCE Customizer.

mceHideSVP

If you get annoyed by the inset window constantly appearing at the lower left of every Media Center screen when you're listening to music or watching TV, use this utility to remove the window (called the *shared viewport*, or SVP) when media playback is stopped. Download it for free from Christoph Buenger Software (www.cbuenger.com/).

MCE Screen Saver

Add a screensaver to your Media Center PC. Download it for free from The Green Button (www.thegreenbutton.com/).

Screensaver Prevention

Sometimes you want your Media Center PC to keep running when its inactive, without going into screensaver mode. Use this utility to prevent the screensaver from starting. Download it for free from The Green Button (www.thegreenbutton.com/).

Sleep Timer

An interesting little utility that closes Media Center after a specified period of inactivity. Download it for free from The Green Button (www.thegreenbutton.com/).

MCE Video Settings

This small utility lets you adjust various video settings on your Media Center PC's TV tuner, including brightness, contrast, saturation, hue, and sharpness. Download it for free from OABsoftware (www.oabsoftware.nl/).

Wizard Reset Utility

Use this utility to reset the Media Center Startup Wizard to its original state. Download it for free from The Green Button (www.thegreenbutton.com/).

Games

Finally, a little fun. They're few and far between for the moment, but Media Center games do exist. Read on to discover a few to check out.

Dragon Maze Media Center Edition

As you can see in Figure 16.19, this is a maze game with a Chinese theme, specially designed to play on the Media Center 10-foot interface. (Sort of; it actually runs in a separate Windows window that sits on top of Media Center, and even then doesn't fill the whole screen.) Download it for free from Sandlot Games (www.sandlotgames.com/).

mcepeaks

A challenging card game for Media Center PCs. Download it for $5 from 10footgames.net (www.10footgames.net/). The company promises that "more exciting games are on the way."

FIGURE 16.19

Play the Dragon Maze game on your living room TV.

Solitaire

If you're hooked on the regular Windows XP version of Solitaire, port your jones to Media Center with this fun little Power Toy. As you can see in Figure 16.20, it looks pretty much like the Solitaire you're used to. Download it for free from Microsoft (www.microsoft.com/downloads/).

FIGURE 16.20

Yippee—now you can play Solitaire in the living room!

Super Slyder Media Center Edition

This is another maze game for Media Center users. Download it for free from Sandlot Games (www.sandlotgames.com/).

Tetris

This is an open source version of the popular falling blocks game, designed for play on any Media Center PC. Download it for free from www.sourceforge.net/projects/dotnetris/.

World Trivia

Trivia games to play on your Media Center PC. Download it for $19.99 from KMS Software (www.mediacentreware.com/).

tip   This chapter has listed only some of the Media Center add-ons that were available as of February 2006. For a more comprehensive, more up-to-date list, see the list of Media Center plug-ins and applications in the Developer's Corner message board at The Green Button website (www.thegreenbutton.com/). Also worth checking out is Microsoft's Media Center Software Plug-Ins page (www.windowmarketplace.com/Results.aspx?collID=96—or just go to the main www.windowsmarketplace.com page and search for "media center").

17

Customizing Windows XP Media Center Edition

If you're a longtime Windows user, you're used to totally personalizing the desktop environment. With Windows XP, you can customize just about any onscreen element—the desktop wallpaper, screen colors, icons, sounds, you name it. With Windows Media Center, however, not so much.

It's not that you can't customize *anything* about Media Center, it's just that Microsoft designed the Media Center interface to give a uniformly satisfying experience for anyone viewing it from 10 feet away. That means standardizing most of the operation and onscreen elements, which takes away your ability to customize those elements.

That said, there are some elements of Media Center that *can* be customized, but not within Media Center proper. Instead, you have to use one of two add-on utilities: Tweak MCE or MCE Customizer. Tweak MCE is an official Microsoft PowerToy, and as such is the customization tool of choice for most users. The other tool, MCE Customizer, is developed by a German firm, and is a little less stable than Tweak MCE. (In fact, MCE Customizer appears to be in a perpetual beta test state.) Both utilities can be downloaded for free, and both let you tweak quite a few settings that aren't normally configurable from within Media Center.

Tweaking Windows Media Center with Tweak MCE

Tweak MCE is the one Media Center add-on that I recommend all users install on their systems—it's that useful. You can download it for free from www.microsoft.com/windowsxp/downloads/powertoys/mcepowertoys.mspx. After it's installed, you launch the program by going to the Media Center Start screen and selecting **More Programs > Tweak MCE**.

As you can see in Figure 17.1, the main Tweak MCE screen organizes its settings into six major categories:

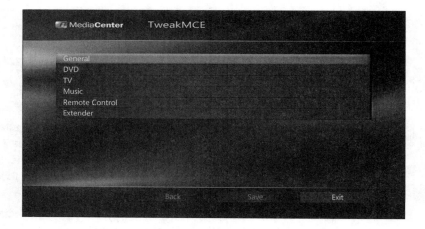

FIGURE 17.1

Tweak MCE's main screen.

- **General**—This category contains just two settings: one for displaying wireless passwords and another for adjusting the overscan on your television display.
- **DVD**—This category lets you turn the Play DVDs function into a My DVDs screen, and also offers a variety of settings for displaying and playing DVDs.
- **TV**—This category lets you adjust various settings related to watching live TV and recording and playing television broadcasts.
- **Music**—This category offers two minor settings related to the display of items on the My Music screen.
- **Remote Control**—This category helps you configure Media Center for use with universal remote controls.
- **Extender**—This category is devoted to the configuration of Media Center Extenders on your system.

We'll look at each of these settings categories in turn.

Tweaking General Settings

The Tweak MCE General screen, shown in Figure 17.2, only has two settings, but one of them is extremely important.

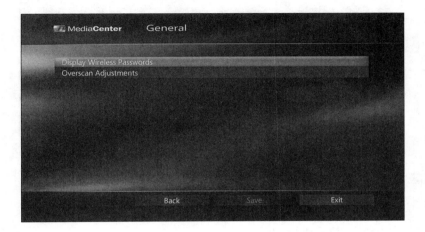

FIGURE 17.2

The settings on the Tweak MCE General screen.

The first setting, however, isn't the important one. The option to **Display Wireless Passwords** is used only when you're setting up your Media Center or Extender over a wireless network, and isn't that important.

The important option, then, is the second one. The **Overscan Adjustments** setting is critical when you're viewing Media Center on a television display that doesn't quite match the resolution settings on your video card. Let's say, for example, that your video card has a resolution of 768 × 1280, but your television has a resolution of 720 × 1280—the standard for 720p displays. What happens to those extra 48 horizontal lines when they're sent to your 720-line TV?

Normally, what you get is called *overscan*—that is, the extra 48 lines overflow the screen and don't get displayed. Although this problem can be rectified with some video cards that offer scalable output, many users have had to deal with not seeing some small part of the Media Center interface.

This is where Tweak MCE's **Overscan Adjustments** setting comes in. As you can see in Figure 17.3, this setting lets you rearrange some of the Media Center screen elements to better fit on a display with noticeable overscan. After you turn on the overscan feature, you can move elements in from either side or from the top and the bottom of the screen. Trust me, this setting is a lifesaver.

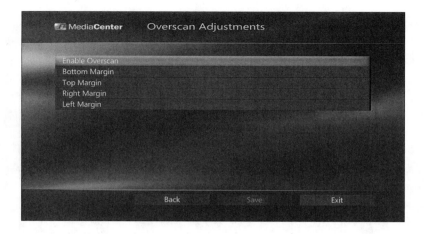

FIGURE 17.3

Adjusting display overscan with Tweak MCE.

Tweaking DVD Settings

Tweak MCE's DVD screen, shown in Figure 17.4, is also important, due to the inclusion of the **Enable My DVDs** option. As first discussed in Chapter 11, "Using Windows XP MCE for DVD Playback and Recording," My DVDs replaces the Play DVD option on the Media Center Start screen, and lets you access ripped DVDs on your hard drive the same way you access digital music in My Music. When you click the **Enable My DVDs** option and then return to the Media Center Start screen, you see the new My DVDs option on the menu. It's a great feature for users who've ripped their DVD library to their Media Center PC's hard drive.

Four of the other options on Tweak MCE's screen affect the way movies are displayed on the My DVDs screen. **Search Depth** determines whether the subfolders under the My DVDs folder are searched for ripped movies; **Search Network Locations** determines whether other computers on your network can be used to feed the My DVDs screen; **Show DVDs in Drives First** tells Media Center to display physical DVDs before ripped ones on the My DVDs screen; and selecting **Show Cache File Location** displays the cache folder when the main DVD file can't be found.

The other three settings have to do with regular DVD playback. **Autostart Enhanced DVD Content** tells Media Center to automatically play the special features associated with some enhanced DVDs; **DVD Notification Timeout** determines how long the Play DVD message is displayed when a new disc is inserted; and **Suppress Eject Prompt** deactivates the onscreen Eject DVD message.

All that said, the important setting on this screen is the **Enable My DVDs** option—but only for those users with DVDs stored on their hard drives.

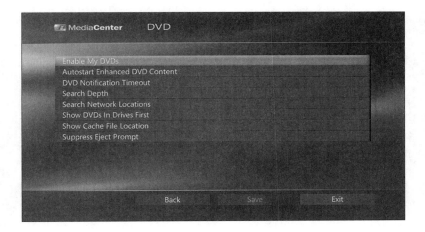

FIGURE 17.4
Adjusting various DVD-related settings—and activating My DVDs—from Tweak MCE's DVD screen.

Tweaking TV Settings

Tweak MCE's TV screen, shown in Figure 17.5, lets you tweak the way various television playback controls work. To me, the most important settings on this screen are **Skip Forward Interval** and **Skip Back Interval**. As you recall from Chapter 10, "Using Windows XP MCE for Television Viewing and Recording," your Media Center remote control has Skip and Replay buttons; by default, the Skip button skips ahead 29 seconds (great for skipping commercials), and the Replay button skips backward 7 seconds (in case you overshoot the start of the regular program). Well, the **Skip Forward Interval** and **Skip Back Interval** settings let you fine-tune these skip/replay intervals. If you'd rather skip ahead 60 seconds or skip back 10 seconds, this is the place to make that adjustment.

The other settings on Tweak MCE's TV screen are less interesting for most users, but do have particular applications. For example, the **Storage Location for Recorded TV** option lets you store your recorded programs in any folder on your hard drive; this is useful if you copy programming for use on a portable video player that can't normally access the default My Recorded TV folder. The **Watched Folders for Recorded TV** lets you add programs stored in other folders to Media Center's recorded TV list.

If you'd like to see an onscreen message before the start of a scheduled recording, select the **Notification Before a Recording Starts** option. You can change how long the More Info panel appears onscreen by using the **More Info Panel Timeout** setting, and if you want to adjust the amount of time the seek bar appears onscreen before fading away, use the **Seek Bar Timeout**, **Seek Bar REW/FWD Timeout**, and **Seek Bar Slow Motion Timeout** settings.

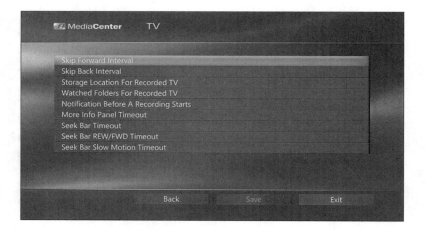

FIGURE 17.5

Adjusting television recording and playback settings on Tweak MCE's TV screen.

Tweaking Music Settings

As you can see in Figure 17.6, Tweak MCE's Music screen doesn't offer a lot of things to tweak. Essentially, you have two options: **Display My Music As Last Viewed** remembers the way you sorted and displayed albums on the My Music screen, and **Show Add to Queue Notification** displays an onscreen confirmation when you add a song to the queue. That's about it for configuring the music settings.

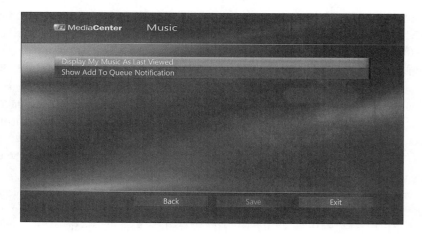

FIGURE 17.6

Tweaking the way My Music works with Tweak MCE's Music screen.

Tweaking Remote Control Settings

Tweak MCE's Remote Control screen, shown in Figure 17.7, is an important one if you're trying to use a universal remote control with your Media Center PC. That's because the standard Media Center remote control and IR receiver aren't particularly compatible with the world of third-party remote control units. If you try to use your universal remote with your Media Center PC and discover that nothing happens, turn to Tweak MCE for the solution.

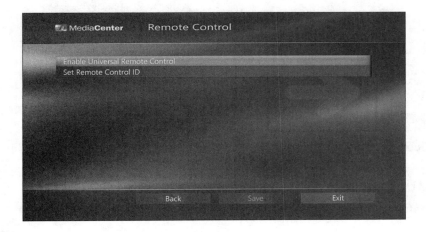

FIGURE 17.7

Configuring Media Center to work with a universal remote via Tweak MCE's Remote Control screen.

The first option on the Remote Control screen is the key one. When you click the **Enable Universal Remote Control** option, Tweak MCE makes the necessary configuration changes that lets Media Center recognize your non–Media Center remote. You can further fine-tune remote control operation by using the **Set Remote Control ID** setting; this might be necessary if your remote still isn't recognized by Media Center.

Tweaking Extender Settings

If you have a Media Center Extender attached to your system, check out Tweak MCE's Extender screen, shown in Figure 17.8. These settings control what you see on the Media Center Extender screen, and how the Extender works on your network.

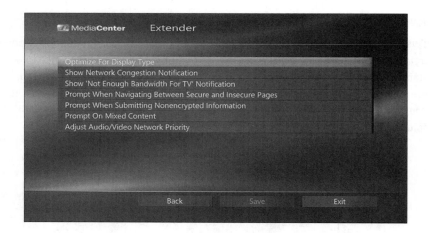

FIGURE 17.8

Configuring various Media Center Extender settings on Tweak MCE's Extender screen.

Table 17.1 details the settings on the Extender screen.

TABLE 17.1 Tweak MCE's Extender Settings

Setting	Description
Optimize for Display Type	Configures the Media Center Extender display for various types of TV screens
Show Network Congestion Notification	Displays a message when the network becomes too busy
Show 'Not Enough Bandwidth for TV' Notification	Displays a message when the network is too busy to display smooth video
Prompt When Navigating Between Secure and Insecure Pages	Asks for permission before displaying web pages that aren't secure
Prompt When Submitting Nonencrypted Information	Asks for permission before submitting information to a nonsecure website
Prompt on Mixed Content	Asks for permission before displaying web pages that mix secure and nonsecure content
Adjust Audio/Video Network Priority	Determines whether Media Center content has priority over other traffic on your network

Customizing Windows Media Center with MCE Customizer

MCE Customizer is a third-party add-in developed by a German programmer. It's distributed free of charge, and can be downloaded from the developer's website (www.mcedev. com/). After it's installed, you launch it by going to the Media Center Start screen and selecting **More Programs > MCE Customizer**.

MCE Customizer organizes its configuration settings into similar categories to those used by Tweak MCE. You access any of the settings in MCE Customizer by first clicking the category in the left menu. The categories include

- **Appearance**—This category hosts settings related to the way Media Center appears onscreen.

- **EPG**—This category contains a single setting related to Media Center's Program Guide.

- **Recording**—This category lets you configure how Media Center records and stores television programs.

- **Repair**—This category lets you reset much of Media Center's key information.

- **Extras**—This category contains a hodgepodge of settings, related primarily to the Media Center remote control, Media Center Extenders, and Media Center's Caller ID function.

- **Settings**—This category, not functioning at the present, promises to let you change the background of the Media Center interface.

- **About**—Click this option to learn more about the MCE Customizer program.

When you explore the program, you'll find that MCE Customizer and Tweak MCE adjust some of the same settings; good minds think alike, apparently. Where MCE Customizer significantly differs from Tweak MCE is that it's an unofficial application, developed by outsiders. This isn't necessarily a bad thing, but sometimes it shows. Whereas Tweak MCE works smoothly within Media Center, MCE Customizer is a little rougher around the edges; it's apparent that Tweak MCE's developers had inside access to Media Center's source code, and MCE Customizer's developers didn't.

That said, MCE Customizer is a useful utility, and one you should explore—particularly if you aren't completely satisfied with the way Media Center looks and acts.

Customizing Appearance Settings

MCE Customizer's Appearance screen, shown in Figure 17.9, lets you configure several aspects of Media Center's appearance. Some of these settings are also available with Tweak MCE; some are exclusive to MCE Customizer.

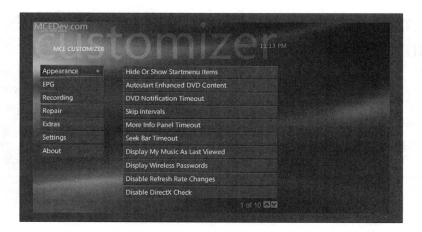

FIGURE 17.9

Configuring various display settings on MCE Customizer's Appearance screen.

The one setting on this page that I find particularly useful is the first one, **Hide or Show Startmenu Options**. Click this option and you see the screen shown in Figure 17.10, which lets you check or uncheck which items you want to display on the Media Center Start screen. This is a great option if have parts of Media Center that you never use, or if you're annoyed by add-in programs that have installed themselves on the Start menu against your wishes.

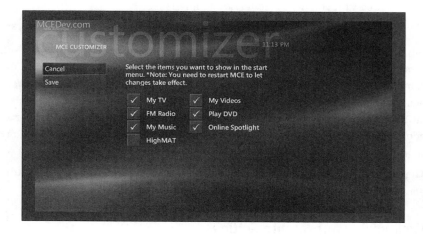

FIGURE 17.10

Selecting which items to display on Media Center's Start menu.

The other options on the Appearance screen are equally useful, if less unique to MCE Customizer. In particular, the following items duplicate similar settings in Tweak MCE:

Autostart Enhanced DVD Content, DVD Notification Timeout, Skip Intervals, More Info Panel Timeout, Seek Bar Timeout, Display My Music As Last Viewed, and **Display Wireless Passwords.**

The final two options are exclusive to MCE Customizer. **Disable Refresh Rate Changes** determines whether the screen is refreshed when you return to the Start screen, whereas **Disable DirectX Check** is a technical adjustment used when viewing some videos or playing some DirectX-enabled PC games.

Customizing EPG Settings

As you can see in Figure 17.11, MCE Customizer's EPG screen has two settings to adjust. When you click **Edit EPG Download Related Information,** you can change the ZIP code used for your program guide listings, as well as change the more technical ClientID setting. The **Reschedule EPG Download** option lets you set a new time to download the electronic program guide data.

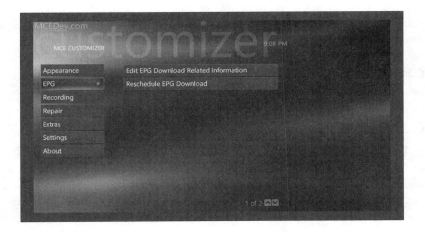

FIGURE 17.11

MCE Customizer's EPG screen.

Customizing Recording Settings

The Customizing Recording Settings screen, shown in Figure 17.12, duplicates some of the settings in Tweak MCE as well as a setting found in Media Center's Settings menu. The duplicated settings are **Choose Temp & Store Path for Recordings** and **Notification Before a Recording Starts** (both from Tweak MCE) and **Recording Pre and Post Padding** (from the regular Settings menu).

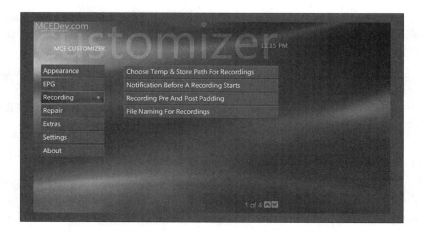

FIGURE 17.12

Customizing settings for recorded TV programs on MCE Customizer's Recording screen.

That leaves one new setting in MCE Customizer, and it's a good one. If you copy recorded programs to a portable video player, you might need to change a program's default filename to something shorter or more understandable. You can do this from MCE Customizer's **File Naming for Recordings** setting. Just click this setting and make the necessary selections; it's an easy change to make.

Customizing the Extras

Just what, pray tell, are the "extras" on MCE Customizer's Extras screen? Well, as you can see in Figure 17.13, there are a lot of them—a dozen in all—and they're really a collection of disparate items. The majority deal with the Media Center remote control and Media Center Extender, although there are some Caller ID functions thrown in, for good measure. As you might expect, many of these settings duplicate those found in either Tweak MCE or Media Center's Settings menu; some, however, are new to MCE Customizer.

Table 17.2 details the settings on the Extras screen.

TABLE 17.2   MCE Customizer's Extras Settings

Setting	Description
Enable Caller-ID	Activates Media Center's onscreen Caller ID function; also found on Media Center's Settings menu
Enable Concurrent Sessions	Lets you run more than one session of Media Center at a time
Use Unbuffered-IO Transfer	Lets you turn off the buffered input/output transfer, which can slow down audio and video streams

TABLE 17.2   Continued

Setting	Description
Enable Universal Remote Control	Configures Media Center to work with universal remote controls; also found in Tweak MCE
Set Remote Control-ID	Configures Media Center for specific remote control types; also found in Tweak MCE
Optimize for Display Type	Configures Media Center Extender displays; also found in Tweak MCE.
Show Network Congestion Notification	Displays a notification message on Media Center Extenders; also found in Tweak MCE
Show 'Not Enough Extenders; Bandwidth for TV' Notification	Displays a notification message on Media Center also found in Tweak MCE
Prompt When Navigating to Insecure Pages	Displays a notification message on Media Center Extenders; also found in Tweak MCE
Prompt When Submitting Nonencrypted Info	Displays a notification message on Media Center Extenders; also found in Tweak MCE
Prompt on Mixed Content	Displays a notification message on Media Center Extenders; also found in Tweak MCE
Start PC with MCE Remote Control	Lets you turn on your PC with the Media Center remote

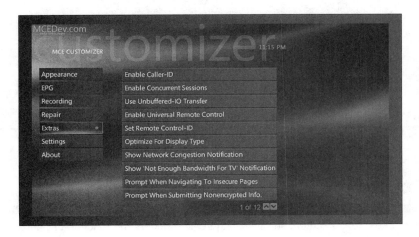

FIGURE 17.13

Configuring a wide variety of settings on MCE Customizer's Extras screen.

To me, the one unique and interesting setting on this page is the last one—**Start PC with MCE Remote Control**. Normally, the only way to turn on a Media Center PC is to push the On button on the front (or back) of the PC's system unit. This is fine when your PC is 10 inches in front of you on a desktop, but a bit of a pain when you're sitting 10 feet away on your living room couch. Activate this setting, however, and you can use the On button on your Media Center remote to turn on your Media Center PC. It's a simple thing, but quite useful.

Customizing Display Settings

MCE Customizer's Settings screen, shown in Figure 17.14, shows a lot of promise—although it's somewhat limited in its scope. To this end, the Settings screen offers the option of changing the background graphic, and the default onscreen language. You can select from English or German-language menus, but the background you select applies only to the MCE Customizer application. It would be nice to be able to change the background for all of Media Center, not just this one app; perhaps in a future version of the program.

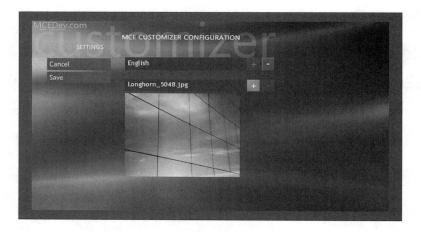

FIGURE 17.14

Changing Media Center's background—or not—on MCE Customizer's Settings screen.

Repairing Selected Settings

MCE Customizer's final screen lets you reset various Media Center settings. The slightly misnamed Repair screen, shown in Figure 17.15, offers the following options.

- **Reset Current MCE Configuration** returns all of Media Center's settings to their default state, before you ran the setup wizard.
- **Reset EPG Data** wipes out the location and provider information for Media Center's Program Guide.

- **Reset WMP Library** erases all references to watched folders and subfolders outside the My Music folder on your hard drive.
- **Reset MCE Error Log** is of particular interest to tech support personal because it wipes clean the otherwise-hidden error log that's created whenever Media Center encounters a problem.

FIGURE 17.15

Resetting Media Center with MCE Customizer's Repair screen.

The Repair screen is useful whenever Media Center gets a little too customized, or when you need to revert to a blank slate state. Otherwise, steer clear—you don't want to undo all the additions and changes you've made to the system!

caution Beware—selecting any of these Repair options can have significant consequences on Media Center's operation.

18

Troubleshooting Media Center Problems

As much as I'd like to tell you otherwise, owning a Media Center PC doesn't always come without a few problems. Unlike most closed-box consumer electronics equipment, a Media Center PC is still a PC, in an "open box" design with components and software from a variety of manufacturers—and not everything always plays well with everything else. In other words, if you're experiencing any problems operating your Media Center PC, you're not alone.

This chapter delves into the topic of Media Center issues. Some of these problems are minor annoyances, some are major inconveniences. Some are easy to fix; some don't have a good fix identified as yet. But they're all possible problems that you might—or, hopefully, might not—encounter on your own system. So, read on to learn more about Media Center problems and how to troubleshoot them.

Keeping Your Media Center System Up-to-Date

First, let's get the obvious out of the way. Media Center, like Windows XP, is an evolving piece of software that is never quite finished. When Microsoft adds a new feature or fixes an identified bug, it issues a patch to update existing systems. For that reason, you should make sure that your system is always up-to-date with the latest software patches.

Because Windows Media Center is part Windows XP and part Media Center interface, you have to update both halves of the equation. We begin with the Windows XP part.

Updating Windows XP

To keep Windows XP updated on your Media Center PC, you'll want to turn on the Windows Update feature. To do so, open the Windows Control Panel and click the Automatic Updates icon. When the Automatic Updates dialog box appears, as shown in Figure 18.1, check the Automatic option, and then click OK.

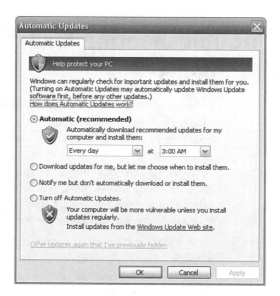

FIGURE 18.1

Activating Windows XP's Automatic Updates feature.

You can manually search for updates by going to Microsoft's Windows Update website (update.microsoft.com/windowsupdate/), shown in Figure 18.2. This page loads a piece of software onto your system so that it can scan your system for necessary updates. After the software figures out what you need, it prompts you to download and install it.

Updating Media Center Edition

As to the Media Center component, the first thing you want to do is ensure is that you have Update Rollup 2 installed on your system. This is the latest update (as of November

2005, anyway) to the Media Center software; it not only fixes a fair number of bugs, it also adds a few of the new features we've discussed in this book. You can find this update at the Windows Update website.

FIGURE 18.2

Scanning your system for necessary updates at the Windows Update website.

The Windows Update site is also where you'll find other patches and updates for Media Center. Check there once a month or so to make sure that your system is completely up-to-date.

Where to Go for Help

Let's say that you're experiencing some sort of problem, major or minor, with your Media Center PC. Where can you go for help?

If you think you have a hardware problem, the first line of defense is your PC manufacturer. Check the manufacturer's website for driver updates, error notices, and the like. And keep the phone number for technical support handy!

note In fact, you should regularly check your manufacturer's website for the latest updates—it's always good to keep abreast of the latest drivers, software versions, and other important information.

Next, there's Microsoft. The Windows XP Media Center Edition 2005 home page (www.microsoft.com/windowsxp/mediacenter/) is a good source of information of all sorts. As you can see in Figure 18.3, this page includes tutorials, FAQs, downloads, and other useful items; this page is always worth checking out.

FIGURE 18.3

Learning more about Media Center on the Microsoft site.

Then there's Microsoft's Knowledge Base, which holds articles related to all sorts of Windows- and Media Center–related problems. You can search the Knowledge Base from Microsoft's Support page (support.microsoft.com/), shown in Figure 18.4. Enter your problem in the search box in the upper left, and then scroll through all the Knowledge Base articles that match your query. Chances are, if it's a problem that someone else has experienced, it will be mentioned in the Knowledge Base.

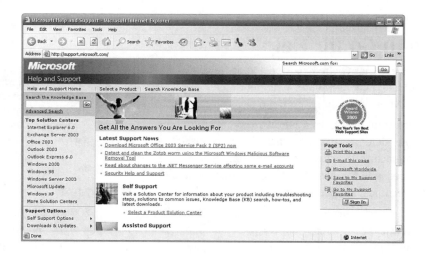

FIGURE 18.4

Searching for answers in the Microsoft Knowledge Base.

Finally, I would be remiss not to mention all the great advice and information at The Green Button website (www.thegreenbutton.com/). As you can see in Figure 18.5, The Green Button includes much expert information, as well as a thriving community of users who band together to help solve each others' problems. Search the site's KnowledgeBase for official information or go directly to the Community forums to interact with other users. I never fail to find my particular problems discussed (if not always solved) by other Green Button users.

FIGURE 18.5
Help and advice from other users at The Green Button.

Common Problems—And Probable Solutions

Now, on to some specifics. Although I can't discuss every possible Media Center problem here (too many problems are hardware-specific), we can examine some of the most common problems, and I can offer some advice on how to fix what's ailing you. Read on to see what is known about your specific problems.

General Problems

First up, let's look at some general Media Center system problems—you know, like when your system crashes or starts to slow down.

System Freezes or Crashes

You're using your Media Center PC as normal, when all of a sudden pressing a button on your remote doesn't get a response. Try all you like, the screen is frozen—or, even worse, the PC goes all fritzy and shuts down. What to do?

There are lots of things that can cause a system shutdown or freeze. Common culprits include bad hardware (including hard disk errors), incorrect or improperly configured software drivers, too little available memory, or conflicts between one program and another. Try rebooting your system and see what happens; try to document what exactly you were doing when the problem occurred.

It's likely that if you experience frequent freezes, you don't have enough memory installed in your system. If you have a 512MB system, upgrade to 1GB; if you have 1GB installed, go for 2GB. Media Center and its associated applications eat a lot of system resources, and the more memory you have, the smoother everything will run.

One thing that many users don't think to look for is an overloaded power supply in your Media Center PC. A power supply that's too small can cause problems with the writing of commands to the operating system, as well as the operation of certain components. Upgrading to a larger power supply can fix a slew of oddball problems.

A related cause of freezes and crashes is too much heat inside your system unit. If you beef up your power supply, make sure that you add the requisite fans/cooling systems. Also, don't put your PC in an enclosed cabinet where heat isn't well dissipated. Provide at least 4"–6" space on the top, sides, and back of the unit to help get rid of the internal heat.

Another possible cause is fluctuating power input, caused by either brownouts or "dirty" power lines. Connect your Media Center PC to a surge suppressor/power cleaner/battery backup device to deliver the cleanest, most consistent power possible to the unit.

Media Center Doesn't Come Out of Standby Mode

Now here's an extremely common problem—so common that I recommend avoiding Standby mode completely. What happens is that you configure your PC (from within Windows) to enter Standby mode after a selected idle period. When you try to wake up your PC, it either doesn't wake up or begins acting abnormally in some fashion.

The problem is that some PC motherboards (especially those used in built-it-yourself systems) appear to be incompatible with the S3 Standby mode. The problem is so widespread I really don't blame the motherboard manufacturers; in the view of many PC builders, Standby mode simply doesn't work. (It's less of a problem with name-brand Media Center PCs, but still something to look out for.)

Possible solutions are to upgrade your motherboard (too expensive; you might as well buy a new PC), apply a patch found on Microsoft's website (which doesn't work most of the time), or just configure your PC not to use Standby mode. In other words, just leave your Media Center PC on all the time. There's no harm in it, and you don't risk the wrath of the standby gods.

Performance Is Sluggish

Operations such as storing a large media collection (music or videos) and watching and recording television programs require a lot of processing power and memory. If you find that the more you do, the slower your Media Center PC runs, it's time to upgrade your system memory. If you have a minimal 512MB, upgrade to at least 1GB. If you're watching and recording HDTV programs, I'd recommend springing for 2GB RAM. The more sluggish your system becomes, the more memory you need to add.

Media Center Remote Doesn't Work (or Works Intermittently)

Assuming that you're using a standard Microsoft Media Center remote control, you probably have either an infrared (*IR*) receiver issue, or a universal serial bus (*USB*) connection issue.

If the IR receiver is having trouble receiving signals from the remote (that is, if the red light on the receiver doesn't light up when you use the remote), try moving the receiver to another location. Moving the receiver out of the light and into a darker location might also help. Also, don't forget the batteries in your remote; weak batteries result in intermittent (and, after a while, no) performance.

Sometimes the problem is in the receiver, not in the signal. I don't know why this is, but when my remote quits working (which it does sometimes), I can fix it by unplugging and then reconnecting the IR receiver's USB cable on the back of the PC. Wait a few seconds before reconnecting, however, to make sure that everything gets reset properly.

If you're having trouble getting a third-party universal remote to work with your Media Center system, check out Tweak MCE or MCE Customizer, both of which let you configure Media Center for universal remote operation. Learn more by referring to Chapter 17, "Customizing Windows XP Media Center Edition."

My Music Problems

Managing a large digital music collection is fraught with potential issues. We discussed some of these issues in Chapter 9, "Using Windows XP MCE for Audio Storage and Playback"; here's a quick review of those and a few other issues.

Media Center Doesn't Recognize the CD

Sometimes when you insert a CD to play or rip, Media Center doesn't recognize it and displays a message to that effect. This can happen if you've temporarily lost your connection to the Internet, or if the album is too old, too new, or too obscure to be in the online database used for CD identification. Assuming that it's not an Internet connection problem, your only recourse is to enter the album information manually.

Wrong or Missing Cover Art

Media Center doesn't always download the right cover art for a ripped CD; sometimes it doesn't download any cover art at all. As discussed in Chapter 9, there are two solutions to this problem. One, you can download or scan your own cover image and copy it into that album's folder as a **folder.jpg** file. Two, you can use the Album Art Fixer program to locate and download the right album art automatically.

Wrong or Missing Track Information

If Media Center doesn't get the track or artist info right, you have to edit that information manually. Use the instructions presented in Chapter 9 to enter the new information for each track from within Media Center. Alternatively, you can edit the information in Windows Media Player (*WMP*), although doing so doesn't work 100% of the time.

Edited Album Information Reverts to Original

Here's a new one. You make your edits to an album or track as just discussed, but later find that Media Center has lost your changes and redisplays the original, incorrect information. There's actually a simple cause and solution for this irritating problem, and it has to do with a setting in Windows Media Player. By default, WMP is configured to always look for new album information on the Web. This means that if you change the info, WMP might still look for that info online, and replace your info with the info it finds—which was wrong, as you recall.

You fix this problem by configuring WMP *not* to automatically update the album and track information every time your PC is connected to the Internet. Exit or minimize Media Center, and then launch Windows Media Player. From within WMP, select **Tools > Options** to display the Options dialog box, as shown in Figure 18.6. Select the **Library** tab and then uncheck the **Retrieve Additional Information from the Internet** option. Click **OK**, and your problem is solved. (And WMP will still retrieve track information when the CD is initially ripped to your PC—just not on any subsequent connections.)

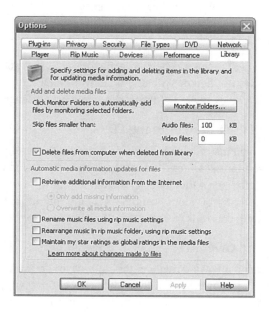

FIGURE 18.6

Configuring Windows Media Player not to update information from the Internet.

Disappearing Albums

I have a rather large digital music collection, and every now and then I'll rip a new CD and then several days later discover that it's not showing up in the My Music album list. I know it's on my hard disk; why isn't it appearing in My Music?

The answer comes from the unfortunate fact that Windows Media Center and Windows Media Player are tied together for the storage and playback of digital music files. If this tie becomes undone, Media Center won't know what WMP is doing and vice versa.

What has happened is that sometime before the new CD was ripped, Media Center and WMP became unsynchronized. So, the album I added in Media Center wasn't recognized by WMP. When I later viewed my album list in Media Center, it accessed the WMP library; because the new album hadn't been officially added to the WMP library, it didn't show up in Media Center's My Music list.

> **tip** Because of the loss-of-synchronization problem, I reboot my Media Center PC every few days; rebooting reestablishes any lost synchronization between Media Center and Windows Media Player.

The solution, when this problem occurs, is to use the Add Music function in My Music (discussed in Chapter 9) to find and select the folder that contains the new album. After it's added to the watch list, the album will appear in the My Music list.

Video Problems

Having trouble with how Media Center looks on your television screen? Then read through the following problems and try the solutions to see whether they help.

Choppy or Stuttering Video Playback

You start watching a television program, and the video begins stuttering (freezing and then unfreezing) or flashing. Sometimes the sound stutters and flashes as well. Annoying, yes, but also a fairly common problem—with a number of possible causes.

The problem in diagnosing this particular problem is that there are so many possible contributing factors. Here are a few things to check:

- It's possible that your PC is using a video card that's incompatible with Windows Media Center. Check the list of compatible cards at www.microsoft.com/windowsxp/mediacenter/partners/dfw/partnerlisting.mspx and upgrade accordingly. You should know that not all video cards are compatible with Media Center, especially older ones. In addition, of the cards on the compatibility list, some work better than others. This shouldn't be a problem if you bought an off-the-shelf Media Center PC, but when you're building your own, you might have to try out several different cards to find one that offers acceptable performance.
- It's also possible that your video card driver is incompatible or out of date. Check with the manufacturer to download the latest version of the driver.

- Another possible cause is that the DVD decoder in your system is incompatible with Media Center, or with your video card, or both. Or maybe the decoder is just a little wonky—or, even worse, maybe you don't even have a decoder installed. You can check

> **note** In spite of its name, the DVD decoder is a piece of software that controls the playback of both DVD and television video.

your DVD decoder by downloading and running the Windows XP Video Decoder Checkup Utility (downloadable from www.microsoft.com/downloads/), shown in Figure 18.7. This utility tells you whether you have the proper MPEG-2 video decoder (AKA *DVD decoder*) installed on your system, and whether the decoder is compatible with Windows XP MCE.

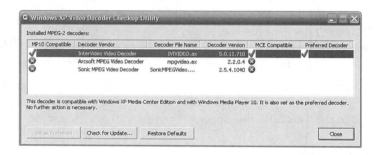

FIGURE 18.7

Using the Windows XP Video Decoder Checkup Utility to check the DVD decoders installed on your system.

MCE Doesn't Display in Widescreen Mode on 16:9 TV

You have a 16:9 widescreen television, yet Media Center displays in a 4:3 square in the center of the screen. What's happening?

Although there can be many causes for this problem (most of which involve incorrect or improperly configured video drivers), the most common cause is the type of video cable you're using. I'm going to bet that if you experience this problem, you've connected your Media Center PC to your TV via S-Video. That's the problem: S-Video doesn't transmit the widescreen video signal. To view MCE in widescreen mode, you have to connect via composite video, DVI, or HDMI. Change the cable, fix the problem.

It's also possible that you have the video resolution set wrong in Windows, or the screen size set incorrectly in Media Center. Go back and revisit all your video settings to make sure that they're set for the proper widescreen aspect ratio.

Television Problems

Now let's examine some TV-specific Media Center problems. (Yes, watching TV can be problematic.)

No TV Signal

If no picture or sound appears onscreen when you switch to live TV, there's probably a problem with the television signal coming into your Media Center PC. Make sure that the output signal from your OTA antenna or cable/satellite box is connected to the antenna input on the back of your PC, using a coaxial cable. If you use an S-Video cable to connect from a cable/satellite box, make sure that you also connect a stereo audio cable. Then run the Set Up TV Signal utility on the TV Settings screen to make sure that your system is properly configured. Remember, a weak signal from the source does you no good.

Stuttering Picture and Sound When Watching HDTV Programs

Although this could be the standard Media Center stuttering picture problem (discussed previously in the section "Choppy or Stuttering Video Playback"), it's just as likely to be a problem with digital television reception. If the digital signal is too weak, the picture doesn't deteriorate as it does with analog signals; instead, the picture stutters and/or freezes. If the signal is extremely weak, you don't get picture or sound at all. A signal on the fringe between acceptable and unacceptable causes all sorts of viewing problems, typified by the continued stuttering or freezing of the picture and sound.

You should use the Digital TV Antenna Strength option on the TV Settings screen to check the signal strength for your digital TV stations. Unless you get all green bars, you could be positioned for viewing problems. And remember—the signal strength can vary depending on time of day and whether any objects (or people) are in close proximity to your digital TV antenna. Moving the antenna just a smidge can greatly affect the signal strength.

Scheduled TV Program Doesn't Record

Here's an annoying fact: If the television signal coming into your Media Center PC is too weak, Media Center won't record any scheduled programs. It won't try to record the weak signal or flash an error message (which would be pointless if you're away from home), it just doesn't make the recording. Which is a good reason to check your signal strength ahead of time.

Also, and this falls into the category of "blindingly obvious," your Media Center PC can't make a recording if it's not turned on. Turn off your PC when you leave home, and nothing gets recorded. 'Nuff said.

Along the same lines, putting your PC into Standby mode could (although it shouldn't) affect its capability to record television programs. Remember all those problems with Standby mode we discussed earlier? They show up here, as well. Follow my advice—disable Standby mode. Please.

Finally, make sure that the Program Guide displays the correct time and channel information. If the Guide is wrong, Media Center records the wrong program. (This is a particular problem twice a year when we go into and out of daylight saving time; that next day after the time change is always a difficult one for television scheduling!)

Program Guide Displays the Wrong Programs or Channels

Now, on to the Program Guide. As just discussed, you need to make sure that the Program Guide is correctly configured for your location and television provider; incorrect setup information results in an incorrect EPG display.

To that end, you should also make sure that the time and time zone are correctly set within Windows XP. The Guide might think it's 8:00 if it's really 7:00 and your computer's system clock is incorrectly set. Again, this is sometimes an issue with daylight saving time.

If the Guide info is really bumfoozled, you might have to delete the current Guide and download a new one. You do this by selecting **Settings > General > Media Center Setup** and choosing not to use the Guide. Then reboot your computer, go back to **Settings > General > Media Center Setup**, and set up the Guide from scratch.

DVD Problems

Some Media Center users experience problems playing or recording DVDs. Here are some of the more common problems and their probable solutions.

DVD Doesn't Play

If you load a DVD in your DVD drive and nothing appears onscreen, you might have to change the type of video cable you use to connect your Media Center PC to your TV. This problem can occur if your Media Center PC is set to a resolution greater than 480p (480 × 640) and connected to your TV via component video cables.

The problem is caused by the copy protection on some DVDs that won't allow higher-resolution playback on a PC connected to a TV via component video cables. The copy protection software thinks that because you're outputting the signal at higher than 480p resolution, you're trying to use the component video cables to bypass the restrictions on digital-to-digital copying. Thus convinced, the software on the DVD simply shuts off the signal—which is not a good thing. Fortunately, there are three solutions to this problem.

First, you can lower the display resolution on your Media Center PC to 480 × 640 pixels. At this lower resolution, playback should be fine.

Second, you can use another type of cable. S-Video works fine (albeit with lower picture quality), as do both the higher-quality DVI and HDMI cables. Anything but component video, in other words.

Finally, you can download and install a *region-free* utility on your PC. This is a small program that works in the background to enable playback of DVDs from any region around the globe. Normally, antipiracy restrictions limit playback to those DVDs produced in the same region as the DVD player or PC; a region-free utility neutralizes this region restriction.

That said, there's another pleasant byproduct of using a region-free utility. In neutralizing the region restrictions, the region-free utility also shuts down other copy protection technologies—like the one that doesn't like component video cables. Install the region-free utility, and you should eliminate the component video DVD playback problem.

Several of these region-free utilities are available over the Internet. For ease of installation and compatibility with most DVD drives, I like DVD Region+CSS Free, which you can download for $39.95 from www.dvdidle.net/. Also good is Remote Selector, downloadable for free from www.remoteselector.com/.

Know, however, that the problem of a DVD not playing isn't relegated to the land of high-resolution video output. A DVD might not play if you have an incorrect or damaged DVD driver installed on your machine, or if you're using an incorrect (or no) DVD decoder. Refer to the "Choppy or Stuttering Video Playback" section, earlier in this chapter, to learn more about DVD decoder software. To resolve a driver problem, check with the manufacturer of your PC or DVD driver to download the latest driver.

Can't Record Some Television Programs to DVD

Here's the deal. Some television programs—especially from digital channels—come with a form of digital rights management (*DRM*) encoded into the program. This DRM encoding places a limit on what you can do with the recorded program. Some DRM constraints let you watch the program only within a specified time period after the initial viewing. Other, more common, constraints prohibit you from making copies of the recorded program to DVD. If you see a screen warning you that you're not allowed to copy the program, that's what's happening.

It's not a fault, it's a feature! (Yeah, right.)

All These Problems—Is It Worth It?

With all the *possible* (emphasis on that word) problems you might encounter with a Media Center PC, is it really worth it to install one in your living room?

In a word, yes.

The problems you might encounter, although unusual for a standard consumer electronics component, are no more than what you typically experience with a desktop PC. Most problems are connection or installation problems and are easily fixed. And, even better, the vast majority of users don't experience any problems at all.

All this is to say that even though a Media Center PC is a leading-edge (some might say *bleeding-edge*) technology investment, it's a sound one. Although living room PCs are relatively rare today, they're becoming increasingly common; as each month goes by, more and more users are adding Media Center PCs to their home entertainment systems. And that's because a Media Center PC adds real value to your system. Not only can it replace several existing components, it adds functionality unavailable previously.

I have a Media Center PC in my home theater system. I use it several hours every day. I wouldn't give it up for anything in the world. Yes, I've experienced a few niggling problems—but not enough to discourage me. It's a terrific investment, and has become an essential component of my leisure activities. I love having all my music available digitally, at the touch of a button, and being able to not just record television shows but also to burn those shows to archival DVDs. There is no other audio/video component that can perform those tasks. To that end, the Media Center PC is unique.

I hope that you have learned more about Media Center PCs by reading this book, and that you've taken—or will soon take—the Media Center plunge. I assure you that you won't regret your decision; you'll wonder how you ever got by without a PC in your living room. It might seem odd at first, but after you start using one, a Media Center PC makes all the sense in the world.

Enjoy!

Index

Numbers

4:3 aspect ratio, Live TV function (Media Center), 218-221

10 Foot World (Online Spotlight), 324-325

10-foot interface (Media Center), 149

16:9 aspect ratio
Live TV function (Media Center), 218-221
no MCE display, troubleshooting, 374

720p HDTV resolution, 261

A

A/V Component Form Factor Media Center PC
Alienware DHS 5, 73
cost range, 73
HP z552, 74-75
Niveus Denali, 72-76
Sony VAIO VGX-XL1 Digital Living System, 76-77

A/V connections, Media Center PC versus desktop PCs, 19

AAC (Apple Audio Compression) format, CDs, ripping, 171

ABC Enhanced TV (Online Spotlight), 309

ABC Family service (Online Spotlight), 309

accessing My File Manager, 287

Add Keyword screen (Media Center), recording via keyword, 231-233

Add Recording screen (Media Center), manual TV recordings, 230-231

add-on programs
caller ID
MCE Caller ID, 340
MCE-YAC, 340
mceTapiRex, 340
computer applications
Hotmail Plus Reader for Media Center, 342
MCE Browser, 341
MCE Outlook, 342
mceContacts, 342
My File Manager, 341
PhotoConnect, 343
DVD-burning
ArcSoft QuickDVD, 336
muvee autoProduce unPlugged, 336
Sonic PrimeTime, 336
Sonic PrimeTime Deluxe, 336
entertainment
In the Movies for MCE, 332
Karatron, 335
Microsoft Media Center Karaoke, 335
My Movies, 332

My Netflix, 332
My Trailers for MCE, 333
MyTV ToGo, 334
MyWebTV, 333
Playlist Editor, 333
Power Compress, 335
Recorded TV, 335
Share Recorded TV, 335
Web Media, 333
WebGuide3, 335
games
  Dragon Maze, 346
  mcepeaks, 346
  Solitaire, 347
  Super Slyder, 348
  Tetris, 348
  World Trivia, 348
home automation
  HAI Home Control, 339
  HomeSeer MCE Plug-In,
    339
  mControl, 339
Internet phone
  MCE SIP Phone, 340
  mcePhone for Skype, 340
lifestyle
  Alarm Clock, 337
  Lottery Results for MCE,
    338
  mceAuction, 337
  My Mapquest for MCE, 337
  My Recipes, 338
Media Center
  MCE Customizer, 344, 357
  MCE Outlook, 283
  MCE Screen Saver, 346
  MCE Video Settings, 346
  mceHideSVP, 345
  My File Manager, 287
  Sleep Timer, 346
  Tweak MCE, 344, 350
news, 328
  MCE RSS Reader, 330
  mNewsCenter, 330
  My NFL Scores for MCE,
    330
  My Portal, 328-329
  My Web News, 329
  MyUK Portal, 328
  ReadNews, 330

remote control
  Media Center
    Communicator, 344
  MediaUFO, 344
  MyRemoteMouse, 343
  Niveus Pocket Remote, 343
  PadOne Media Controller,
    344
  Rudeo Control, 344
TheGreenButton.com, listings
  of, 348
weather
  mceWeather, 331
  My Weather, 331
  Simply Weather, 331
WindowsmarketPlace.com,
  listings of, 348
advancing CD tracks, 176
Ahanix D5 Media Center Enclosure
  (case), 78-79
Akimbo service (Online Spotlight),
  307
Alarm Clock add-on, 337
Album Art Fixer, downloading,
  190-192
Album Cover view, CDs, playing,
  174
albums
  art
    fixing, 189-192
    manual file replacement,
      192
  digital music information,
    editing, 187-188
  playing, 185
Alienware DHS 5 A/V Component
  Form Factor Media Center PC, 73
AMD chips, 81
analog stereo, left/right audio
  output connections, 111-113
Antec Overture II (case), 79
antenna input for Media Center
  PC, 94
  cable line connections, 96-97
  coaxial signal splitter, 95
  digital cable box connections,
    97, 99
  HDTV connections, 95
  moving for better reception
    (Media Center Extender), 300

over-the-air (OTA) connections,
  95
satellite receiver connections,
  99-100
AOL Music on Demand (Online
  Spotlight), 315
AOL Pictures (Online Spotlight),
  315
AOL Radio (Online Spotlight), 315
Appearance category (MCE
  Customizer), 357
  options, setting, 357-359
Apple iPod, non-WMA
  compatibility, 29
appointments
  management of (MCE Outlook),
    283
  viewing (MCE Outlook), 284
ArcSoft QuickDVD
  downloading, 253
  DVDs, burning, 251-253, 336
  Online Spotlight, 326
aspect ratios (TV)
  16:9, 218-221
  4:3, 218-221
ATI HDTV Wonder ATSC tuner
  card, 84
ATI Radeon X850 video card, 84
ATSC tuner for high-definition
  television (HDTV), 47
auctions, mceAuction add-on
  program, 337
audio cards for Media Center PC
  cost ranges, 84
  Sound Blaster Audigy 2, 84
audio connections
  Media Center Extender, 294
  Media Center PC, 108
    analog stereo connectors,
      111-113
    coaxial digital, 110
    HDMI, 109
    multichannel analog audio,
      112
    optical digital, 109-110
    stereo mini-jacks, 112
  versus desktop PCs, 91-94
audio files, accessing via Media
  Center Extender on living room
  system, 63-64

audio output connections
  digital versus optical, selecting
    for Media Center PC, 35–36
  digital video recorder (DVR)
    specifications, 52
audio settings
  configuring (Media Center),
    138–141
  Media Center, configuring,
    168–172
    sound effects, configuring,
      142
audio/video components for Media
  Center PC, 37–38
auto updates for Media Center
  PCs, 366
automatic playlists, creating
  (Windows Media Player),
  202–203
automatic software updates,
  configuring (Media Center), 143
Autostart Enhanced DVD Content
  option (MCE Tweak utility), 352
auxiliary rooms (Media Center
  Extender)
  accessing audio/video files for
    home theater system, 63–64
  necessary components for, 62

B

backgrounds for Start page (Media
  Center), 150
backup hard disks for Media
  Center PC, 37
bit rates, CD ripping, 171
building Media Center PC from
  scratch
  advantages of, 77–78
  component price estimates,
    86–87
  component selection options,
    78–86
  general assembly instructions,
    87–88
  necessary skill levels, 78
built-in amplifiers (speakers), 92
burning
  CDs (Media Center PC), 31–32,
    205–207
    mixed album sources
      (Media Center), 207–208

third-party software
  applications, 208
digital photos to CDs (Media
  Center), 271–274
DVD movies
  ArcSoft QuickDVD, 251–253
  Media Center PC, 248–251
  Roxio My DVD, 254
  Sonic Easy Media Creator,
    254
  Sonic PrimeTime, 251
  Sony Click-to-DVD
    program, 253
  Ulead DVD MovieFactory,
    254
recorded television programs
  to DVDs, 48–50
videotaped home movies to
  DVDs, 48–50

C

cable lines, connecting to Media
  Center PC, 96–97
calendars, appointments
  management of (MCE Outlook),
    283
  viewing (MCE Outlook), 284
caller ID
  configuring (Media Center),
    144
  add-ons
    MCE Caller ID, 340
    MCE-YAC, 340
    mceTapiRex, 340
canceling scheduled TV
  recordings, 239
captions
  configuring (Media Center),
    144
  slideshows, displaying, 262
cases (Media Center PC), 79
  Ahanix D5 Media Center
    Enclosure, 78–79
  Antec Overture II, 79
  nmediapc HTPC BA & S
    models, 79
  Silverstone LC11M, 79
CD/DVD drives, selecting for
  Media Center PC, 34

CDs
  burning, 31–32
  changers, 43
  copying from hard disks,
    205–208
  copying to hard drives, 176
  cover art, displaying, 24
  digital photos, burning to,
    271–274
  digital rights management
    (DRM), 44
  drives
    cost ranges, 83
    selecting for Media Center
      PC, 34
    vendor listing, 83
  DVD-Audio type, inability to
    play via Media Center PC,
    24–25
  edited albums revert to
    original, troubleshooting, 372
  Media Center, third-party
    burning software, 208
  missing from library,
    troubleshooting, 373
  missing or wrong cover art,
    troubleshooting, 371
  missing or wrong track
    information, troubleshooting,
    372
  MSN Music Store, 176
  non–recognition,
    troubleshooting, 371
  players, Media Center PC
    capability, 8–9
  playing, 24–25, 173–176
  recorders, Media Center PC
    capability, 9
  ripping
    bit rates, 171
    file format options, 170–171
    format selection, 27–28
    hard disk space
      requirements, 171–172
    Media Center configuration,
      170–172
  ripping
    Media Center PC, 25–28
    Windows Media Player,
      172–173

ripping services (MusicShifter),
27
SACD type, inability to play via
Media Center PC, 24–25
standard audio type, playing,
24
changer units (DVDs), 255
channels
listings
adding (Program Guide),
212
editing (Program Guide),
211–212
Live TV function (Media
Center)
changing, 222
inset window view, 222
pausing live programming,
222–223
program information,
viewing, 222
recording programs,
224–227
switching to avoid interference
(Media Center Extender), 300
chat sessions, launching (Media
Center Messenger), 277–280
CinemaNow service (Online
Spotlight), 306
closing Media Center, 163–164
PC shutdowns, 164–165
CNET Download.com, Hotmail Plus
Reader for Media Center, 281
coaxial digital cable
audio output connections, 110
signal splitters and amplifiers,
95
Comedy Central MotherLoad
(Online Spotlight), 311
commercials, skipping over in
recordings, 240
Component video, output
connections (Media Center PC),
101–102, 105
components of Media Center PC
audio cards, 84
cases, 78–79
CD drives, 83
CPUs, 81
general assembling
instructions, 87–88
hard disk drives, 82

input devices, 85
memory modules, 81–82
motherboards, 80
power supply options, 79–80
price estimates, 86–87
TV tuner cards, 84
video cards, 84
Windows XP Media Center
software, 86
Composite video, output
connections (Media Center PC),
101–102, 106–108
computer application add-ons
Hotmail Plus Reader for Media
Center, 342
MCE Browser, 341
MCE Outlook, 342
mceContacts, 342
My File Manager, 341
PhotoConnect, 343
configuring
Media Center
audio settings, 168–172
automatic software
updates, 143
caller ID/instant messaging,
144
captions, 144
digital slideshows, 144
download options, 143
DVD language playback,
144
graphical visualizations for
music, 144
initial setup, 121–128
Internet connections, 142
minimum component
specifications, 32–37,
50–55
parental controls, 143
privacy settings, 143
remote desktop, 143
sound effects, 142
window behaviors, 142
wireless networking, 143
Media Center Extender,
297–298
slideshows
displaying pictures in
subfolders, 262
random order, 262

show captions, 262
show song information
during show, 262
transition effects, 263
transition times, 263
TV recorder (Media Center),
224
audio language, 227
disk space issues, 225–226
life of recording, 227
number of recordings, 227
quality issues, 225–226
start/stop settings, 227
TV series issues, 227
Windows Media Player,
CD-ripping settings, 172–173
connecting
antenna input, 94
cable line connections,
96–97
coaxial signal splitters, 95
digital cable box
connections, 97–99
HDTV connections, 95
over-the-air (OTA)
connections, 95
satellite receiver
connections, 99–100
audio output, 108
analog stereo, 111–113
coaxial digital, 110
HDMI, 109
multichannel analog audio,
112
optical digital, 109–110
stereo mini-jacks, 112
external peripherals, 118–119
keyboards, 117
Media Center Extender,
293–294
audio, 294
ethernet networks, 296
home networks, 296–297
multiple room setup, 62
video, 294
Wi-Fi networks, 297
Microsoft Xbox as Media
Center Extender, 66
Microsoft Xbox 360 as Media
Center Extender, 67
mouse, 117

networks, 114
  via ethernet (Media Center PCs), 114–115
  via Wi-Fi (Media Center PCs), 116–117
  remote control for Media Center PCs, 117
  video output
    Component video, 101–102, 105
    Composite video, 101–102
    DVI, 101–104
    HDMI, 101–102
    S-video, 101–102, 106–108
connections, Media Center PC versus desktop PCs, 91–94
contact management (MCE Outlook)
  appointments
    management of, 283
    viewing, 284
  contacts, viewing, 284
Contrast tool, digital photos, fixing (Media Center PC), 270
controlling DVD changers in Media Center PC, 42–43
Copy DVD function (Media Center), 243
copying
  CDs to hard drives, 176
    ripping process, 25–28
  DVDs to hard drives, 44–45
  files/folders via My File Manager, 288–289
  recorded TV programs to DVDs, 243
cover art for CDs, displaying (Media Center PC), 24
CPUs (Media Center PC)
  AMD chips, 81
  Intel chips, 81
crashes, troubleshooting, 369–370
Create CD/DVD function (Media Center PC), digital photos, burning to CDs, 271–274
Create CD/DVD utility (Media Center PC), 248–251
Crop tool, digital photos, resizing (Media Center PC), 270

D

deleting
  digital photos from My Photos folder, 266
  recorded TV programs, 240–241
Dell Dimension E510 Desktop Media Center PC, 71
Desktop Media Center PC
  Dell Dimension E510, 71
  Sony RA-940, 71–72
desktop PCs versus Media Center PC
  A/V connections, 19
  connections, 91–94
  interface viewing, 16–17
  noise levels, 18–19
  remote control operations, 17–18
  unit design, 19
  uses, 15–16
devices, potential interference, avoiding (Media Center Extender), 300
digital audio, Media Center PC specifications, 32–33
  backup hard drives, 37
  hard disk drives, 34
  microprocessors, 33
  networking connections, 36
  noise reduction methods, 37
  optical drives, 34
  output connections, 35–36
  RAM, 33
digital audio connections, 35–36
digital audio jukeboxes, Media Center PC capability, 13–14
digital cable boxes, connecting to Media Center PC, 97–99
Digital Media Converter
  downloading, 255
  DVR-MS format (DVDs), converting to MPEG format, 254–255
digital media servers
  Escient FireBall Movie Manager, 20
  versus Media Center PC, 20–21

digital music
  downloading
    file format issues, 177–179
    MusicGiants Network, 178
  Media Center
    album art, fixing, 189–192
    album art, manual file replacement, 192
    display and sort options, 179–182
    editing album information, 187–188
    editing song information, 185–188
    playing albums, 185
    playing individual songs, 185
    playlists, creating, 195–198
    playlists, playing, 194–195
    scrolling through, 183
    searching, 184–185
  playing (Media Center PC), 13–14
  Playlist Editor, playlists, creating, 198–199
  watch list, adding to My Music folder (Media Center), 168–170
  Windows Media Player
    automatic playlists, creating, 202–203
    playlists, creating, 200–201
    playlists, editing, 203–205
digital photos
  burning to CDs, 271–274
  deleting (My Photos folder), 266
  editing tools
    accessing, 268
    Contrast tool, 270
    Crop tool, 270
    disadvantages, 268
    Red Eye tool, 269
  folder storage options, 265, 268
  full-screen view, 264
  picture properties, displaying, 264
  picture thumbnails, viewing, 263

slideshows
  configuring, 262
  viewing, 261
  viewing in slideshow format,
    14
digital rights management (DRM),
  377
  CD/DVD usage, 44
digital slideshows, configuring
  (Media Center), 144
digital television recorder (DTR),
  224
  configuring, 224
    audio language, 227
    disk space issues, 225–226
    life of recording, 227
    number of recordings, 227
    quality issues, 225–226
    start/stop settings, 227
    TV series issues, 227
  MSN Remote Record Service,
    signup process, 235
  programs, recording while
    watching, 234
  recording entire season series,
    228–230
  scheduled recordings
    canceling, 239
    reviewing, 237–238
  scheduling recording from
    Program Guide, 227–228
  searching for programs to
    record in Media Center, 230
digital video recorders (DVRs),
  Media Center PC specifications,
  50–51
  audio output connections, 52
  hard disks, 51–52
  microprocessors, 51
  networking connections, 53
  noise reduction methods, 54
  optical drives, 52
  RAM, 51
  television programming,
    recording, 48
  TV tuners, 52
  video output connections, 53
DISCover My Games (Online
  Spotlight), 322
Discovery Media Center (Online
  Spotlight), 308

Display My Music as Last Viewed
  option (MCE Tweak utility), 354
Display Wireless Passwords option
  (MCE Tweak utility), 351
download options, configuring
  (Media Center), 143
downloading
  digital music
    format issues, 177–179
    MusicGiants Network, 178
  DVD rippers
    DVD Decrypter, 256
    Flash DVD Ripper, 256
    ImTOO DVD Ripper, 256
    Magic DVD Ripper, 256
    Xilisoft DVD Ripper, 256
  MCE Outlook, 283
  music
    format considerations,
      28–29
    sound quality, 29
  My File Manager, 287
  videos from Internet, 45
Dragon Maze add-on, 346
DVD Decrypter, downloading, 256
DVD-Audio CDs, inability to play
  on Media Center PC, 24–25
DVD-burning programs add-ons
  ArcSoft QuickDVD, 336
  muvee autoProduce unPlugged,
    336
  Sonic PrimeTime, 336
  Sonic PrimeTime Deluxe, 336
DVDs
  burning
    ArcSoft QuickDVD, 251–253
    Media Center PC, 248–251
    recorded television
      programs to, 48–50
    Roxio My DVD, 254
    Sonic Easy Media Creator,
      254
    Sonic PrimeTime, 251
    Sony Click-to-DVD
      program, 253
    Ulead DVD MovieFactory,
      254
  changers, 255
    controlling (Media Center
      PC), 42–43

Niveus Ice Vault 200 Disc
  Changer, 43, 255
Sony VAIO XL1 Digital
  Living System, 43
copying recorded programs to,
  243
decoder problems, 374
digital rights management
  (DRM), 44
drives for Media Center PC
  cost ranges, 83
  vendor listing, 83
DVR-MS format, conversion to
  MPEG format, 254–255
LaCie Bigger Disk Extreme,
  disk storage capabilities, 255
language playback, configuring
  (Media Center), 144
naming (Media Center PC), 249
non–playing, troubleshooting,
  376–377
playback options (Media
  Center PC)
  FWD button, 246
  Pause button, 246
  Pause+FWD button, 246
  Pause+REW button, 246
  Play button, 246
  Replay button, 246
  REW button, 246
  seek bar, 247
  Skip button, 246
  Stop button, 246
players/recorders, Media
  Center PC capability, 8–9
playing (Media Center PC), 42,
  245, 247
recorded TV programs,
  troubleshooting, 377
recording (Media Center PC),
  248
recording time per disc, 250
rippers
  DVD Decrypter, 256
  Flash DVD Ripper, 256
  ImTOO DVD Ripper, 256
  Magic DVD Ripper, 256
  Xilisoft DVD Ripper, 256
ripping to hard drives, 44–45
  data storage options, 44
  legal ramifications, 255
  popular utilities, 255

process of, 256-257
space requirements, 255
time per disc, 257
DVI (digital visual interface), 53, 91
    video output connections, 101-104
DVR-MS format (Media Center DVDs), converting to MPEG format, 254-255
DVRs (digital video recorders). *See* digital video recorders (DVRs)

E

editing
    digital music
        album information, 187-188
        song information, 185-188
    digital photos, 268-270
    playlists in Windows Media Player, 203-205
electronic program guides (EPGs)
    television tuners (Media Center PC), 10-11, 46
    versus TiVo, 11
email
    Hotmail Plus Reader for Media Center
        account requirements, 281
        downloading, 281
        Inbox screen, 282
        installing, 281
        launching, 281
        limited features, 281
        reading new messages, 282
    new messages, composing (MCE Outlook), 285-286
Enable My DVDs option (MCE Tweak utility), 352-353
Enable Universal Remote Control option (MCE Tweak utility), 355
entertainment programs add-ons
    In the Movies for MCE, 332
    Karatron, 335
    Microsoft Media Center Karaoke, 335
    My Movies, 332
    My Netflix, 332
    My Trailers for MCE, 333
    MyTV ToGo, 334
    MyWebTV, 333
    Playlist Editor, 333
    Power Compress, 335
    Recorded TV, 335
    Share Recorded TV, 335
    Web Media, 333
    WebGuide3, 335
Escient FireBall Movie Manager, 20
ethernet connections for Media Center PC, 36
    setting up, 114-115
exiting Media Center, 163-164
    PC shutdowns, 164-165
Extender screen (Tweak MCE utility), 355-356
Extender. *See* Media Center Extender
external amplifiers (speakers), 92
external hard disk for Media Center PC backups, 37
external peripherals, connecting to Media Center PCs, 118-119
Extras category (MCE Customizer), 357, 360-362

F

fast-forwarding, CD playback, 176
file formats for CDs
    AAC (Apple Audio Compression), 171, 177-179
    MP3, 170-171
    WMA (Windows Media Audio), 170, 177-179
    WMA Lossless (Windows Media Audio Lossless), 171, 177-179
files (My File Manager)
    accessing, 287
    copying, 288-289
    folder contents
        copying, 288-289
        viewing, 287
filtering Program Guide options, 214-215
FireWire connections, viewing tape through Media Center PC, 46
firmware, updating for better reception (Media Center Extender), 301
fixing
    album art (Media Center), 189-192
    digital photos
        contrast problems, 270
        red eye problems, 269
Flash DVD Ripper, downloading, 256
FM radio, listening via Media Center PC, 31, 36
folders
    copying (My File Manager), 288-289
    digital photos, storing, 265, 268
    viewing (My File Manager), 287
food, My Recipes add-on program, 338
Fox Sports for Media Center (Online Spotlight), 320
FWD button, DVD transport options (Media Center PC), 246

G

GalleryPlayer (Online Spotlight), 323
game add-ons
    Dragon Maze, 346
    mcepeaks, 346
    Solitaire, 347
    Super Slyder, 348
    Tetris, 348
    World Trivia, 348
Game xStream (Online Spotlight), 321-322
Games (Online Spotlight), 304
    DISCover My Games, 322
    Game xStream, 321-322
general troubleshooting tips
    remote control operation, 371
    sluggish performance, 370
    standby mode freezes, 370
    system freezes or crashes, 369-370
graphical visualizations during music playback, configuring (Media Center), 144, 175

H

HAI Home Control home automation add-on, 339
hard disks
  CD-ripping, space issues, 27-28
  CDs, copying from (Media Center), 205-208
  contents, viewing (My File Manager), 287
  cost ranges, 82
  digital video recorder (DVR) specifications, 51-52
  DVDs, ripping, 44-45, 255
  external, connecting (Media Center PC), 118-119
  RAID, 34
  recommended sizes, 82
  space issues, selecting for Media Center PC, 34, 171-172
  storage space, Media Center PC versus TiVo, 12
  vendor listing, 82
hardware (Media Center PC), component selection specifications, 32-37, 50-55
HDMI (high-definition multimedia interface), 53, 91
  audio output connections, 109
  video output connections, 101-102
HDTV (high-definition television)
  720p resolution, 261
  antenna, connecting to Media Center PC, 95
Help Center (Media Center), 151-152
help resources
  Microsoft Knowledge Base website, 368
  The Green Button website, 369
  Windows XP Media Center Edition website, 367
high-definition television
  ATSC tuner (Media Center PC), 47
  viewing (Media Center PC), 47
home automation programs add-ons
  HAI Home Control, 339
  HomeSeer MCE Plug-In, 339
  mControl, 339

home movies, burning to DVDs, 48-50
home networks
  Media Center Extender, 14
  connecting, 296-297
  ethernet type, 296
  Wi-Fi type, 297
  Media Center PC, connection options, 36
home theater systems
  general connection process, 54-55
  Media Center Extender, connecting, 64-65
  typical components, 54
HomeSeer MCE Plug-In home automation add-on, 339
Hotmail Plus Reader for Media Center
  downloading, 281
  email account requirements, 281
  Inbox screen, reading new messages, 282
  installing, 281
  launching, 281
  limited features, 281
Hotmail Plus Reader for Media Center add-on, 342
HP z552 A/V Component Form Factor Media Center PC, 74-75
HP zd8230us Notebook Media Center PC, 70-71

I - J - K

ImTOO DVD Ripper, downloading, 256
In the Movies for MCE entertainment add-on, 332
Inbox screen
  Hotmail Plus Reader for Media Center, reading new messages, 282
  new messages, composing (MCE Outlook), 285-286
individual songs, playing (Media Center), 185
infrared (IR) remote control receivers, 94

input devices for Media Center PC
  Gyration Media Center Remote & Keyboard, 86
  remote controls, 85
instant messaging
  configuring, 144
  launching (Media Center Messenger), 277-280
Intel chips, 81
Intel D955XBK motherboard, 80
InterActual (Online Spotlight), 311
interfaces
  Escient FireBall Movie Manager, 20
  Media Center PC versus desktop PCs, 16-17
  Windows XP Media Center Edition, 19-20
Internet
  connections, configuring (Media Center), 142
  phone programs add-ons
    MCE SIP Phone, 340
    mcePhone for Skype, 340
  video programming, downloading, 45
Internet radio
  listening to, 29-31
  sound quality, 30
  XM Radio Online, 30
IR (infrared) bugs, digital cable boxes, connecting, 99

Karatron entertainment add-on, 335
keyboards
  connecting, 117
  Gyration Media Center Remote & Keyboard, 86
KMS Software (Online Spotlight), 325
Kodak Share (Online Spotlight), 323

L

LaCie Bigger Disk Extreme, disk storage capabilities, 255
launching
  instant messaging via Media Center Messenger, 277-280

Media Center
  with PC activation, 162
  within Windows XP, 162
Lifestyle (Online Spotlight), 304
  10 Foot World, 324-325
  ArcSoft QuickDVD, 326
  GalleryPlayer, 323
  KMS Software, 325
  Kodak Share, 323
  Sonic PrimeTime, 326
lifestyle programs add-ons
  Alarm Clock, 337
  Lottery Results for MCE, 338
  mceAuction, 337
  My Mapquest for MCE, 337
  My Recipes, 338
Linksys Media Center Extender,
59
listening
  Internet radio, 29-31
    FM tuning, 31
    sound quality, 30
    XM Radio Online, 30
  music in other rooms (Media
    Center Extender), 61
live television
  electronic programming guide
    (Media Center PC), 46
  viewing (Media Center PC),
    46-47
Live TV function (Media Center)
  4:3 aspect ratio display,
    218-221
  16:9 aspect ratio display,
    218-221
  channels, changing, 222
  inset window view, 222
  launching, 217-218
  live programming
    pausing, 222-223
    recording, 224-227
  program information, viewing,
    222
  zoom modes, 219-221
Live365 (Online Spotlight),
312-313
looping CD playback (Media
Center), 176
Lottery Results for MCE add-on,
338

M

Magic DVD Ripper, downloading,
256
management features, 285
manual updates for Media Center
PCs, 366
maps, My Mapquest for MCE
add-on program, 337
MCE Browser add-on, 341
MCE Caller ID caller ID add-on,
340
MCE Customizer add-on, 344
  Appearance category, options,
    setting, 357-359
  EPG category, options, setting,
    357-359
  Extras category, 357
    options, setting, 360-362
  Recording category, options,
    setting, 357-360
  Repairs category, 357
    options, setting, 362-363
  Settings category, 357
    options, setting, 362
MCE Outlook, 342
  downloading, 283
MCE RSS Reader news add-on,
330
MCE Screen Saver add-on, 346
MCE SIP Phone Internet phone
  add-on, 340
MCE Video Settings add-on, 346
MCE-Software.com, 283, 287
MCE-YAC caller ID add-on, 340
mceAuction add-on, 337
mceContacts add-on, 342
mceHideSVP add-on, 345
mcepeaks add-on, 346
mcePhone for Skype Internet
  phone add-on, 340
mceTapiRex caller ID add-on, 340
mceWeather weather add-on, 331
mControl home automation
  add-on, 339
Media Center Communicator
  add-on, 344
Media Center Extender
  audio/video files, accessing via
    Media Center PC, 63-64
  back panel connections, 294
  configuration settings, 299
  configuring, 297-298
  connections, 293-294
    audio, 294
    ethernet networks,
      296-297
    home networks, 296-297
    video, 294
  function of, 58
  high-definition TV
    programming, non-playback
    of, 298
  home network functionality, 14
  independent operation of, 67
  instant messaging, 59
  Linksys Media Center
    Extender, 59
  maximum number in use
    simultaneously, 58
  memory requirements, 60
  Microsoft Xbox/Xbox 360
    connecting, 66-67
    kit costs, 66
    using as, 65-66
  multiple, placing throughout
    home, 62
  music, listening in other rooms,
    61
  My Music option, 298
  My Pictures option, 298
  My TV option, 298
  Network Performance Tuner,
    performance and diagnostics
    tool, 301-302
  number in use, performance
    considerations, 68
  performance improvement tips,
    299-301
  placing in home theater
    system, 64-65
  primary uses, 293-294
  processor requirements, 60
  Settings screen, 299
  Setup Key screen, 297-298
  standard-definition TV
    programming, 298
  Start screen, 298
  streaming music and TV
    programming to multiple
    rooms, 58-59
  supported media types, 58

television
    set connections, 294
    watching in other rooms,
      61
    versus Media Center PC
      features, 67
    wireless network
      troubleshooting
        antenna relocation, 300
        device interference, 300
        firmware updates, 301
        network upgrades, 301
        recording at lower quality
          levels, 301
        switching channels, 300
Media Center Messenger versus
  Windows Messenger, 278-280
Media Center PC
    A/V component form factor
      type
        Alienware DHS 5, 73
        cost range, 73
        HP z552, 74-75
        Niveus Denali, 72-76
        Sony VAIO VGX-XL1 Digital
          Living System, 76-77
    Add Keyword screen,
      recording via keyword,
      231-233
    Add Recording screen, manual
      TV recordings, 230-231
    add-ons
      MCE Customizer, 344,
        357-363
      MCE Screen Saver, 346
      MCE Video Settings, 346
      mceHideSVP, 345
      Sleep Timer, 346
      Tweak MCE, 344, 350-356
    alternatives, 20-21
    antenna inputs
      cable line connections,
        96-97
      connections, 94-95
      digital cable box
        connections, 97-99
      HDTV connections, 95
      over-the-air (OTA)
        connections, 95
      satellite receiver
        connections, 99-100

appearance of with other
  media components, 37
Apple iPod incompatibility, 29
audio/video components,
  required, 37-38
audio output, connecting,
  108-113
audio settings, configuring,
  138-141, 168-172
automatic updates (Windows
  Update feature), 143, 366
building from scratch
  advantages of, 77-78
  component price estimates,
    86-87
  component selection
    options, 78-86
  necessary skill levels, 78
buying versus building, 88
caller ID/instant messaging,
  configuring, 144
caller ID add-on programs
  MCE Caller IDS, 340
  MCE-YAC, 340
  mceTapiRex, 340
capabilities
  CD/DVD player, 8-9
  digital audio jukeboxes,
    13-14
  digital video recorder
    (DVR), 11-12
  slideshow viewer, 14
  television tuner, 10-11
captions, configuring, 144
CDs
  advancing to next tracks,
    176
  Album Cover view, 174
  burning, 31-32
  copying from hard disks,
    205-208
  copying to hard drives, 176
  fast-forwarding through
    playback, 176
  graphic visualizations,
    viewing, 175
  infinite looped playback,
    176
  pausing playback, 175
  playing, 24-25, 173-176
  random track playback, 176

ripping configuration,
  25-28, 170-172
stopping playback, 175
track listings, viewing, 174
closing, 163-164
  PC shutdowns, 164-165
components, general
  assembling instructions,
    87-88
computer application add-on
  programs
  Hotmail Plus Reader for
    Media Center, 342
  MCE Browser, 341
  MCE Outlook, 342
  mceContacts, 342
  My File Manager, 341
  PhotoConnect, 343
configuration options
  audio output connections,
    35-36
  external hard disk for
    backups, 37
  FM radio tuning, 36
  hard disk space, 34
  microprocessors, 33
  minimum specifications,
    32-37, 50-55
  networking connections, 36
  optical drives, 34
  RAM, 33
  video output connections,
    36
desktop type
  Dell Dimension E510, 71
  Sony RA-940, 71-72
digital music
  album art, fixing, 189-192
  album art, manual file
    replacement, 192
  display and sort options,
    179-182
  editing album information,
    187-188
  editing song information,
    185-188
  playing albums, 185
  playing individual songs,
    185
  playlists, creating, 195-198
  playlists, playing, 194-195
  scrolling through, 183
  searching, 184-185

digital photos
  burning to CDs, 271-274
  editing tools, 268-270
  folder storage options, 265, 268
  full-screen view, 264
  picture information view, 264
  picture thumbnails view, 263
download options, configuring, 143
DVD changers, controlling, 42-43
DVD transport buttons, 246
DVD-burning add-on programs
  ArcSoft QuickDVD, 336
  muvee autoProduce unPlugged, 336
  Sonic PrimeTime, 336
  Sonic PrimeTime Deluxe, 336
DVDs
  burning, 248-251
  naming, 249
  playing, 42, 245-247
  recording, 248
entertainment add-on programs
  In the Movies for MCE, 332
  Karatron, 335
  Microsoft Media Center Karaoke, 335
  My Movies, 332
  My Netflix, 332
  My Trailers for MCE, 333
  MyTV ToGo, 334
  MyWebTV, 333
  Playlist Editor, 333
  Power Compress, 335
  Recorded TV, 335
  Share Recorded TV, 335
  Web Media, 333
  WebGuide3, 335
external peripherals, connecting, 118-119
games add-on programs
  Dragon Maze, 346
  mcepeaks, 346
  Solitaire, 347
  Super Slyder, 348
  Tetris, 348
  World Trivia, 348

general connection guidelines, 38-39
graphical visualizations for music, configuring, 144
hard disks, storage space advantages over TiVo, 12
high-definition television, viewing, 47
home automation add-on programs
  HAI Home Control, 339
  HomeSeer MCE Plug-In, 339
  mControl, 339
home theater systems
  connection diagram, 54
  general connection process, 54-55
initial configuration, 121-128
instant messaging, launching, 277-280
Internet connections, configuring, 142
Internet phone add-on programs
  MCE SIP Phone, 340
  mcePhone for Skype, 340
Internet radio
  listening to, 29-31
  sound quality, 30
  XM Radio Online, 30
keyboards, connecting, 117
launching
  with PC activation, 162
  within Windows XP, 162
lifestyle add-on programs
  Alarm Clock, 337
  Lottery Results for MCE, 338
  mceAuction, 337
  My Mapquest for MCE, 337
  My Recipes, 338
live television
  4:3 aspect ratio display, 218-221
  16:9 aspect ratio display, 218-221
  channels, changing, 222
  electronic programming guide, 46
  inset window view, 222
  launching, 217-218

pausing live programming, 222-223
program information, viewing, 222
recording programs, 224-227
viewing, 46-47
zoom modes, 219-221
manual updates (Windows Update feature), 366
MCE Customizer
  Appearance category, 357-359
  EPG category, 357-359
  Extras category, 357, 360-362
  Recording category, 357-360
  Repair category, 357
  Repairs category, 362-363
  Settings category, 357, 362
Media Center add-on programs
  MCE Customizer, 344, 357
  MCE Screen Saver, 346
  MCE Video Settings, 346
  mceHideSVP, 345
  Sleep Timer, 346
  Tweak MCE, 344, 350
mouse, connecting, 117
network connections, 114
  ethernet, 114-115
  Wi-Fi, 116-117
news add-on programs, 328
  MCE RSS Reader, 330
  mNewsCenter, 330
  My NFL Scores for MCE, 330
  My Portal, 328-329
  My Web News, 329
  MyUK Portal, 328
  ReadNews, 330
Online Spotlight, 303
  Games, DISCover My Games, 322
  Games, Game xStream, 321-322
  International options, 304
  Lifestyle, 10 Foot World, 324-325
  Lifestyle, ArcSoft QuickDVD, 326
  Lifestyle, GalleryPlayer, 323

How can we make this index more useful? Email us at indexes@samspublishing.com

Lifestyle, KMS Software, 325

Lifestyle, Kodak Share, 323

Lifestyle, Sonic PrimeTime, 326

Music & Radio, AOL Music on Demand, 315

Music & Radio, AOL Pictures, 315

Music & Radio, AOL Radio, 315

Music & Radio, Live365, 312-313

Music & Radio, MSN Music, 314

Music & Radio, MTV Overdrive, 316

Music & Radio, mtvU, 316

Music & Radio, Musicmatch for Media Center, 314

Music & Radio, Napster for Media Center, 314

Music & Radio, VH1 VSPOT, 317

Music & Radio, XM Satellite Radio Online, 311-312

News & Sports, Fox Sports for Media Center, 320

News & Sports, MSNTV Today, 318

News & Sports, NewsGator Online, 319

News & Sports, NPR for Media Center, 321

News & Sports, Reuters, 318

Showcase, 304

TV & Movies, ABC Enhanced TV, 309

TV & Movies, ABC Family service, 309

TV & Movies, Akimbo service, 307

TV & Movies, CinemaNow service, 306

TV & Movies, Comedy Central MotherLoad, 311

TV & Movies, Discovery Media Center, 308

TV & Movies, InterActual, 311

TV & Movies, Movielink service, 305-307

TV & Movies, TitanTV, 309-310

TV & Movies, TVTonic service, 307-308

web browser requirements for some installations, 305

noise reduction methods, 37

notebook type, 70-71

parental controls, configuring, 143

privacy settings, configuring, 143

Program Guide

adding channel listings, 212

editing channel listings, 211-212

filtering options, 214-215

navigating, 210-211

recording entire series, 228-230

scheduling recordings from, 227-228

searching channel listings, 216

setting up, 127-134

viewing, 209-210

remote control add-on programs

Media Center Communicator, 344

MediaUFO, 344

MyRemoteMouse, 343

Niveus Pocket Remote, 343

PadOne Media Controller, 344

Rudeo Control, 344

remote control features, 117, 148-149

slideshows

configuring, 262

music accompaniment, 275

pausing, 275

playing, 274-275

stopping, 275

viewing, 261

Sony VAIO XL1 Digital Living System, 43

Start page

10-foot interface, 149

appearance of, 149

background of, 150

Help Center, 151-152

inset window, 151

More Programs menu, 160

My DVDs activation, 257-258

My Music menu, 159

My Pictures menu, 154

My TV menu, 155, 158

My Videos menu, 154

Online Spotlight menu, 153

Play DVD deactivation, 257-258

Play DVD menu, 152-153

Radio menu, 159

scrolling menu, 150

Settings menu, 160

Shut Down control, 151

television programming, recording, 48

television signal, setting up, 127-134

third-party CD burning software, 208

troubleshooting areas

choppy video playback, 373-374

disappearing album library, 373

edited albums revert to original (My Music), 372

failure to play DVDs, 376-377

inability to record TV to DVDs, 377

missing or wrong cover art for music, 371

missing or wrong track information for music, 372

music CD non–recognition, 371

no MCE widescreen mode, 374

no TV signal, 375

Program Guide display errors, 376

recording TV program failure, 375

remote control operation, 371

sluggish performance, 370

standby mode freezes, 370

stuttering picture/sound in HDTV, 375

system freezes or crashes, 369-370

TV display resolution, setting up, 134-138

TV programs

recording while watching, 234

searching for recording purposes, 230

Tweak MCE

DVD settings, 352-353

general settings, 351

main screen appearance, 350

Media Center Extender settings, 355-356

Music settings, 354

Remote Control settings, 355

TV settings, 353

Update Rollup 2 installations, 366

versus desktop PCs

A/V connections, 19

interface viewing, 16-17

noise levels, 18-19

remote control operations, 17-18

unit design, 19

uses, 15-16

versus Media Center Extender features

home theater arrangement, 63-64

versus TiVo

electronic program guide (EPG), 11

hard disk storage space, 12

versus Windows Media Player, song information changes, 186-187

video files

playing, 258-260

viewing details of, 258-260

video output, connecting, 101-108

videotaped home movies, viewing, 46

weather add-on programs

mceWeather, 331

My Weather, 331

Simply Weather, 331

window behaviors, configuring, 142

wireless networking, configuring, 143

MediaUFO add-on, 344

memory modules for Media Center PC

recommended sizes, 81

vendor listing, 82

menus (Media Center Start page)

More Programs, 160

My Music, 159

My Pictures, 154

My TV, 155, 158

My Videos, 154

Online Spotlight, 153

Play DVD, 152-153

Radio, 159

Settings, 160

messages, composing (MCE Outlook), 285-286

microprocessors

Media Center Extender requirements, 60

Media Center PC, digital video recorder (DVR) specifications, 51

selecting for Media Center PC, 33

Microsoft Knowledge Base website, 368

Microsoft Xbox, using as Media Center Extender, 65-66

Microsoft Xbox 360, built-in Media Center Extender technology, 59, 67

minimizing Media Center, 163

mixed CDs, creating (Media Center), 207-208

mNewsCenter news add-on, 330

motherboards for Media Center PC

cost range, 80

Intel D955XBK, 80

vendor listing, 80

mouse

Media Center PCs

connecting, 117

Gyration Media Center Remote & Keyboard, 86

MyRemoteMouse add-on, 343

Movielink service (Online Spotlight), 305-307

movies on DVDs

burning

ArcSoft QuickDVD, 251-253

Media Center PC, 248-251

Roxio My DVD, 254

Sonic Easy Media Creator, 254

Sonic PrimeTime, 251

Sony Click-to-DVD program, 253

Ulead DVD MovieFactory, 254

naming (Media Center PC), 249

playing (Media Center PC), 42, 245-247

recording (Media Center PC), 248

MP3 format, CDs, ripping, 170-171

MPEG format, conversion from DVR-MS format of Media Center DVDs, 254-255

MSN Music (Online Spotlight), 314

MSN Music Store, 176

MSN Remote Record Service, signup process, 235

MSNTV Today (Online Spotlight), 318

MTV Overdrive (Online Spotlight), 45, 316

mtvU (Online Spotlight), 316

multichannel analog audio, audio output connections, 112

multiple Media Center Extenders, placing throughout home, 62

music

CDs

burning, 31-32

ripping, 25-28

downloading

format considerations, 28-29

sound quality, 29

listening to in other rooms (Media Center Extender), 61

My Music menu (Start page), 159

playing (Media Center PC), 24-25

slideshows, playing during, 275

streaming to other room via Media Center Extender, 58-59

Music & Radio (Online Spotlight), 304

AOL Music on Demand, 315

AOL Pictures, 315

AOL Radio, 315

Live365, 312-313

MSN Music, 314

MTV Overdrive, 316

mtvU, 316

Musicmatch for Media Center, 314

Napster for Media Center, 314

VH1 VSPOT, 317

XM Satellite Radio Online, 311-312

Music screen (Tweak MCE utility), 354

MusicGiants Network digital music download service, 178

Musicmatch for Media Center (Online Spotlight), 314

MusicShifter service, CD-ripping services, 27

muvee autoProduce unPlugged DVD burner add-on, 336

My Documents folder (Windows), digital photo storage, 265, 268

My DVDs menu

activating (Tweak MCE PowerToy), 257-258

versus Play DVD function, 257-258

My File Manager

accessing, 287

downloading, 287

drive contents, viewing, 287

files/folders

copying, 288-289

viewing, 287

My File Manager add-on, 341

My Mapquest for MCE add-on, 337

My Movies entertainment add-on, 332

My Music folder

album art

file replacement, 192

fixing, 189-192

album view

displaying alphabetically, 179-180

displaying by artist, 179-180

displaying by genre, 181-182

displaying by songs, 181

editing, 187-188

albums, playing, 185

digital music watch list, adding folders to, 168-170

individual songs, playing, 185

scrolling through, 183

searching, 184-185

song information

editing, 185-188

typical errors, 186

troubleshooting tips

CD non-recognition, 371

disappearing album library, 373

edited albums revert to original, 372

missing or wrong cover art, 371

missing or wrong track information, 372

My Netflix entertainment add-on, 332

My NFL Scores for MCE news add-on, 330

My Photos folder, pictures, deleting, 266

My Pictures folder, digital photos

playing all in slideshows, 274-275

storage of, 265, 268

My Pictures menu, Start page (Media Center), 154

My Playlists folder

creating, 195-198

viewing, 194-195

My Portal news add-on, 328-329

My Recipes add-on, 338

My Trailers for MCE entertainment add-on, 333

My TV menu, Start page (Media Center), 155, 158

My Videos screen (Media Center PC), 154

files, viewing details of, 258-260

playing, 258-260

My Weather weather add-on, 331

My Web News news add-on, 329

MyRemoteMouse add-on, 343

MyTV ToGo utility, 242, 334

MyUK Portal news add-on, 328

MyWebTV entertainment add-on, 333

N

naming DVD movies, 249

Napster for Media Center (Online Spotlight), 314

navigating

My Music folder (Media Center), 183

Program Guide, 210-211

Network Performance Tuner, performance and diagnostics tool, 301-302

networks

digital video recorder (DVR) specifications, 53

Media Center Extender

connecting, 296-297

ethernet type, 296

Wi-Fi type, 297

Media Center PCs

connecting via ethernet, 114-115

connecting via Wi-Fi, 116-117

News & Sports (Online Spotlight), 304

Fox Sports for Media Center, 320

MSNTV Today, 318

NewsGator Online, 319

NPR for Media Center, 321

Reuters, 318

news programs add-ons, 328

MCE RSS Reader, 330

mNewsCenter, 330

My NFL Scores for MCE, 330
My Portal, 328-329
My Web News, 329
MyUK Portal, 328
ReadNews, 330
NewsGator Online (Online
Spotlight), 319
Niveus Denali A/V Component
Form Factor Media Center PC,
72-76
Niveus Ice Vault 200 Disc
Changer, 43, 255
Niveus Pocket Remote add-on,
343
nmediapc HTPC BA&S cases, 79
noise levels (Media Center PC)
versus desktop PCs, 18-19
notebook Media Center PC, 70-71
Notification Before a Recording
Starts option (MCE Tweak
utility), 353
NPR for Media Center (Online
Spotlight), 321
NTSC tuner, standard-definition
television, 47

O

Online Spotlight, 303
Games, 304
DISCover My Games, 322
Game xStream, 321-322
installations, web browser
requirements, 305
International options, 304
Lifestyle, 304
10 Foot World, 324-325
ArcSoft QuickDVD, 326
GalleryPlayer, 323
KMS Software, 325
Kodak Share, 323
Sonic PrimeTime, 326
Music & Radio, 304
AOL Music on Demand, 315
AOL Pictures, 315
AOL Radio, 315
Live365, 312-313
MSN Music, 314
MTV Overdrive, 316
mtvU, 316
Musicmatch for Media
Center, 314

Napster for Media Center,
314
VH1 VSPOT, 317
XM Satellite Radio Online,
311-312
News & Sports, 304
Fox Sports for Media
Center, 320
MSNTV Today, 318
NewsGator Online, 319
NPR for Media Center, 321
Reuters, 318
Showcase, 304
TV & Movies, 304-305
ABC Enhanced TV, 309
ABC Family service, 309
Akimbo service, 307
CinemaNow service, 306
Comedy Central
MotherLoad, 311
Discovery Media Center,
308
InterActual, 311
Movielink service, 305-307
TitanTV, 309-310
TVTonic service, 307-308
optical audio connections, 35-36
optical drives for Media Center PC
audio output connections,
109-110
digital video recorder (DVR)
specifications, 52
selecting, 34
over-the-air (OTA) antenna,
connecting to Media Center
PC, 95
Overscan Adjustments option
(MCE Tweak utility), 351

P

PadOne Media Controller add-on,
344
parental controls, configuring
(Media Center), 143
Pause button, DVD transport
options (Media Center PC), 246
Pause+FWD button, DVD transport
options (Media Center PC), 246
Pause+REW button, DVD transport
options (Media Center PC), 246

pausing
CD playback (Media Center),
175
live TV programming (Media
Center), 222-223
slideshows (Media Center PC),
275
performance
Media Center Extender,
improvement tips, 299-301
sluggish, troubleshooting, 370
PhotoConnect add-on, 343
picture information of digital
photos, viewing, 264
Picture Settings screen (Media
Center PC), 262
Show Caption, 262
Show Pictures in Random
Order, 262
Show Pictures in Subfolders,
262
Show Song Information Suring
Slide Show, 262
Transition Time, 263
Transition Type, 263
picture thumbnails of digital
photos, viewing, 263
Play button, DVD transport options
(Media Center PC), 246
playback of recorded programs
deleting, 240-241
saving, 240
viewing, 239
playing
CDs
Media Center, 173-176
Media Center PC, 24-25
digital music
entire albums (Media
Center), 185
individual songs (Media
Center), 185
DVD movies, 42, 245-247
slideshows, music in
background (Media Center
PC), 274-275
video files, 258-260
Playlist Editor
add-on, 333
digital music playlists,
creating, 198-199

playlists
    automatic, creating (Windows
        Media Player), 202–203
    burning to CDs, 207–208
    digital music
        creating (Media Center),
            195–198
        creating (Playlist Editor),
            198–199
        creating (Windows Media
            Player), 200–201
        editing (Windows Media
            Player), 203–205
        playing (Media Center),
            194–195
    portable devices (MyTV ToGo
    utility), 242
Portable Media Center, media
    files, transferring to portable
    devices, 242
Power Compress entertainment
    add-on, 335
power supplies for Media Center
    PC
        cost range, 79–80
        fan versus fanless, 79–80
        vendor listing, 79–80
powered speakers
    built-in amplifiers, 92
    external amplifiers, 92
previewing digital photos, editing
    changes, 268
pricing Media Center PCs,
    custom-built, 86–87
privacy settings, configuring
    (Media Center), 143
Program Guide (Media Center)
    channel listings
        adding, 212
        editing, 211–212
        searching, 216
    configuring (Media Center),
        127–134
    filtering options, 214–215
    navigating, 210–211
    recording entire series,
        228–230
    recordings, scheduling,
        227–228
    viewing, 209–210
    wrong display,
        troubleshooting, 376

programming live television
    pausing (Media Center),
        222–223
    recording (Media Center),
        224–227
properties of video files, viewing
    (Media Center PC), 258–260

R

Radio menu, Start page (Media
    Center), 159
RAID (Redundant Array of
    Inexpensive Disks), 34
RAM (random access memory)
    Media Center Extender
        requirements, 60
    Media Center PC
        digital video recorder (DVR)
            specifications, 51
        selecting for, 33
random slideshow settings, 262
random tracks, CD playback
    (Media Center), 176
ReadNews news add-on, 330
rebooting PCs after Media Center
    shutdowns, 164–165
recorded programs
    burning to DVDs, 48–50
    copying to DVDs, 243
    deleting, 240–241
    saving, 240
    television, troubleshooting,
        375
    transferring to portable
        devices, 242
    viewing, 239
        skipped commercials, 240
Recorded TV entertainment
    add-on, 335
recorder (Media Center)
    audio language, 227
    disk space issues, 225–226
    life of recording, 227
    number of recordings, 227
    quality issues, 225–226
    start/stop settings, 227
    TV series issues, 227
recording
    DVD movies in Media Center
        PC, 248

live TV programming (Media
    Center), 224–227
    at lower quality levels,
        performance improvements
        (Media Center Extender), 301
    programs while watching, 234
    TV programs to DVDs, digital
        rights management
        (DRM), 377
    TV series, entire seasons,
        228–230
Recording category (MCE
    Customizer), 357–360
Red Eye tool, digital photos, fixing
    (Media Center PC), 269
remote control
    add-ons
        Media Center
            Communicator, 344
        MediaUFO, 344
        MyRemoteMouse, 343
        Niveus Pocket Remote, 343
        PadOne Media Controller,
            344
        Rudeo Control, 344
    Media Center PCs, 85, 148–149
        connecting, 117
        troubleshooting, 371
        versus desktop PCs, 17–18
Remote Control screen (Tweak
    MCE utility), 355
remote desktop, configuring
    (Media Center), 143
Remote Record (Media Center)
    installing, 234
    MSN Service signup process,
        235
    scheduling recordings from
        other PCs, 234–237
Repairs category (MCE
    Customizer), 362–363
replacing
    digital music, album art files
        (Media Center), 192
    Play DVD function with My
        DVDs function, 257–258
Replay button, DVD transport
    options (Media Center PC), 246
resizing digital photos with Crop
    tool, 270
resolution of television display,
    configuring (Media Center),
    134–138

Reuters (Online Spotlight), 318
reviewing scheduled TV recordings, 237-238
REW button, DVD transport options (Media Center PC), 246
ripping
    CDs
        bit rates, 171
        file format options, 170-171
        format selection, 27-28
        hard disk space (Media Center PC), 27-28, 171-172
        Media Center PC, 25-26, 170-172
        MusicShifter service, 27
        time per CD, 176
        time per disc calculations (Media Center PC), 26-27
        title retrieval, 176
        Windows Media Player configuration, 172-173
    DVDs to hard disks, 44-45
        legal ramifications, 255
        popular utilities, 255
        process of, 256-257
        space requirements, 255
        time per disc, 257
Roxio My DVD program, 254
Rudeo Control add-on, 344

S

S-video, output connections, 36, 101-102, 106
S/PDIF audio connection (Sony/Philips Digital Interface), 109
SACD CDs, inability to play on Media Center PC, 24-25
SAM-Consult, Media Center add-ons
    MCE Outlook, 283
    My File Manager, 287
satellite receivers, connecting to Media Center PC, 99-100
saving recorded TV programs, 240
scheduling
    manual TV recordings, 230-231

recordings
    canceling, 239
    from Program Guide (Media Center), 227-228
    reviewing, 237-238
    via keyword, 231-233
    TV recordings from another PC (Remote Record), 234-237
Search Depth option (MCE Tweak utility), 352
Search Network Locations option (MCE Tweak utility), 352
searching
    channel listings (Program Guide), 216
    digital music, 184-185
    Program Guide for recording purposes, 230
seek bar, DVD playback (Media Center PC), 247
Set Remote Control ID option (MCE Tweak utility), 355
Settings category (MCE Customizer), 357, 362
Setup Wizard, Media Center configuration, launching, 122-126
Share Recorded TV entertainment add-on, 335
Show Add to Queue Notification option (MCE Tweak utility), 354
Show DVDs in Drives First option (MCE Tweak utility), 352
Showcase (Online Spotlight), 304
Shut Down control, Start page (Media Center), 151
signal amplifiers, coaxial signal splitters, 95
Silverstone LC11M (case), 79
Simply Weather weather add-on, 331
Skip Back Interval option (MCE Tweak utility), 353
Skip button, DVD transport options (Media Center PC), 246
Skip Forward Interval option (MCE Tweak utility), 353
skipping commercials from recorded programs, 240
Sleep Timer add-on, 346

slideshows
    configuration settings, 262
        displaying pictures in subfolders, 262
        random ordering, 262
        show captions, 262
        show song information during show, 262
        transition effects, 263
        transition times, 263
    digital photos, viewing, 261
    music, listening to, 275
    pausing, 275
    playing, 274-275
    stopping, 275
Solitaire add-on, 347
songs
    digital music information, editing (Media Center), 188
    displaying in slideshows, 262
Sonic Easy Media Creator, DVDs, burning, 254
Sonic PrimeTime, 326, 336
    downloading, 251
    DVDs, burning, 251
    versions, cost range, 251
Sonic PrimeTime Deluxe DVD burner add-on, 336
Sony Click-to-DVD program, 253
Sony RA-940 Desktop Media Center PC, 71-72
Sony VAIO VGX-XL1 Digital Living System, 76-77
Sony VAIO XL1 Digital Living System (Media Center PC), 43
sorting digital music, 179-182
Sound Blaster Audigy 2 audio card, 84
Sound Blaster Audigy Z 2S audio card, 25
sound effects, configuring (Media Center), 142
sound quality of downloaded music, 29
speakers
    audio settings, configuring (Media Center), 138-141
    powered
        built-in amplifiers, 92
        external amplifiers, 92
standard audio CDs, playing (Media Center PC), 24

standby modes, frozen, troubleshooting, 370
Start page (Media Center)
10-foot interface, 149
appearance of, 149
background of, 150
Help Center, 151-152
inset window, 151
More Programs menu, 160
My Music menu, 159
My Pictures menu, 154
My TV menu, 155, 158
My Videos menu, 154
Online Spotlight menu, 153
Play DVD menu, 152-153
Radio menu, 159
scrolling menu, 150
Settings menu, 160
Shut Down control, 151
stereo mini-jacks, audio output connections, 112
Stop button, DVD transport options (Media Center PC), 246
stopping
CD playback (Media Center), 175
slideshows (Media Center PC), 275
Stored Location for Recorded TV option (MCE Tweak utility), 353
streaming music/TV programming to other rooms (Media Center Extender), 58-59
stuttering picture (HDTV), troubleshooting, 373-375
Super Slyder add-on, 348
system freezes, troubleshooting, 369-370

T

tags, digital music information
editing (Media Center), 185-187
typical errors (Media Center), 186
television
720p HDTV resolution, 261
cable line inputs, connecting to Media Center PC, 96-97

digital cable boxes, connecting to Media Center PC, 97-99
display resolution, configuring (Media Center), 134-138
DVD does not play, troubleshooting, 376-377
electronic programming guide (Media Center PC), 46
HDTV
antenna inputs, connecting to Media Center PC, 95
stuttering picture/sound, troubleshooting, 375
viewing (Media Center PC), 47
inability to record to DVDs, troubleshooting, 377
Live TV function (Media Center)
aspect ratio displays, 218-221
channels, changing, 222
inset window view, 222
launching, 217-218
pausing live programming, 222-223
recording live programming, 224-227
viewing program information, 222
zoom modes, 219-221
manual recordings, scheduling, 230-231
Media Center Extender connections, 294
My TV menu (Start page), 155, 158
MyTV ToGo utility, 242
no signal, troubleshooting, 375
over-the-air (OTA) antenna inputs, connecting to Media Center PC, 95
Program Guide
adding channel listings, 212
editing channel listings, 211-212
filtering options, 214-215
navigating, 210-211
searching channel listings, 216

Program Guide
setting up (Media Center), 127-134
troubleshooting, 376
viewing, 209-210
programs
recording while watching, 48, 234
searching for recording purposes, 230
recorded programs
burning to DVDs, 48-50
deleting, 240-241
failures, troubleshooting, 375
saving, 240
transferring to portable devices, 242
viewing, 239-240
recordings, scheduling
from another PC (Remote Record), 234-237
via keyword, 231-233
from Program Guide, 227-228
satellite receivers, connecting to Media Center PC, 99-100
scheduled recordings
canceling, 239
reviewing, 237-238
series, recording entire season (Program Guide), 228-230
signal setup, NTSC/ATSC tuning (Media Center), 127-134
streaming to other room via Media Center Extender, 58-59
viewing (Media Center PC), 46-47
watching in other rooms (Media Center Extender), 61
Tetris add-on, 348
TheGreenButton.com
help resources, 369
Media Center add-on listing, 348
thumbnails of digital photos, viewing, 263
TitanTV (Online Spotlight), 309-310

TiVo
    hard disks, storage space
        disadvantages to Media
        Center PC, 12
    versus Media Center PC
        electronic program guide
        (EPG), 11
        hard disk storage space, 12
Touch Up page menu (My Pictures
    folder), 268
track listings for CDs, viewing, 174
transferring recorded TV programs
    to portable devices, 242
transition effects in slideshows,
    263
transition times in slideshows,
    applying, 263
troubleshooting
    Media Center
        choppy video playback,
        373-374
        disappearing album library,
        373
        DVD does not play,
        376-377
        edited albums revert to
        original (My Music), 372
        inability to record TV to
        DVDs, 377
        missing or wrong cover art
        for music, 371
        missing or wrong track
        information for music, 372
        music CD nonrecognition,
        371
        no TV signal, 375
        no widescreen mode, 374
        Program Guide display
        errors, 376
        recording TV program
        failure, 375
        remote control operation,
        371
        sluggish performance, 370
        standby mode freezes, 370
        stuttering picture/sound in
        HDTV, 375
        system freezes or crashes,
        369-370
    Media Center Extender,
        wireless networks
        antenna relocation, 300

        device interference, 300
        firmware updates, 301
        recording at lower quality
        levels, 301
        switching channels, 300
        upgrades, 301
TV & Movies (Online Spotlight),
    304-305
    ABC Enhanced TV, 309
    ABC Family service, 309
    Akimbo service, 307
    CinemaNow service, 306
    Comedy Central MotherLoad,
    311
    Discovery Media Center, 308
    InterActual, 311
    Movielink service, 305-307
    TitanTV, 309-310
    TVTonic service, 307-308
TV screen (Tweak MCE utility),
    353
TV tuner cards
    digital video recorder (DVR)
    specifications, 52
    Media Center PC
        cost ranges, 84
        vendor listing, 84
    NTSC format versus ATSC
    format, 84
TVTonic service (Online Spotlight),
    45, 307-308
Tweak MCE add-on, 344
    DVD screen, 350-353
    Extender screen, 350,
    355-356
    General screen, 350-351
    main screen appearance, 350
    Music screen, 350, 354
    Remote Control screen, 350,
    355
    TV screen, 350, 353

U - V

Ulead DVD MovieFactory, 254
Update Rollup 2 (Media Center PC)
    DVD changer controls, 42-43
    software update, 366
updating Media Center
    automatic method (Windows
    Update feature), 366

    manual method (Windows
    Update feature), 366
upgrading wireless networks
    (Media Center Extender), 301

VH1 VSPOT (Online Spotlight), 317
video
    choppy playback,
    troubleshooting, 373-374
    downloading from Internet, 45
    no MCE widescreen mode,
    troubleshooting, 374
    video card compatibility
    problems, 373
video cards
    cost ranges, 84
    vendor listing, 84
video connections
    Media Center Extender, 294
    Media Center PC
        Component video, 101-102,
        105
        Composite video, 101-102,
        106-108
        DVI, 101-104
        HDMI, 101-102
        S-video, 101-102, 106
        versus desktop PCs, 91-94
video files
    accessing via Media Center
    Extender on living room
    system, 63-64
    playing (Media Center PC),
    258-260
    viewing details of (Media
    Center PC), 258-260
video output connections
    DVI, 53
    HDMI, 53
    Media Center PC, digital video
    recorder (DVR) specifications,
    53
    selecting for Media Center
    PC, 36
videotapes
    burning to DVDs, 48-50
    viewing (Media Center PC), 46
viewing
    contacts list (MCE Outlook),
    284
    high-definition television
    through Media Center PC, 47

live television on Media Center
PC, 46-47
Program Guide, 209-210
recorded TV programs, 239
commercial skipping, 240
scheduled TV recordings,
237-238
videotaped home movies, 46

W

Watched Folders for Recorded TV
option (MCE Tweak utility), 353
watching television in other
rooms (Media Center Extender),
61
weather programs add-ons
mceWeather, 331
My Weather, 331
Simply Weather, 331
Web Media entertainment add-on,
333
WebGuide3 entertainment add-on,
335
websites
CNET Download.com, 281
MCE-Software.com, 283, 287
Microsoft Knowledge Base,
help resources, 368
Microsoft Windows Update,
366
MusicGiants Network, 178
MusicShifter.com, 27
TheGreenButton.com
help resources, 369
Media Center add-on
listing, 348
Windows XP Media Center
Edition, help resources, 367

WindowsMarketPlace.com,
Media Center add-on listing,
348
Wi-Fi connections, 36
differing standards, data speed
rates, 116-117
Media Center PC
setting up, 116-117
versus desktop PCs, 93-94
widescreen mode (television), no
MCE display, troubleshooting,
374
window behaviors, configuring
(Media Center), 142
Windows Marketplace, Media
Center add-ons listing, 348
Windows Media Player
CD track/album information,
update settings, 372
CD-ripping options,
configuring, 172-173
digital music
automatic playlists,
creating, 202-203
playlists, creating, 200-201
playlists, editing, 203-205
update settings, 372
versus Media Center, song
information changes,
186-187
Windows Messenger versus Media
Center Messenger, 278-280
Windows XP
launching with Media Center
with PC activation, 162
launching within, 162
Windows XP for Home Users,
Service Pack 2 Edition, 122

Windows XP Media Center Edition
website, help resources, 367
wireless networks (Media Center
Extender)
antennas, relocating, 300
channels, switching, 300
configuring, 143
device interference, avoiding,
300
firmware, updating, 301
upgrading, 301
WMA (Windows Media Audio)
format
Apple iPod incompatibility, 29
CDs, ripping, 27-28, 170
WMA Lossless (Windows Media
Audio Lossless) format, CDs,
ripping, 27-28, 171
World Trivia add-on, 348

X - Y - Z

Xbox Media Center Extender kit,
66
Xilisoft DVD Ripper, downloading,
256
XM Radio Online, 30
XM Satellite Radio Online (Online
Spotlight), 311-312

zoom modes, Live TV function
(Media Center), 219-221